Cambridge Studies in Management

15

The quest for productivity

Cambridge Studies in Management

Formerly Management and Industrial Relations series

Editors
WILLIAM BROWN, *University of Cambridge*
ANTHONY HOPWOOD, *London School of Economics*
and PAUL WILLMAN, *London Business School*

The series focusses on the human and organizational aspects of management. It covers the areas of organization theory and behaviour, strategy and business policy, the organizational and social aspects of accounting, personnel and human resource management, industrial relations and industrial sociology.

The series aims for high standards of scholarship and seeks to publish the best among original theoretical and empirical research; innovative contributions to advancing understanding in the area; books which synthesize and/or review the best of current research, and aim to make the work published in specialist journals more widely accessible; and texts for upper-level undergraduates, for graduates and for vocational courses such as MBA programmes. Edited collections may be accepted where they maintain a high and consistent standard and are on a coherent, clearly defined, and relevant theme.

The books are intended for an international audience among specialists in universities and business schools, undergraduate, graduate and MBA students, and also for a wider readership among business practitioners and trade unionists.

The quest for productivity

A case study of Fawley after Flanders

BRUCE W. AHLSTRAND

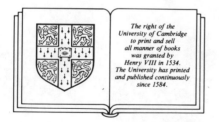

The right of the
University of Cambridge
to print and sell
all manner of books
was granted by
Henry VIII in 1534.
The University has printed
and published continuously
since 1584.

CAMBRIDGE UNIVERSITY PRESS

Cambridge
New York   Port Chester
Melbourne   Sydney

Published by the Press Syndicate of the University of Cambridge
The Pitt Building, Trumpington Street, Cambridge CB2 1RP
40 West 20th Street, New York, NY 10011, USA
10 Stamford Road, Oakleigh, Melbourne 3166, Australia

© Cambridge University Press 1990

First published 1990

Printed in Great Britain by the University Press, Cambridge

British Library cataloguing in publication data

Ahlstrand, Bruce
The quest for productivity: a case study of Fawley after Flanders.
1. Great Britain. Industrial relations. Productivity bargaining. Management aspects
I. Title
658.3'154

Library of Congress cataloguing in publication data

Ahlstrand, Bruce W.
The quest for productivity: a case study of Fawley after Flanders
Bruce W. Ahlstrand.
        p.   cm. – (Cambridge Studies in Management: 15)
Bibliography.
ISBN 0-521-36380-2
1. Productivity bargaining – Great Britain – Case studies.
2. Productivity bargaining – England – Fawley. 3. Flanders, Allan D.
I. Title. II. Series.
HD4946.G7A34 1990
331.11'8'0942 – dc20   89-9809 CIP

ISBN 0 521 36380 2

Contents

Contents

Contents

Contents

Tables

To my parents Berit and Eric
and to the memory of E. Batstone

Acknowledgements

I would like, first, to thank the many stewards, workers and managers at Esso's Fawley Refinery who shared their experiences of productivity bargaining with me. With good grace, they not only tolerated my presence, but were also always willing to recall events from the past and explain more recent developments. I can only hope that I have written about them fairly and honestly. In particular, I would like to thank Mr John Harryman, Employee Relations Manager, for giving me approval to proceed with the research, and Mr Robin Schneider, Industrial Relations Advisor, who acted as my regular contact at Fawley.

I owe an enormous debt to my supervisors, Dr Eric Batstone and Lord McCarthy of Nuffield College, Oxford, for their kind and helpful supervision over the four-year period of this research. They managed to provide more encouragement, enthusiasm and insight than I had any right to expect. Discussions with them invariably helped me to better understand the issues I was trying to address. Dr Batstone died shortly after the completion of this research. His memory will always be with me. His work continues with the work of his students.

I would like to thank Mr John Purcell of Templeton College, Oxford for his careful reading and detailed comments on the final draft of this work. I am grateful to him for the opportunity to work as his research associate over the past year and a half. Mr Arthur Marsh of St Edmund Hall, Oxford has contributed to the substance of this research by drawing upon his memories of the Blue Book era.

I am grateful to the Canadian Citizenship Institute for providing me with a scholarship for this research. Thanks must also be extended to Nuffield College for funding my field work activity.

Allan Flanders' study of the Fawley Blue Book agreement is powerful, and it is easy to see why it has become a classic within the field of British industrial relations. I hope that, in this 'second' instalment, I have not fallen too far short of Flanders' high standard. Although some of my findings differ from the conclusions drawn by Flanders some twenty-five years ago, I have the deepest admiration for his work.

Finally, I must thank my wife Maeve for wise editorial advice and valuable comments on earlier drafts.

1

Introduction

The Fawley experiment stands as a practical demonstration
that management can evolve and act upon higher standards.
Will other progressive managements follow this lead? If enough
of them do, the outcome will not be limited to their own firms.
They will be setting new norms of industrial conduct from
which society will then permit no retreat. (Allan Flanders' final
words on the Fawley Refinery 'Blue Book' productivity deal,
1964: 255–6)

Background to the research

Nearly three decades ago, in February 1960, the first historic productivity
agreement, known as the 'Blue Book', was concluded at Esso's Fawley
Refinery near Southampton. The Fawley Blue Book deal was to spark a
productivity bargaining revolution within Britain. More than any other
single management initiative in the past twenty-five years, the Blue Book
has perhaps had the greatest and longest lasting impact on the management of industrial relations in Britain. Allan Flanders described this first
agreement as '... without precedent or even proximate parallel in the
history of collective bargaining in Great Britain' (1964: 13). Klein has
pointed out that 'some commentators thought that it put the company
(Esso) into the ranks of the classic innovators like Hawthorne and Glacier
...' (1976: 2).

The enthusiasm with which the Blue Book agreement was met in the
1960s is strangely reminiscent of the excitement associated with Japanese
management techniques today. Fawley Refinery was seen to hold the
answers to an elusive productivity problem in much the same way that
Japan is today. While at present all 'good' academics, consultants and
practitioners have their heads tilted to the Japanese experience, it was only
some twenty-five years ago that all heads were directed towards Fawley.

1

The same kind of ritualistic trips that are being made to Japan today were then being made to Fawley. Fawley was to represent '. . . the hallowed ground of productivity bargaining: it has almost become a national shrine, with overseas visitors being urged to pay a visit to the Esso Refinery' (McKersie, 1966: i).

The notoriety and celebrity status accorded the Blue Book productivity deal has led to the nature and substance of this productivity agreement being generally well known. Before the Blue Book, labour productivity at Fawley Refinery had compared unfavourably with performance at other Esso refineries elsewhere in the world. Fawley was seen by management to be plagued by restrictive practices, job demarcations and wage drift (in the form of systematic overtime to compensate for low earnings). Fawley was caught in what Bill Allen, the Emerson consultant who worked with Fawley management in devising the Blue Book, referred to as a 'half-pay and half-effort' syndrome.

To work a way out of these 'problems' Fawley management offered large increases in wage rates to all its employees of the order of 40 per cent in return for the workers' and unions' consent to certain defined changes in their existing working practices. Pay was, in other words, to be linked to productivity through a mutually agreed revision in the nature and methods of work. According to Clegg,

> the novelty of the 1960 (Blue Book) agreements at Esso's Faw-
> ley refinery was not that this was the first occasion on which
> work practices were mentioned in an agreement, or that it was
> the first exchange of alterations in work practices for increases
> in pay. What was new was the negotiation with workshop
> representatives of all unions concerned of a series of changes in
> work practices throughout the plant and their embodiment in a
> formal agreement with the unions. (Clegg, 1970: referred to by
> McKersie and Hunter, 1973: 8)

In some ways, the Fawley experiment stood as a great symbol or example of the potential for the reform of British management and for that matter of the entire system of British industrial relations. Indeed, Fawley became a convenient laboratory setting for the construction of a new model of industrial relations, a model that promised the transition from a system of chaos and confusion to one of order and stability. The advent of productivity bargaining was seen to promise no less than a revolution in management's ability to manage. Both the celebrated Royal Commission on Trade Unions and Employers' Association, known as the Donovan Commission, and the National Board for Prices and Incomes were to draw on the Fawley experience as a platform for the development of their own particular strategies for industrial-relations reform in Britain.

Even during the striking of the original Blue Book agreement, the managers at Fawley themselves sensed that they were involved in a fairly revolutionary change in the conduct of their industrial relations and, as a result, invited Allan Flanders, then an industrial relations lecturer at Oxford University, to document the process and provide an independent assessment of its results in order to ensure proper recording for posterity. It was Flanders who was to coin the term 'productivity bargaining' to describe Fawley's management innovation in collective bargaining. The coining of the term 'productivity bargaining' and Flanders' volume on the Blue Book deal, *The Fawley Productivity Agreements: A Case Study of Management and Collective Bargaining*, helped to ensure the future importance of productivity bargaining within Britain as well as establishing Allan Flanders '... almost overnight (as) the outstanding theorist of industrial relations in Britain and, many would say in the world ...' (H. Clegg's May 1974 introduction to *Management and Unions* by A. Flanders, 1975: 7). Referring to Flanders' work on Fawley, Brown claims that 'there can have been few books which have had such rapid and powerful effects upon thinking about policy' (1974: 420).

Flanders' imagination was clearly captured by the possibility of a case study of Fawley's innovation in collective bargaining. Flanders suggested, in fact, that the Blue Book case study '... had the fascination of reproducing in a microcosm many of the factors affecting present day management and collective bargaining in this country' (Flanders, 1964: 17). For Flanders, the Blue Book story held crucial importance for the notion of strategy in the management of industrial relations and it was '... in the last resort based upon a single theme – the growth of managerial initiative in labour relations' (1964: 100).

For Flanders, however, productivity bargaining was to be about something even more than '... convictions about the responsibilities of management'; it was also to provide for more 'democracy from below'. For Flanders, productivity bargaining provided the platform for a new 'pluralist' based strategy for control – a platform which could be used by management groups throughout Britain. Productivity bargaining, therefore, was seen by Flanders as integrating union representatives into the management decision-making process and thereby 'reconciling planning with democracy'.

Using the very same case study technique as Flanders, this research provides a critical analysis of 'Fawley after Flanders'. Like Blackler's and Brown's (1980) study, *Whatever Happened to Shell's New Philosophy of Management?*, this research seeks to discover 'whatever happened to

Fawley's productivity bargaining'. The research endeavours to explore the evolution of Esso's industrial-relations strategy from 1960 to 1985 at Fawley. In doing so, the research seeks to shed light on how a major company, one which became a symbol or hope for reform, reacted and responded, over the years, to the complex problems that bore on British industrial relations.

In August of 1983 I made my first trip to Fawley with a view to negotiating research access with the local employee relations manager. With access successfully negotiated, the possibilities for the research were immediately exciting. I hoped, for instance, that this research would have direct relevance to the recent strategy debate in industrial relations. The more I thought about Fawley as a possible site at which to investigate the meaning of the notion of strategy for industrial relations, the more appropriate it seemed. It was, after all, Fawley Refinery which had been one of Britain's first firms '... consciously and consistently ... to apply a "philosophy" of industrial relations, in trying to solve administrative problems ...' (Lupton, 1966: 46). Moreover, no social science researcher had been in Fawley since Flanders, and it was perhaps time to conduct an examination of productivity bargaining and industrial-relations management at the refinery.

Fawley revisited: case study findings from the Blue Book to 1985

Upon my first visit to Fawley Refinery, it became immediately clear that productivity bargaining had not withered away at Fawley after the famous Blue Book productivity deal. The Blue Book was not a one-off negotiation; rather, it represented the first of a long string of productivity deals (some 21 productivity deals were struck over the 25 years covered by the case study). Instead of diminishing in importance over the years, productivity bargaining had been accorded a special place in Fawley's industrial relations and had come, in fact, to define the very essence of Esso Fawley's industrial-relations strategy.

As this research progressed, it became apparent that productivity bargaining had established itself as something even more than a management technique; it had become a fixture of the Fawley management culture. Both Fawley management and workers were always more than willing to define or interpret Fawley's industrial relations directly within the context of productivity bargaining. As one of the Fawley managers put it to me when I informed him I was doing a study on industrial-relations strategy at Fawley: '... oh, you must be here to study our productivity bargaining.'

Much of the folklore associated with the productivity bargaining process at Fawley could be linked back to the original Blue Book deal itself. Fawley managers, union representatives and workers alike remember (some more fondly than others) the Blue Book experiment. The relative employment stability at Fawley has meant that there were still employees who remembered the Blue Book era. These people were quickly and readily identified for me; these were the 'story-tellers', the custodians of the Blue Book folklore. Like most folklore, however, the story line was to take different twists and turns depending on which story-teller I was speaking to.

The Blue Book agreement was not, therefore, simply an artefact of the past. It existed within the minds of story-tellers and was transmitted by them to the new managers, to union representatives and to the workers. In this way, the Blue Book was to have a central effect on shaping the content and nature of Fawley's current industrial-relations strategy. The puzzle of unravelling the meaning and significance of the original Blue Book agreement was presented early in the research, when, in one of my first interviews with a shop steward, he hesitatingly mentioned that '... Flanders' study of the Blue Book was ok. But you have to remember that this was only his interpretation.' When asked what he meant by this, the steward replied that '... Flanders' interpretation was not always the same as management's and it certainly wasn't the same as ours.'

Over time, it became clear to me that productivity bargaining at Fawley was not always what it seemed. Case study findings revealed that there were in fact a number of myths associated with productivity bargaining at Fawley: (1) the myth of Fawley management's success in attaining the stated objectives of the productivity agreements, (2) the myth of Fawley management's success in transforming the internal work-force into one of 'full-effort and full pay', thereby isolating Esso Fawley workers from the broader labour market and, finally, (3) the myth of achieving union partnership in decision-making or 'joint control'.

For example, my reassessment of the Blue Book deal revealed quite a significant creep back to the old working practices of the pre-Blue Book period. Each successive productivity agreement underwent the same fate as the original Blue Book deal – a gradual creep back to old pre-Blue Book working practices. There was to be little adaptive learning on the part of Fawley management in the use of the productivity bargaining technique. In short, some twenty-one generations of productivity agreements failed quite dramatically to meet their stated objectives at Fawley Refinery.

Marxian scholars such as Cliff (1970) and Topham (1969), having feared that a 'full effort' strategy would transform British labour into exploited efficiency automatons, turned out to be totally mistaken. For

5

Marxian scholars, however, the creep back to old working practices and the defusing of management controls could be interpreted as a major triumph of labour over capital. Just as workers have been found to be able to 'run rings' around piecework payment systems so, too, are they able to 'run rings' around a strategy based on productivity bargaining (see Brown, 1973 on the case of piecework bargaining). While the case study results may seem to give some small comfort to those of the Marxian persuasion, to others hopeful of reform, like Flanders, the results are less positive. For such reformists, the picture would not be an attractive one; workers are still eking out a living on a 'half-time' wage while at the same time suffering the indignity and humiliation of being underemployed, working only 'half' a job. British efficiency and productivity, in comparison with other Western industrialized countries, continues its downward spiral.

It will be seen that Allan Flanders' own hope for Fawley, that productivity bargaining would lead to the incorporation of the union into the heart of the management decision-making process, was also dashed. With respect to the 'pluralist' myth of joint management–union control, the case study findings indicate that Fawley management, in the post-Blue Book period, came to pursue a decidedly 'anti-union' labour relations strategy. The use of productivity bargaining as a device for extending union participation ended up being turned on its head to aid and abet management in *eliminating* collective bargaining rights and introducing individual 'staff status' contracts.

The evaluation and analysis of Fawley management's productivity bargaining and wider industrial-relations strategy is conducted within the context of a *tripartite structure*, i.e. from within rational, political and symbolic interpretations. The value of looking at organizations and management interventions from different perspectives, metaphors or frames of reference has recently (Bolman and Deal, 1984; Morgan, 1986) been highlighted within organizational theory. Morgan has argued, for instance, that our theories and explanations of organizational life are based on metaphors that lead us to capture the nature of organizational life in different ways, each permitting powerful, distinctive but essentially partial kinds of insight. For Morgan, the logic of multiple metaphorical analysis is found in the idea that

> new metaphors may be used to create new ways of viewing
> organizations which overcome the weaknesses and blindspots
> of traditional metaphors, offering supplementary or even con-
> tradictory approaches to organizational analysis. (1980: 612)

Morgan (1986) identifies eight metaphors which have pervaded organizational theory: organization as machine; as organism; as brains; as culture; as political system; as psychic prison; as flux and transformation; and as instrument of domination.

Bolman and Deal (1984) have also endorsed this multiple analytical frame of analysis and provide a somewhat neater categorization of perspectives. They suggest that it is possible to identify four relatively coherent perspectives or 'frames' within organizational theory: the rational frame, the human resources frame, the political frame and the symbolic frame. For Bolman and Deal these 'frames' are windows on the world which filter out some things while highlighting others. Our interpretation of organizational reality changes as the frame or filter changes. Bolman and Deal have summarized their four frames as follows:

> *Rational systems theorists* emphasize organizational goals, role and technology. They look for ways to develop organizational structures that best fit organizational purpose and the demands of the environment.
>
> *Human resource theorists* emphasize the interdependence between people and organizations. They focus on ways to develop a better fit between people's needs, skills, and values and the formal roles and relationships required to accomplish collective goals and purposes.
>
> *Political theorists* see power, conflict, and the distribution of scarce resources as the central issues in organizations. They suggest that organizations are very like jungles and that managers need to understand and manage power, coalitions, bargaining and conflict.
>
> *Symbolic theorists* focus on problems of meaning in organizations. They are more likely to find serendipitous virtue in organizational misbehaviour and to focus on the limits of managers' abilities to create organizational cohesion through power or rational design. In this view, managers must rely on images, luck, and sometimes the supernatural to bring some semblance of order to organizations. (1984: 2–3)

This multiple perspective approach is still germinal and has not yet penetrated the industrial-relations discipline. The tripartite structure (rational, political and symbolic interpretations) employed in this research was adopted retrospectively and unfolded naturally in an attempt to answer vexed questions raised by the case study. No single perspective or frame was seen to be adequate in itself to resolve these questions. Each of the three perspectives provide different insights into Fawley's productivity bargaining and wider industrial-relations strategy.

At the rational level, an attempt is made to evaluate the effectiveness of the many generations of Fawley's productivity agreements. Here an attempt is made to assess the extent to which Fawley management was able to attain its stated objectives. A major research finding is that there is a discrepancy between the assumed effectiveness of the deals and the actual effectiveness of the agreements. The agreements are found to be far less effective than portrayed by scholars and the popular press. In order to answer the question why the agreements were not succeeding, a political frame of analysis is employed.

The failure of the agreements at the level of stated objectives leads us to ask why the agreements were still being perpetuated year after year. Why, in other words, did Fawley management persist in the use of productivity bargaining technique in spite of its obvious failure? It is argued that, at a hidden level of meaning, productivity bargaining had deep and important symbolic functions. At this deeper level, the significance of productivity bargaining is interpreted within its function as ritual, rhetoric and myth.

Research outline

This research investigates the evolution of Fawley Refinery's industrial-relations strategy from the striking of the Blue Book productivity agreement to 1985. Fawley's industrial-relations strategy is defined directly through the process of productivity bargaining.

Chapter 2 discusses the notion of strategy as it relates to industrial relations at a more general theoretical level. It suggests that there are three possible approaches to the notion of strategy for industrial relations: the rational approach, the political approach and the symbolic approach. Each of these operates from a different assumption about the model of man and image of organization. Examples from the literature relating to the rational, political and symbolic approaches are reviewed and discussed.

Chapter 3 discusses the notion of strategy for industrial relations within the specific British context. It argues that the productivity bargaining technique is closely linked to the strategic planning process. The productivity bargaining technique is defined and distinguished from traditional collective bargaining, from payment by results systems and from unilaterally imposed change. The history and evolution of the productivity bargaining technique is explored. Productivity bargaining is seen to have continued importance within British industrial relations to the present day. More than any other technique or strategy, productivity bargaining has come to define the very essence or heart of British industrial relations.

Chapter 4 reviews the three major control implications of productivity bargaining: (1) that productivity bargaining implies the movement from a 'low-wage and low-effort' strategy to a 'high-effort and high-pay' strategy (implicit in this strategy was a movement towards labour market 'internalization'), (2) that productivity bargaining implies a shift to a new pluralist strategy of 'joint control' and (3) that productivity bargaining implies an increasing bureaucratization or formalization of the employment relationship.

Chapter 5 sets up the background for the case study. It discusses the research methodology employed in the case study analysis; it reviews the business environment within the refining industry from 1960 to 1985 – both generally and within Esso; finally, it sets up the case study by reviewing the general organizational and industrial-relations structure at Fawley Refinery.

Chapters 6, 7, 8 and 9 are devoted to an evaluation of Fawley's productivity bargaining strategy from 1960 to 1985. Chapter 6 takes a second look at the Blue Book agreement and re-evaluates its effectiveness over a longer time frame than was covered by Flanders' analysis. Chapter 7 reviews the second generation productivity deals struck at Fawley from 1967 to 1971. Chapter 8 evaluates what could be termed Fawley's third generation of productivity deals, that is, those negotiated between 1972 and 1980. For the most part, this third generation of productivity deals was defined by the so-called open-ended or non-detailed productivity deals. Chapter 9 analyses those productivity agreements that were struck at Fawley in the early 1980s and provides some insights into how management attempted to use productivity bargaining as a means of coping with the recession. Despite twenty-five years of productivity bargaining, the case study data reveal quite significant failure of Fawley's productivity bargaining at the 'rational' level, that is, at the level of stated objectives. The case study data stand as a vivid testimony to the difficulties associated with the operation of a rationally based change strategy.

Chapter 10 examines two subsidiary industrial-relations 'strategies' at Fawley – both offshoots of the dominant productivity bargaining based strategy. The first of these relates to Fawley's 'staff status' initiative (which meant the long-term withdrawal of collective bargaining rights from the site) and the second to the increased use of contractor labour. Both of these 'strategies' can be seen as attempts to overcome the problems associated with the failure of productivity bargaining.

Chapter 11 reconsiders the three control implications of productivity bargaining as laid out in chapter 4. First, Fawley Refinery is seen to have failed to realize its 'full-pay and full-effort' strategy. It has only haltingly and unevenly moved in this direction. The intention of having a highly paid and highly skilled internal work-force never materialized. Ironically, however, Fawley chose to create a large pool of expensive contractor labour, partly in order to overcome the deficiencies of its twenty-five years of productivity bargaining. Secondly, the notion that productivity bargaining achieved the higher pluralist ideal of 'joint control' was seen to be a myth, with research revealing that the objective of 'joint control' was not as alive in the minds of management at Fawley as many believed. In fact, productivity bargaining was used to introduce 'staff status' contracts for various groups at Fawley – contracts which actually meant the relinquishing of collective bargaining rights at Fawley. Thirdly, the notion of increased management control through the formalization of the employment contract did not come about, since – where formalization did take place – it rarely worked to the management's advantage.

Chapter 12 reveals some of the problems associated with operating a rational 'productivity bargaining' based strategy for industrial relations at the levels of design, negotiation, implementation and day-to-day operation. In so doing, this chapter demonstrates the relevance of the political approach for understanding industrial-relations strategy.

Chapter 13 uncovers the hidden meanings of Fawley's productivity bargaining based strategy and demonstrates the relevance of the symbolic approach to industrial-relations strategy. It is proposed, for example, that the productivity bargaining process became an important symbolic activity for (1) reducing uncertainty and anxiety in the face of a turbulent business environment, (2) projecting impressions of efficiency and achievement to various target groups (partly as a rhetorical device with which to create or maintain managerial legitimacy) and (3) enhancing careers (as an important 'rite of passage').

Chapter 14 is a concluding chapter which discusses the notion of strategy for industrial relations at the theoretical level as well as at the practical level of Fawley Refinery.

2

The search for industrial-relations strategy

Introduction

The 'strategy' debate has established itself as a new vogue within industrial relations (see, for instance, Thurley and Wood, 1983). It has been claimed, in fact, that a 'strategic' approach '... for the analysis and explanation of managerial actions in industrial relations ... is clearly fruitful and seems superior to other approaches ...' (Thurley and Wood, 1983: 221). Similarly, the notion of industrial-relations strategy has recently become an important organizing concept within industrial sociology, specifically within the so-called 'labour process' school (ignited initially by Braverman, 1974). This debate has taken many forms and has been significant enough for some (e.g. Salaman, 1981) to claim the ascendance of a new organization theory.

This chapter seeks to examine the meaning and significance of strategy for industrial relations. It is argued that it is possible to define, not one, but three rather distinct approaches to industrial-relations strategy: the rational approach, the political approach and the symbolic approach. Research on industrial-relations strategy has, for the most part, been limited to the rational and the political perspectives; the symbolic perspective has not yet been developed within industrial relations.

Once it is understood that there are different models of man and images of organization which underlie the various approaches to industrial-relations strategy, it becomes clear that there can be no one definition of strategy for industrial relations but rather a number of definitions. For example, the rational approach to strategy stresses long-term planning and the adoption of various prescriptive formulae, while the political approach stresses the emergent nature of strategy, incorporating the notion of accommodation and conflict, and, finally, the symbolic approach views strategy not in terms of what is happening but rather through the underlying *meaning* of what is happening.

11

The rational approach

Most of industrial-relations research on strategy has assumed a rational model of man. By viewing organizations as rational entities, with rational goals, rational decisions and rational people, industrial-relations strategy has for the most part been accepted as fulfilling its rational purposes. The rational view assumes an element of consciousness to strategy, that is, it represents a desired approach to some future action. This assumption is based on the view that industrial-relations strategies, plans and policies function according to their formal blue-prints, that rules and procedures will be followed and that actual activities conform to the prescriptions of formal structure. For practitioners, the appeal of the idea of strategy is the belief that industrial questions are best solved by using a long-term rational approach (Thurley and Wood, 1983: 222).

According to the rational perspective, industrial-relations problems can be remedied or overcome by careful planning and forethought. From this perspective, industrial-relations strategy has been concerned both with goals (for example, productivity improvement) as well as with the means of achieving them (for example, through productivity bargaining). The focus of the rational approach is one of means–ends. In this context, the term rationality refers to the extent to which a series of actions is organized in such a way as to lead to predetermined goals with maximum efficiency (Scott, 1981: 57–8).

The rational approach assumes the existence of a dominant managerial élite which is charged with the responsibility of designing, implementing and day-to-day monitoring of the strategy. There is seen to exist, in other words, a monolithic management group which is conscious of its economic interests and which is suitably equipped and organized to realize them. The approach assumes that management or the dominant coalition is a homogeneous group or is organized around a relatively coherent and unambiguous set of aims.

Moreover, industrial-relations researchers whose work could be classified under the rational model make great play of the need for managers to have the proper educational training to allow them to deal with industrial-relations problems in a systematic, impartial and rational fashion. Education is seen to be critical in the sense that it provides the proper tools to analyse conditions, monitor the effects of actions and explain the rationality of the strategy in question. In this way, management's failure to conduct industrial relations at a strategic level is often attributed to a lack of proper education or training. The success of strategic management in industrial relations is often seen to depend on the ability to persuade (or educate) management itself that emphasis on strategic planning is essential.

Those who make pleas for a strategic approach within the context of the rational perspective tend not to treat as problematic the difficulties associated with the design, implementation or day-to-day operation of a particular strategy. The dominant managerial élite is seen to be capable of altering significantly the tone and nature of industrial relations, of maintaining stability where it exists and even of reducing conflict.

The rational approach to strategy can be found in a wide-ranging and diverse set of writings within industrial relations. It is evidenced perhaps most vividly within the so-called British industrial-relations 'reformist' movement of the 1960s. This movement, somewhat less homogeneous than some would impute, is associated primarily with the work of the Royal Commission on Trade Unions and Employers' Associations from 1965 to 1968 (also known as the Donovan Commission) and later with the work of the Commission of Industrial Relations which was set up in the 1970s upon the recommendation of the Donovan Commission.

The rational approach to strategy does not, however, begin and end with the reformists. There are other bodies of thought which depend upon a rational model of man and image of organization for their view of industrial-relations strategy. Interestingly, the rational model can also be seen to underpin much of the recent vogue literature on industrial-relations strategy (Thurley and Wood, 1983; Purcell and Sisson, 1983; Timperley, 1980) as well as recent work within radical sociology, most notably the labour-process tradition. It is useful to review briefly the rational perspectives of the reformist movement, of the more recent industrial-relations strategy debate and of radical sociology (strange bedfellows though they may be) to help our understanding of the rational approach to strategy in industrial relations.

The rational approach and the reformist movement

The reformist group believed that academics should play not only an active role in the diagnosis of the nation's industrial-relations problems, but also in the management of change itself. Indeed, this was to be reflected in the high level of participation by the 'Oxford' school in various reform bodies (H.A. Clegg was one of the Donovan Commission's members, Allan Flanders submitted written evidence to the Donovan Commission and was a member of the Commission of Industrial Relations, W.E.J. McCarthy was the Commission's research director). Academics were not to be embarrassed by social intervention, or for that matter by providing lessons for management. There was to be a certain positive quality to their work. These were the 'lone rangers', the 'hired guns' who were placed in charge of the reconstruction of British industrial relations. British industrial relations had a problem – and it needed to be solved.

An early call for the strategic management of industrial relations came from the reformist movement which began in the 1950s with the work of the so-called Oxford school of industrial relations. The picture painted by the reformist school of industrial relations in Britain after the Second World War is now a familiar one. By making *ad hoc* concessions to shop stewards and by submitting to worker pressure, British management was seen to have fostered a guerilla warfare over wages and working conditions (Flanders, 1975). During this period the problems of British management were to be found in

> ... unofficial strikes and earnings drift; in under-utilization of labour and resistance to change; in the growth of systematic overtime and the demoralization of incentive pay schemes; in inequitable and unstable factory pay structures; in a general decline in industrial discipline; in an undermining of external regulation by industry-wide and other agreements; and in a weakening of control by trade unions and employers' associations over their members. (Flanders, 1975: 196)

As a result, workplace industrial relations were seen to be characterized by a '... chaotic state of relations between managements and shop stewards ...' having been '... formed by drift rather than by design' (Flanders, 1975: 195).

The work of Allan Flanders, a reformist and one of the doyens of the Oxford school of industrial relations, is particularly illustrative of the rational approach to strategy in industrial relations. Inspired by his work and observations about productivity bargaining at Fawley Refinery, Flanders was to make an impassioned plea for strategic thinking in the management of industrial relations, for a need for '... line management to face up to the problems of labour policy, actively and consciously, rather than avoiding them as had been its habit' (1964: 100). Flanders argued that management ought to take the initiative in proposing changes in working practices to improve productivity and that it ought not simply to respond or wait for trade-union demands.

According to Flanders, management's inefficiency was seen to exist at the three levels of (1) training, (2) management structure and (3) ideology. First, managers were not considered to be well prepared for the social aspects of their job due to an '... almost complete ignorance of the social sciences ...' (Flanders, 1975: 171). Secondly, the separation of personnel management from management in general was seen to have inhibited managerial initiative; personnel management was rarely '. . . given a place in the formulation of policy or in forward planning because it was not thought necessary to define objectives and look ahead in industrial relations' (ibid.: 172). Thirdly, Flanders blamed the prevailing management ideology '. . . which rejected any division or sharing of authority within the firm' (ibid.: 172).

Flanders believed, further, that the '. . . responsibility for the reconstruction of workplace relations must fall primarily on the managements of individual companies. This is especially true of large companies' (1975: 208). According to Flanders, this was a lesson that British managers desperately needed to learn: '*Management learns to manage by being forced to accept the full responsibilities of management* . . . it is probably the greatest challenge confronting British management' (Flanders, 1975: 61). Management education was to figure prominently, therefore, in Flanders' formula for reform. Speaking of the Fawley 'Blue Book' productivity agreement, Flanders went so far as to suggest that, 'apart from its direct and immediate effect on labour relations, the Fawley Blue Book has also to be viewed as an exercise in management education' (1975: 63).

The Royal Commission on Trade Unions and Employers' Associations which was set up by the Labour government in the mid-1960s and is known as the Donovan Commission also saw the challenge of reform as primarily one of education. The problems of excessive informality, fragmentation and local bargaining were seen to be mainly a reflection of management itself. Faced with an increase in shop-steward power, British management was seen simply to be '. . . unprepared to cope constructively with this situation' (Flanders, *The Times*, 9 June 1968, 'The case for the package deal'). As Clegg, a member of the Donovan Commission, put it:

> The job to be done, therefore, was educational, beginning with the Donovan Report itself, and subsequently to be carried on by the new Commission (the Commission on Industrial Relations). When managers and trade unionists saw that current ideas were out of touch with reality, and had become a prop for outworn institutions, they would be ready to carry out the reforms that were needed. (1976: 454)

The Donovan Commission itself had faith in the rational process. For the members of this commission, their task was simply a matter of isolating those methods and techniques which were best suited to reforming industrial relations. The problems and difficulties confronted by British industry were seen to be

   . . . primarily due to the widespread ignorance about the most

sensible and effective methods of conducting industrial relations, and to the very considerable obstacles to the use of
sensible and effective methods contained in our present system.
(Donovan Commission, para. 204, CF. Shop Stewards and
Workshop Relations, para. 230)

The reformists were not content, therefore, merely to extol the virtues of
management education; they were also to offer a number of prescriptive
techniques which were to hold promise of the reconstruction of British
industrial relations. If only managers would become aware of, and begin
to apply, new sophisticated managerial techniques such as manpower
planning, job evaluation and productivity bargaining, then reform would
be achieved.

In the 1970s, the Commission on Industrial Relations (C.I.R.) was set
up on the recommendation of the earlier Donovan Commission. Like the
Donovan Commission, the Commission on Industrial Relations itself
came to place emphasis on consciousness and deliberateness on the part of
management in reforming industrial relations. The Commission on Industrial Relations was most explicit in making the call for more careful and
long-term industrial-relations planning on the part of all managers:

A company's industrial relations policy should form an integral
part of the total strategy with which it pursues its business
objectives. In this way it will not only define the company's
course of action with regard to particular industrial issues; it
will also reflect the interaction of industrial relations with policies in other areas, such as production, marketing or finance.
(Commission on Industrial Relations, 1973: 4)

The Commission on Industrial Relations believed that industrial-
relations policies could easily be neglected by senior management. The
message developed by the commission was simple. The development and
implementation of clear and well-defined industrial-relations policies and
plans would lead to a more orderly management of industrial relations. As
the commission put it: 'A total corporate strategy needs to include a policy
defining the company's industrial relations objectives and the principles
which should guide management in its every-day pursuit of them' (Commission on Industrial Relations, 1973: 5).

While it is difficult to distil from the many writings of the reformist
group any one particular message, the theme of planning figures centrally
in most of the writing. Flanders noted for instance:

The kind of reconstruction to which I have referred is in the
last resort an exercise in planning. It is planning by consent

applied not only to the use of manpower but to the whole social structure of the plant; the social counterpart to invest-ment planning. One cannot expect shop stewards to behave in an orderly fashion within a disordered framework. Consistency should be the *sine qua non* of management policy in labour relations, but consistency is impossible without planning and firms cannot be compelled to plan. (1975: 208)

This planning theme was perhaps most elegantly and well developed by McCarthy and Ellis (1973) who argued that the 'challenge from below' needed to be 'directed at managers in a more precise and predictable way'. They urged that collective bargaining should become increasingly future-oriented in character, so that a link could be established between collective bargaining of a 'predictive' kind and corporate planning. The central aim of this form of predictive bargaining was to '. . . change the emphasis of bargaining from recriminations over the past to planning for the future' (ibid.: 102). Major aspects of the 'wage–work' bargain were to be costed and attempts were to be made '. . . to assess their relative contribution to other known parts of the corporate plan' (ibid.: 104). The logic for a new 'predictive' bargaining was based on the belief that 'corporate plans cannot be changed overnight, and attempts to monitor and assess the impact of all aspects of the wage–work equation on other parts of the business take a considerable time' (ibid.: 109). It is important to stop and reflect on the sheer power of such pleas – especially as they have pre-dated by so many years current fashionable pleas for more strategy in industrial relations (for example, Thurley and Wood, 1983).

The reformist tradition, however disparate it may have been, was clearly a heroic tradition. No less than the future of the nation was at stake:

Progress depends on our ability as a nation to see our problems in the industrial relations field as they really are, which would then put us in a better position to solve them. If we fail in this, and we have not been very successful so far, one can only say that the future is very grim. (Flanders, 1972: 15)

It provided an analysis of the problems of British industrial relations and a prescription for reform based on a desire and deep will to change structures and systems. Much of the prescription was based on a plea or call for strategy in industrial relations. The work of the reformists was rooted in a deep desire to seize the industrial relations 'problems' of the day and put things right. The approach was not based on a piecemeal and *ad hoc* prescription for change, but rather on a wider strategy. It assumed an element of consciousness to strategy and put forward a desired approach to future action. It was predominantly based on a rational model of man and image of organization.

For the reformists, much of the blame for a 'chaotic' state of industrial relations could be placed squarely on the shoulders of management. What is interesting for our analysis of strategy in industrial relations is the extent to which the reformist tradition saw the 'chaotic state' of industrial relations as being remedied by rational analysis and problem-solving.

The rational approach to industrial-relations strategy has not, as I have suggested, been confined to the reformist tradition. It can be found in much of the industrial-relations literature. It underpins, for instance, much of the more recent strategy debate in industrial relations (e.g. Timperley, 1980; Thurley and Wood, 1983).

The rational approach and recent industrial-relations debates on strategy

It is curious, in itself, to note that the strategy debate has had something of a resurgence within industrial relations in the 1980s – so much so that it could be said that it has established itself as the current orthodoxy. Some two decades after the plea for more strategy in industrial relations was made by the reformists, the plea for strategic thinking in industrial relations is being made once again.

The reason for this new major call for more strategy in industrial relations is not, however, totally clear. One could argue that such a resurgence can be attributed to the 'challenge from without', to the crisis faced by capital in the recession. This would explain the attention that has been focussed (descriptively) on the ways in which capital has managed its way out of the recession and (prescriptively) on how capital ought to be managing its way out of the crisis. Alternatively, one could argue, however, that this resurgence of interest in the notion of industrial-relations strategy has had more to do with the failure of British management to take heed in the first place of the reformists' plea in the early 1960s. Or, it could be suggested that this resurgence has had more to do with the inherent problems relating to the application of a strategic approach to industrial relations. The recent interest in strategy, then, suggests a failure of management to live up to Flanders' hope that management would '... face up to the problems of labour policy, actively and continuously ...' (1964: 100).

Regardless of the reasons for this resurgence, much of this second wave or call for strategy in industrial relations assumes the same rational model of man and image of organization as the reformist tradition. For example,

The search for industrial-relations strategy

Thurley and Wood's definition of industrial-relations strategy itself attributes a decided rationality to management:

> Industrial relations strategies refer to long term policies which are developed by the management of an organization in order to preserve or change the procedures, practice or results of industrial relations activities over time. (1983: 198)

Timperley's definition also approaches the issue of strategy from the rational perspective:

> The elements of this (strategic) approach would be a concern with a longer time-horizon, a concern with a consistent coherent view of the future (not simply ad hoc recommendations) ... and, perhaps most importantly of all, a clear reinforcement of management's role in managing and decision-making. (1980: 40)

These definitions are 'means–ends' directed. They assume not only consciousness and deliberateness on the part of the management, but also that management is capable of identifying long-term desirable goals and of implementing and sustaining them. The language and tone of this second strategy wave is, in fact, reminiscent of the first reformist wave. What is even stranger is that the notion of industrial-relations strategy is sometimes being passed off as if it were being developed for the first time. Timperley notes, for instance, that a strategic approach '. . . has certainly not been characteristic of industrial relations either theoretically or practically' (1980: 40). Moreover, Thurley and Wood claim:

> Reform of industrial relations does require a new strategic approach from management, but this inevitably goes far beyond industrial relations itself. There has to be a corporate managerial capacity and will to formulate strategies and carry them through. Only major organizational changes in structure, recruitment and development could provide such a capacity and only major political changes at least within the large company sector could provide the will for this. (1983: 224)

Thurley and Wood go on, in fact, to place the same kind of stress on the role of education as did the earlier reformists.

> All the major problems – wage inflation, job inflexibility and over-manning, lack of job security and consequent defensive attitudes, inter-union conflict at the steward level, inadequate reward systems and career routes, lack of internal qualification

systems – are rooted in organization of production and the processes of recruitment to management, its lack of training, the conflict between functional and line staff and the way that top management takes decisions. (1983: 224)

The major industrial-relations problems to which they refer, for example job inflexibility, and the solution which is offered (a new strategic approach), are both so strangely reminiscent of the earlier reformist movement that it makes one wonder *whatever happened to the 'old' strategic approach*. It makes one wonder, in fact, about the real meaning that strategy has held for British industrial relations over the years.

It should be noted, however, that the more recent strategy debate has not been a simple parody of the reformist position. Purcell (1981), for instance, appears to have taken the debate in a new direction by making a call for paying greater attention to the complex relationship between corporate headquarters, divisions and plants in relation to strategy formulation and application.

The rational approach and the radical school

The rational view of industrial-relations strategy is not restricted to industrial relations. Such a view is also to be found within industrial sociology and, more specifically, within the so-called labour process school and amongst radical critics of key industrial-relations reforms of the 1960s. The notion of strategy has come to be the organizing concept within the so-called labour process debate. Like the prolonged quest for the Holy Grail, much of this debate has been located around a feverish attempt at defining or labelling a dominant strategy for labour relations. This has resulted in the production of a series of well-packaged and neat theories.

There is a seemingly endless string of such theories. For example, Braverman (1974) has asserted the primacy of management strategy through scientific management, while Friedman (1977) argues for the need to supplement scientific management with human relations and neo-human relations interventions. R. Edwards (1979) indicates the need to include the notion of bureaucratic control through the use, amongst other things, of internal labour markets, while still others have been content to discover hybrids of already uncovered strategies (for example, Littler's (1982) discovery of Bedauxism as a mutation of scientific management).

While the labour process school's analysis of management strategy has focussed on exposing management's exploitative strategies rather than on providing management prescription, it does, nevertheless, share with the

20

two traditions discussed above a fundamentally rational model of man and image of organization. It assumes a deliberateness and consciousness on the part of the management; indeed, much of the criticism aimed at the current labour process school has been directed at this assumption. The labour process school is considered to have given management too much credit regarding its effectiveness by viewing the capitalist class as '. . . a class "for itself", fully conscious of its economic interests and organized and conspiring to realize them' (Wood, 1982: 14). The assumption that much of the school has operated from, therefore, is that '. . . management . . . (is) . . . omniscient, conspiratorial and able, at least for a certain period of time, to get its own way – that is, to solve successfully its problem of control' (Wood, 1982: 16).

At the same time it has been suggested that much of the labour process school (with the possible exception of Friedman, 1977) has neglected, or not treated seriously enough, the dimensions of class struggle and consciousness. Braverman's (1974) work has been particularly prone to such attack, and it has been widely suggested that he underestimates the extent to which workers are able to reshape the content of management strategies, either by blocking them totally or by reshaping them at the margins, but somehow always deflecting management intention to some extent. This critique has itself resulted in a revisionist labour process position whereby political factors have been directly incorporated into the analysis (see Knights and Willmott, 1986).

What is perhaps most strange about the current labour process tradition is that it ignores an earlier and quite rich tradition of work which has amply demonstrated management inability to operate an effective control strategy. Brown's work on piecework payment systems and on 'custom and practice' is, for instance, a testimony to '. . . powerful workforces interacting with uncoordinated managements' (1972: 61). For Brown, 'custom and practice' is often a '. . . product of management error and worker power' (1972: 61). Much of the wage payment literature (Gowler, 1969; Lupton and Gowler, 1972) is yet another affirmation of the instability of management controls.

The rush by the labour process school to label the dominant all-powerful management strategy has led such theorists into a panacea quest. The assumption pervading such writings is that if one strategy has not magically succeeded in subordinating labour to capital once and for all, then there would simply be another, more sophisticated strategy around the corner to do the job. Many writers in the labour process school have tended, in fact, to see labour-relations strategies as following unproblematically from the stated objectives of a firm. As Batstone et al. note, according to the labour process school, management is

... often viewed in a crudely functionalist way (cf. Salaman, 1982) as a kind of transmission belt converting the imperatives of the 'law of value' into strategies for the exploitation of labour, according to the type of firm or the historical stage of capitalist development. (1984: 2)

The labour process school's tendency to impute management rationality where it does not always exist, leads us to consider those writers who neither assume high levels of management organization nor the unproblematic design of management strategies. The following section looks at industrial-relations strategy as it is viewed, not by those writers who believe in a rational model of man but by those embracing what could be called a political model of man or image of organization.

The political approach

Much of the substance of the political approach to industrial-relations strategy has been born out of a critique of the rational approach. Within the political approach, stress is placed on the complex set of interactions that take place between various actors in the organization over the design, implementation and day-to-day operation of any one particular strategy. The political approach has sought to '... rescue research on strategic choice and change from its habitual focus on rational analytical schemas of intentional process and outcome ...' (Pettigrew, 1985: 19). In doing so, the approach interprets organizations as political entities, with political goals, political decisions and political people. As a result, industrial-relations strategies are seen as products of complex political processes.

The political approach rejects the rational model of problem-solving which, as we have seen, emphasizes both the content of a particular strategy and the outcome that is being sought. Instead, the political approach focusses on how outcomes are achieved and on how various impediments affect such outcomes. From the political perspective, strategies are not the product of a conscious, deliberate and well thought-out process. According to the political model, strategies have no prior logic. Rather, strategies are emergent and evolve over time (Mintzberg, 1978). They evolve as a result of a complex process of negotiation, compromise and accommodation amongst a number of competing groups within the organization. Accordingly, there can be no one single grand rational strategy which transforms chaos into order or inefficiency into efficiency. This is partly because rationality is always seen to be relative to the specific interests of the actors involved. According to the political approach, the multiplicity of interests and cognitive frameworks of the various actors in the system precludes any possibility of any one grand strategy.

While the rational approach assumes the existence of a dominant managerial élite, the political approach highlights the fragmented and disparate nature of the management group. The political approach sees the firm as a 'dispersed social agency' in which the dominant group will always be composed of competing groups with competing objectives. The firm, in other words, is characterized as '... an entity through which a number of often competing and ambiguous practices of calculation and assessment pass' (Thompson, 1982: 233). The design of any one strategy, therefore, while optimizing the objectives or goals of one group, may result in the sub-optimization of the goals of another group. As Cressey et al. point out, there are

> ... dangers of attributing the idea of managerial strategy to management as a collectivity ... The internal cohesion of management is itself a matter for investigation, as are the conditions in which that cohesion breaks down. The cohesion may itself be quite precarious and given the reality of managerial politics, may shift from issue to issue, with different alliances and coalitions. (1985: 141)

Rationality is not, however, completely vacuumed out of the political approach; there remains what might be called a contingency and coalition-based rationality. While it is not accepted that there is one overriding rational logic to which the organization is ultimately committed, there is instead a multiplicity of rational motives each of which is group or coalition based and each of which is seen to carry its own internal logic. It is through these logics and their interaction over time, that strategies are seen to emerge. To see strategy within these terms requires a sensitivity to the micro-politics of organizational life. Moreover, this approach requires an analysis of strategy over a time frame by *post factum* examination.

The political approach to strategy has perhaps been best articulated outside of the industrial-relations discipline and most notably within organizational theory (March and Simon, 1958; Cyert and March, 1963; Pfeffer and Salancik, 1974; Tushman, 1977; Mintzberg, 1978; Pettigrew, 1972, 1973, 1977, 1985). Pettigrew's (1985) study of organizational change in I.C.I. is exemplary of this approach and of the difficulties of making fundamental change in organizations. He stresses the theme of continuity in change situations and conjures up the image of the 'waxing and waning' of particular strategies over time (1985: 447). According to Pettigrew, the value of such an approach is that it '... directs attention towards the factors which facilitate and hinder change and to the reasons why political energy is often released within the firm at even the prospect, never mind the reality, of change' (1985: 42). He sees organizations as consisting of coalitions of decision-makers characterized by conflict and tension that exists between such coalitions. Bargaining and coalition formation are seen to play a central part in organizational life.

Another study revealing the political nature of strategy is Blackler's and Brown's (1980) entertaining account of Shell's attempt at introducing a new philosophy of management to its refineries. Blackler and Brown reject Hill's (1976) earlier autobiographical account of Shell's attempt to introduce a new philosophy of management and conclude that the exercise failed, 'rather spectacularly', to introduce a new philosophy of management to Shell.

Formal strategies, even though they may be produced by management, may have little or no real meaning. Such formal strategies are seen to take on new meanings once they are translated into action. What might once have been seen to be a coherent and well thought-out plan becomes transformed into a pale shadow of itself when it enters and passes through the real world of complex competition (conducted simultaneously at overt and covert levels) between various groups and coalitions. Management intentions are not seen, therefore, to be transformed easily and unproblematically into reality. The best of management plans may fade away, either through managerial lethargy, through internal management squabbling and bickering or by action directed against such plans by subordinate groups.

The political approach to strategy has not, however, remained strictly within the boundaries of organizational theory, but has found its way into industrial-relations literature. Much of the early work on 'custom and practice' (e.g. Brown, 1972, 1973) can, of course, be seen as part of this tradition. Armstrong's and Goodman's (1979) and Brewster's and Richbell's (1983) more recent research on managerial and supervisory custom and practice is also representative of the political approach. Their work provides interesting examples of micro-politics in action within management groups themselves. Batstone et al.'s (1984) study of the British post office is a further illustration of such an approach. The authors trace in detail the evolution of the post office from a public service organization to a commercial organization in response to political pressures. The study reveals the ambiguities of management strategies in state enterprises, and the effects of those ambiguities on labour relations. The study is a fine example of '. . . intra-management bargaining and micro-political struggles that make the outcome of the process of change uncertain and at the very least negotiable' (1984: 286). Labour-relations strategy at the post office was resultingly seen to be '. . . uncertain, provisional and complex'.

The search for industrial-relations strategy

Apart from highlighting micro-politics within the management group, the political approach to strategy also tries to stress the role of subordinate groups in both the determination and the distortion of management strategy. With respect to the determination of management strategy, Littler (1982) has shown, for instance, that working-class consciousness and resistance constituted a major ground for alternative strategies of work design. In this way, management strategies are seen as a *joint* product of capital and labour. In Littler's words:

> Actual shopfloor behaviour and relationships must be seen then not as consequences of the unilateral imposition by management on a passive workforce of specifications and prescriptions, but a two-way exchange in which an accommodation concerning the meaning and relevance of such prescriptions is achieved . . . . (1982: 42)

Worker resistance, itself, can potentially take many complex forms, both organized and unorganized. It is clearly important, for instance, to understand more fully the role of organized labour in shaping or reshaping the content of any one management strategy. Managements operating within a unionized context are not free operators in making change, but rather, are forced to work through a system of joint regulation. As Batstone notes:

> If there is union opposition, then broader changes will be difficult, and change will in any event be constrained by the system of joint regulation. In short, the difficulties of transforming the broader pattern of regulation may serve to discourage management from grand strategies of change . . . (forthcoming: 44)

Management strategies can also be repelled at informal levels – in the form of indirect subversion. Much of 'negotiated order' theory (Strauss et al. 1963; Bucher and Stelling, 1969; Benson, 1977; Day and Day, 1977) reveals how organizational arrangements are being continuously negotiated and adapted through the day-to-day encounters of participants. Day and Day (1977: 130), for instance, discuss the way in which formal structures are replaced by informal structures whereby the involved parties develop tacit agreements that enable them to carry out their work. Rules are often cited selectively and stretched or 'fudged' by persons or groups pursuing their own vested interests. The fudging of rules may even take place with the tacit approval of the management group. In this instance, management enters the subversion process either because controls are too tight and conflict with production demands (Bensman and

Gerver, 1963) or because controls need to be relaxed in order to secure cooperation and harmony on the shop floor (Gouldner, 1954).

It could be argued, in fact, that workers have often been able to use management strategies to their own ends. Crozier (1964), for instance, has amply demonstrated how rules can be turned back on their makers, while more recently Batstone et al. (1984) have shown how bureaucratization and the fuller specification of rules (often seen as an important management control device) have provided the basis for worker control of both an individual and collective nature. As Batstone notes:

> Workers may achieve a considerable influence and control over management through involvement in the creation and application of rules – they may mobilize institutional agreements in their favour. Rules also provide a gauge for the actions of management, as well as providing a form of worker defence against changes in management demands. Furthermore, they often provide a fruitful area of continual negotiation – rules may be mutually inconsistent, arguments can develop concerning priority of application and, for example, whether the spirit or the letter of rules should be followed ... (Batstone, forthcoming: 31)

The political approach has, no doubt, provided important qualifications for the use of the notion of strategy in industrial relations. It has put to question the idea of a monolithic management structure capable of designing and implementing optimal management strategies. Instead, the organization is redefined in terms of a multiplicity of competing interest groups and coalitions. The political perspective stresses the potential of various groups to reshape the content of management strategies. It places stress not only on the power of labour to circumvent the best of management intentions, but also highlights tensions and conflict within the management group itself.

The political perspective is not presented as a higher order approach, but simply as another perspective or view of strategy. It could, in fact, be suggested by some that the approach has gone too far in its political definition of organizational life, depicting a model of man or image of organization that is either totally irrational, incompetent or a mere victim of circumstance. The net negative organizational effects of situational and political action on the part of various actors may be somewhat exaggerated. There is a temptation to interpret 'fiddling' at the margins as more significant than it might actually be. Moreover, it could be argued that the approach has underestimated the extent to which homogeneity of interests exist. The very definition of organization implies a certain degree of collaboration and community.

The symbolic approach

The symbolic approach represents yet another perspective on strategy, but has not yet been developed in relation to the notion of strategy within industrial relations. Borrowed from social anthropology, the symbolic approach to organizational life is still in its germinal state and can be found only amongst a small number of writers working in allied fields such as organizational theory (see, for instance, Pondy et al., 1983).

The symbolic approach goes one step further than the political perspective in removing rationality from strategic decision-making. Exponents of the symbolic approach reject the idea that organizational life can be represented in terms of deterministic relationships, favouring the view that organizational life is fashioned by members in a way that is meaningful to them. This approach stresses that organizational phenomena should be researched in a way that reveals their inner and hidden nature. From a symbolic perspective, organizational activities are understood not so much by what they do as by what they represent. It is through the medium of symbolic processes that individuals engage and give meaning to their world. Symbolism is concerned with the way in which individuals create and sustain significant patterns of meaningful action, rather than merely the way in which people act. As a term of reference, a symbol has been defined as

> ... a sign which denotes something much greater than itself, and which calls for the association of certain conscious or unconscious ideas, in order for it to be endowed with its full meaning and significance. (Morgan et al., 1983: 4–5)

From the symbolic perspective, organizational structures, activities and initiatives are interpreted in terms of secular myths, rituals and ceremonies. The symbolic approach seeks to explore the function that myths, rituals and ceremonies play in day-to-day organizational life. For example, it has been argued that rituals and ceremonies serve '... to socialize, to stabilize, to reduce anxieties and ambiguities, and to convey messages to external constituencies' (Bolman and Deal, 1984: 159). Furthermore, myths can serve to provide an organizational smoke-screen behind which problems within organizational systems may be hidden.

A symbolic frame suggests that organizational activities and initiatives may have meaning and significance above and beyond the purely rational functions normally attributed to such phenomena. In the symbolic frame,

27

the real meaning of an element lies not with its overt stated goals, objectives and functions, but rather with the 'messages' and 'impressions' that these convey. As Morgan et al. point out:

> It is not sufficient for activities to be performed, so that given ends are fulfilled; it is the nature of the way in which they are performed that is sometimes all important, for the manner of performance reinforces or contravenes a whole range of symbolic meaning associated with the event in question. (1983: 20)

Within the symbolic perspective, what appears to be the case often is not the case. For instance, while, at a rational level, certain management initiatives appear to be directed at the attainment of some definite objective, these management initiatives may, at the symbolic level, have an entirely different meaning. The significance of a formal planned change programme, for example, may be found not so much in the extent to which change is actually achieved, but rather in the message that is being transmitted or beamed to other actors that 'something is being done' or that 'management is on top of the situation'. Bolman and Deal note, for example, that the very act of planning '. . . has become a ceremony that an organization must conduct periodically to maintain its legitimacy' (1984: 177).

Whether or not a particular activity or initiative actually produces results vis-à-vis its stated objectives may not be important in itself. Within the symbolic frame, it is the message or signal which is conveyed to key actors in (or outside of) the organization which is important. Therefore, while certain management initiatives may be failing desperately at their rational or stated objectives level, these initiatives may still be providing a latent function or purpose. As Bolman and Deal note:

> Even if processes do not produce results, they still are important. They serve as rituals and ceremonies that provide settings for drama, opportunities for self-expression, forums for airing grievances, and arenas for negotiating new understandings and meanings. (1984: 175)

Much of the hidden meaning of various management initiatives may have less to do with rational goals, such as productivity improvement, than with establishing the legitimacy of the management groups involved in such programmes.

The notion of strategy is itself rich in symbolism. The very proclamation that one is engaged in a strategic activity evokes images of being in control, or 'at the helm'. The simple act of devising or producing a strategy stands as a declaration to others that it is indeed possible to tame or resolve seemingly unresolvable problems. In this way, rituals and ceremonies are used, according to Bolman and Deal, '. . . to create order, clarity, and predictability, particularly in dealing with problems that are too complex, mysterious, or random to be controlled in any other way' (1984: 158). Thus, from a symbolic approach, grand management strategies may be nothing more than coping devices for dealing with seemingly unmanageable problems. Their meaning is found not at the level of stated objectives, but rather in the way in which these strategies are used by management when dealing with uncertainty and confusion. A symbolic frame of reference implies an interpretive research method. The hidden and often obscure nature of organizational happenings means that the researcher can only really provide one interpretation of a situation amongst a number of possible interpretations.

Conclusions

This chapter has reviewed three approaches to the notion of strategy for industrial relations: the rational, the political and the symbolic. Each of these approaches is based upon different ideas and assumptions about the underlying model of man or image of organization. The following research investigates the evolution of a 25-year productivity bargaining based strategy at Esso's Fawley Refinery, using the substance and analytical power of each of these three approaches to strategy.

The fact that the industrial relations terrain is filled with 'problems and issues' which appear to be 'complex, mysterious and random' might suggest that industrial relations are ripe for symbolic analysis. The elusive 'problem' of labour productivity, for example, seems to fit neatly within these terms. As I have suggested, the symbolic approach is only in its germinal stage; its analytical power has yet to be tested within industrial relations. It is presented here, alongside the rational and political approaches, as a further way of understanding the meaning of industrial-relations strategy.

3

The nature and development of productivity bargaining in Britain

Introduction

This chapter argues that the meaning of strategy for industrial relations – within the specific British context – is inextricably bound to the productivity bargaining process. In the 1960s and for many years subsequently, productivity bargaining was presented as a technique which held the answer to a previously unanswerable and elusive productivity problem.

Productivity bargaining took on more importance, however, than a mere technique; it was also to become a rich and powerful symbol of the reassertion of management control. Productivity bargaining captured the imagination of both academics and practitioners alike, who came, in fact, to associate productivity bargaining with the birth of strategy in British industrial relations. The advent of productivity bargaining gave substance to the notion of a strategy for industrial relations; it became an organizing construct around which all that was bad and potentially good for industrial relations could be put to debate.

This chapter seeks, first, to develop the importance of productivity bargaining for the notion of strategy in British industrial relations. Productivity bargaining is seen as an attempt within British industrial relations to make the break from an *ad hoc* to a more systematic management of industrial relations. Secondly, this chapter defines productivity bargaining, contrasting the particular features of the technique against those of traditional collective bargaining, payment-by-results systems and unilaterally imposed change.

Thirdly, this chapter traces the early beginnings of productivity bargaining and the expansion of the technique throughout Britain. It is demonstrated that productivity bargaining is not merely an artefact of the 1960s, but rather, that it has remained engrained within the life of British organizations. There has, in other words, been a continuing theme within British industrial relations around the pay, productivity and working practices nexus (White, 1981). The power of productivity bargaining as a symbol for reform and structural change is evidenced by the extent to which British managers have time and time again turned back to the productivity bargaining process in moments of crisis. Indeed, British management has shown an unshakeable faith in productivity bargaining. However good or bad the technique may be, productivity bargaining has, in many ways, come to define the very essence and heart of British industrial relations.

It has been commonplace (McKersie and Hunter, 1973) to identify two distinct phases of productivity bargaining, one from 1960 to 1966 and the other from 1967 to 1970. Curiously, the industrial-relations literature has ignored productivity bargaining in the post-1970 period. This chapter attempts to fill this gap in history, not only by demonstrating that productivity bargaining never disappears, but also by identifying two further surges of activity, from 1977 to 1979 and from 1981 to 1985.

Productivity bargaining and the growth of the managerial initiative in Britain

The role of British management during the inter-war period can perhaps best be described in terms of the idea of craft control and the abrogation of management to manage. During this period, British management was considered to be dependent not on its own skills, but rather on the skills of foremen and the long-standing crafts (Batstone, 1986). This historical legacy has meant that more 'pro-active' managerial initiatives like scientific management have had only a marginal impact in Britain (Littler, 1982, was only able to discover some 245 firms which claimed to use a hybrid of scientific management – Bedauxism). The post-World War II period and subsequent years of full employment only served further to entrench craft control in Britain. By the end of the 1950s management practice came to be defined, in fact, for the most part by *'ad-hocery'* (Marsh, 1981: 34).

Flanders himself was highly critical of British management in the post-World War II period. He asserted that top management in Britain 'preferred to have as little as possible to do with labour relations'; labour relations was 'looked upon ... as a nuisance, a disturbance diverting their energies away from what they regard as the more important aspects of their work' (1964: 251). Flanders argued that the problems of British trade unions had a 'common cause', that of reliance upon employers' associations and national negotiations to determine the main terms of employment and to provide procedures for disputes. For Flanders, this meant that

> ... plant bargaining has developed, not as a deliberate policy, but haphazardly as a result of the pressures of the moment. It has been forced upon employers and unions, at first largely against their will by the logic of the prevailing industrial relations situation. (1967: 30)

'Frissons of doubt' about the universal wisdom of such a negative approach to industrial relations began to surface in the late 1950s; partly as a result of the work of the British Productivity Council, which drew examples of different approaches from British and American firms (Marsh, 1981: 34). As Britain turned into the 1960s these 'frissons of doubt' were, however, to be transformed into firmly held convictions about the need to seize the initiative in the management of industrial relations.

The striking of the Blue Book productivity agreement in 1960 at the Esso Fawley Refinery was to symbolize the first 'shot' by management in the attempt to seize this initiative. This single shot was to send shock waves throughout British industry and was to open a lengthy debate, not only about the problems of British industrial relations but also about ways and methods of resolving these problems. The Esso experiment addressed industrial-relations problems that were endemic to British industry, notably low labour productivity and persistently high levels of overtime work. The popular press itself actively picked on this debate. The most influential of these journalistic accounts of Britain's productivity problem was undoubtedly William Allen's famous newspaper article in 1964, entitled 'Is Britain a half-time country, getting half-pay for half-work under half-hearted management?' (*The Sunday Times*, 1 March 1964). Allen, the architect of the Blue Book agreement, depicted British industry as being characterized by over-manning and high levels of systematic overtime. Britain was, according to Allen, caught in a half-effort and half-pay syndrome. In a later article entitled 'Britain in blinkers', Allen was to indict British management further: '... the attitude is now apparent to all, and the concern of everyone: viz., the unwillingness of management (with a few notable exceptions during the last 5 years) ... to attempt to solve the problem of labour inefficiency' (*The Sunday Times*, 12 June 1966).

At the same time that Allen and others were exposing the problems of British efficiency, Flanders' account of the Blue Book agreement at Fawley Refinery surfaced; this account pointed out the problems of one particular firm and explained how management had made an attempt to resolve these problems. Flanders' account of the Fawley experiment and his coining of the term 'productivity bargaining' was to bring substance to the productivity debate. It is hard to overestimate the impact of Allan

Flanders' contribution to the diffusion of the productivity bargaining technique within Britain. As McKersie and Hunter have noted, Flanders' book on Fawley's Blue Book productivity agreement '... received a great deal of publicity and was quickly followed up by a number of journalistic impressions and assessments ... (and) ... it is difficult to imagine that without the work of Flanders the concept of productivity bargaining would have been so well established in so short a time' (1973: 50).

Fawley's experiment with productivity bargaining stood as a symbol of what could be done; while exhortations had been made in the past to improve productivity, little action had been taken. The Fawley experiment provided British management with an apparently concrete and tangible method for improving productivity. This method was to be hailed as the embodiment of forward thinking and progressive industrial-relations management. It was to be held up almost instantly as the greatest promise for reform:

> Following the Donovan Commission's analysis, with the argument taken somewhat further by Alan Fox and myself, one might say, without exaggeration, that comprehensive productivity agreements are a principal means for creating a new social order in industry. The old social order, founded mainly on a structure of national agreements, has, as we know, crumbled because it could not cope with the range and types of conflict surging up with increased workers' power and rising levels of expectation on the shop floor. (Flanders, 1972: 14)

For Flanders, the reason for favouring productivity bargaining was clear: 'The most telling argument in favour of productivity bargaining is the lack of a practical alternative' (Flanders, 1964: 245). As a technique, productivity bargaining promised to rationalize British industrial relations. The Donovan Commission report itself stressed the value of productivity bargaining and its underlying philosophy of linking pay to productivity:

> A genuine productivity agreement offers solutions to many of the typical problems of industrial relations. It raises standards of supervision and of managerial planning and control. It closes the gap between rates of pay and actual earnings. It permits negotiation on performance. It enables demarcation difficulties to be eliminated or reduced. It concentrates decisions at the level of the company or factory. It formalizes and regulates the position of the shop steward. (Donovan Commission, 1968: 84)

Furthermore, productivity bargaining was directly incorporated into various incomes policies by permitting pay increases above the 'norm', provided that such increases were associated with an improvement in productivity. The technique was also endorsed by the National Board for Prices and Incomes (see Reports No. 23, 1966 and No. 36, 1967).

There was, in fact, a direct equivalence to be drawn between productivity bargaining and strategic planning. Productivity bargaining was to be directly contrasted to the *ad hoc* management of industrial relations:

> Previous attempts to secure increases in productivity, through incentive schemes like piece-work, or simply by the more efficient use of existing resources of manpower, had mainly taken place on an *ad hoc* basis. Productivity bargaining systematically located such attempts within the broad context of the wage–work bargain. (Nightingale, 1980: 320)

Many managers, politicians and academics alike, came to associate productivity bargaining with

> ... the abandonment by management of a typically defensive posture in favour of a greater initiative in labour and the utilization of labour: greater attention to comprehensive planning, again especially with regard to the workforce and its development ... (McKersie and Hunter, 1973: 5)

For McKersie and Hunter, by far the most important impact of productivity bargaining upon managerial style was the emergence of '... planning as a key function. Planning can be seen both as a necessary prerequisite for productivity bargaining and as an important result of the exercise itself' (1973: 322). The association of productivity bargaining with strategy in industrial relations was made forcefully by Daniel:

> It focusses the attention of management, particularly line management, on the use of manpower and human resources. It induces cost consciousness by providing new indices of performance and by introducing new methods of measuring work, productivity and performance. It gives management an awareness of techniques of measuring work; job evaluation, work study and operations research. It recognizes and emphasizes managerial responsibility for industrial relations and brings a far wider range of managers into the process. Instead of at worst accepting methods of working and industrial relations as an immutable constraint, or at best the responsibility of a specialist industrials relations department, they have for the

first time been made to recognize the industrial implications of what were formerly regarded as purely technical or financial issues. In doing so it has forced line managers to accept the obvious tenet that the use of human resources is a prime management responsibility at all levels. (1970a: 27)

The pioneers of productivity bargaining at Fawley were also to stress the link between productivity bargaining and strategy:

> Productivity bargaining starts from the assessment of an oper-
> ating problem and the statement of objectives based on careful
> management study. It is more susceptible to systematic treat-
> ment. It can only come through management initiative and
> study and must be a success in the eyes of both the Company
> and unions. (Evidence to the Royal Commission on Trade
> Unions and Employers' Associations, May 1966: 2)

Flanders himself came to define productivity bargaining directly within these terms – as first and foremost a *strategic* process. He even suggested that, if it was not comprehensive and did not have a long-term focus, then it was not productivity bargaining. There was, therefore, a deep and rich association between productivity bargaining and the notion of strategy itself.

Marxian scholars were also quick to make an association between productivity bargaining and strategy. The Marxian school took pains to emphasize that '... far from being an isolated "gimmick", it (productivity bargaining) was part of a total attack on the living standards and organization of rank and file workers' (Nightingale, 1976: 49). Topham came to refer to productivity bargaining directly in terms of a '... grand management strategy' (1969: 86). Cliff describes this 'total attack' in the following lyrical terms:

> ... productivity bargaining is not an accident but part of a
> determined offensive by the employing class which has as its
> final aim the shifting of the balance of forces in industry signifi-
> cantly in its favour. The attack is a total one – in other words it
> seeks to bring all the weapons into the field against the worker.
> (1970: 11)

Cliff suggests, moreover, that '... at the end of the process they (management) will have a far better understanding of how their own factory really operates – of unofficial working practices and of workers' *ad hoc* methods of undermining the management authority' (1970: 23). Productivity bargaining, from the Marxian view, was decidedly conspiratorial. It was to evoke images of a well-coordinated assault by the state and capital on labour.

The definition of productivity bargaining

Over the twenty-five years of its development, productivity bargaining has assumed a variety of forms. Each of these variants, however, emphasizes the two key notions of change and exchange. Workers agree to make a number of changes in working practices (which are to lead, hopefully, to more productive working) in exchange for higher levels of pay or other benefits. A large number of definitions of productivity bargaining have been produced over the years (see Stettner, 1969: 2–3 who lists seven of these). For the purposes of this research Fox's broadly based definition of productivity bargaining will be used:

> ... a method by which substantial wage increases and/or other improvements in the terms of employment are financed not through higher costs or prices, but by agreed changes in the work system which result in labour being used more effectively. (1966: 447)

This is a relatively broad definition of productivity bargaining which encompasses the four different types of productivity bargaining that will be described in this chapter. First, however, this chapter demonstrates how productivity bargaining differs from traditional collective bargaining, payment-by-results systems and unilaterally imposed change.

Productivity bargaining: a sub-type of collective bargaining

Productivity bargaining differs from other forms of collective bargaining in that it actively seeks to change working practices, while more traditional collective bargaining '... involves management and employee representatives in negotiating the norms which regulate the contract of employment, without reference to the norms which regulate production methods and the utilization of capital and labour' (Fox, 1971: 173). As Towers notes, productivity bargaining is

> ... clearly in a different category to traditional collective bargaining where improved benefits are sought by trade union negotiators as a matter of right, without any strings attached, with the actual size and distribution of these benefits being determined by the use of external criteria (e.g. the cost of living, comparability with similar occupations elsewhere, and profit levels) and negotiation variables which have generally

little to do with the more efficient utilization of resources. (1972: 25)

Daniel has seen the distinction between collective bargaining and productivity bargaining in terms of the difference between the making of rules versus the changing of rules:

> At its simplest then productivity bargaining can be seen as an aspect of wage–work bargaining ... More properly, in the sense that collective bargaining can be seen to be essentially a rule-making process, productivity bargaining is a rule-changing process in which the rules governing remuneration are re-negotiated in relation to the rules governing working practices. (1970a: 2)

The distinction between other forms of collective bargaining and productivity bargaining has become less sharp over the years, as it has become common practice to include productivity provisions in collective agreements as a matter of course. Productivity provisions are often, for instance, integrated into collective agreements in difficult negotiations as last minute 'deal clinchers'. In this way, Brown has argued that negotiated changes in working practices had become so common that '... to some extent ... we are all productivity bargainers now' (1974: 421).

Productivity bargaining in contrast to payment by results

Productivity bargaining can also usefully be contrasted to the notion of 'wage–effort' bargaining (coined by Behrend in 1957). As Marsh notes, '... the phrase "productivity bargaining" was created to contrast with "effort bargaining", the process by which workers sold their efforts in return for payment by results' (1972: 93). McKersie and Hunter point out that, while both productivity bargaining and payment by results systems are concerned with relating work to payment, productivity bargaining differs in that it '... places the consideration of ways of improving productive performance directly in the context of wage bargaining' (1973: 4).

The distinction between payment by results schemes and productivity bargaining lies for the most part in the degree to which each is concerned with 'effort'- or 'work'-related changes. In this regard Corina has noted:

> The latter (payment by results) may not necessarily involve any change in working practices or conditions but may concentrate essentially on stimulating greater effort. A productivity agreement makes a contribution in circumstances where working

37

practices need reform rather than where the chief aim is to encourage greater effort. (1967: 88)

However, as payment-by-results systems are often based on some form of work study (Brown, 1981), it is possible that they may also involve some adjustments to work methods. Such adjustments would bring payment-by-results schemes closer to the definition of productivity bargaining. Therefore, the distinction between productivity bargaining and payment-by-results schemes would appear to lie, for the most part, in the scope and *degree of change* to working methods. As Stettner points out:

> It (payment by results) relates to a particular job at a particular time with a particular productive method; it has no effect on the overall organization of work ... Hence it (productivity bargaining) is broader than PBR and encompasses changes in methods of work, in work allocation, in labour practices and in flexibility of labour. (1969: 4–5)

It is for this reason that Flanders took great pains to convey the message that, in order for productivity bargaining to be distinctive, it needed to be 'comprehensive', in the sense that it needed to encompass a full review of work methods and processes and not just marginal changes which are a feature of payment by results systems.

In making the distinction between productivity bargaining and payment by results schemes, it is worth noting that productivity bargaining tends to be '... a once-for-all method of relating increases in pay to increases in productivity ...' while payment by results systems operate such that '... rewards to labour may fluctuate from week to week as output or productivity varies' (McKersie and Hunter, 1973: 5). Smith makes a similar distinction and suggests that

> whereas ... PBR earnings are used to directly influence the level of worker effort and therefore the level of productivity of the production process, the increase in earnings given to workers in productivity agreements was an 'enabling' pay increase which would provide a controlled basis from which to secure improvements in the effectiveness with which labour is used. (1973: 120)

The distinction between productivity bargaining and payment by results schemes has more relevance than mere definitional semantics; it also serves to provide clarity which can be used as a basis for more precise payment systems research and bargaining trend analysis. *The New Earnings Survey*, for example, lumps both productivity bargaining and various forms of payment by results systems under the loose umbrella term 'payment by results', thereby disguising the extent to which these two broad-based techniques are actually used.

Productivity bargaining in contrast to unilaterally imposed change

Productivity bargaining can also be compared to unilaterally imposed change. Clearly, productivity as such can be improved by changes which are largely within the unilateral control of management but such changes cannot in themselves be defined as productivity bargaining. Stettner (1969: 4) makes the important point that a change in production methods does not in itself qualify as a productivity bargain; rather, it must be a change which is mutually agreed with workers resulting from a bargaining process. This distinction would serve to exclude such 'productivity' based changes as the 1979–80 Leyland 'Blue Paper' which represented a set of changes which were simply imposed by management fiat (Willman and Winch, 1985).

Types of productivity bargaining

As productivity bargaining developed over the years, it began to assume a number of different forms, although each of these continues to emphasize the pay, productivity and working practices nexus. The productivity bargaining literature has defined four main types of productivity bargaining as follows: (1) the comprehensive-detailed agreements, (2) the partial agreements, (3) the open-ended or indirect agreements and, finally, (4) the framework agreements.

The 'comprehensive-detailed' type of productivity agreement

The prime example of a classic comprehensive-detailed agreement is the Fawley Blue Book productivity agreement, the agreement which the Donovan Commission took as its model for industrial-relations reform. Towers describes the comprehensive-detailed type of productivity agreement as '. . . covering the whole of the plant, including radical changes in working practices, in return for higher benefits of both a financial and non-financial nature, with the whole deal written up into a formal, written, fixed-duration agreement' (1972: 25).

Sometimes referred to as the 'listing' approach, comprehensive-detailed agreements involve setting out, in precise detail, the required changes in working practices. The pre-negotiation phase is crucial to the comprehensive-detailed approach as it assumes that, before change can be made, a

39

careful audit of the current organization of work needs to be conducted. Fawley's Blue Book productivity agreement is instructive in this case. At Fawley, management and a team of consultants conducted a diagnosis of operations which took approximately eighteen months before their proposals were placed with the unions. It was precisely this type of 'comprehensiveness' that Flanders himself so heavily defended:

> Comprehensive productivity agreements tackle the problem at its roots. They are a means of diminishing the informality, autonomy and fragmentation of local bargaining, and of contracting areas of unilateral regulation by management and workers in favour of joint control by collective agreement. (Flanders, 1975: 70–1)

The cruder types of comprehensive-detailed agreements came eventually to be seen as a 'horse-trading' activity whereby detailed changes to working practices were being sold for the highest price. As a result, it was even thought that workers might begin to create new restrictive practices in order to sell these away at future auctions (Daniel, 1970a: 14–20). Ironically, it was also thought that the detailed set of work rules generated by the agreements might result in a new set of demarcations and rigidity (Daniel, 1970a: 14–20).

The 'partial' type of productivity agreement

Partial agreements have been defined in the 'pure' sense as relating to a limited set of changes made to working practices and affecting only a limited group of workers (Stettner, 1969). This type of agreement generally comes to be employed when managers have neither the time nor the resources to engage in a total restructuring of the workplace. They are also seen to provide managers with an ability to apply a sequentially based strategy, with management first picking off those groups of workers that might prove more amenable than others to striking a deal (McKersie and Hunter, 1973: 28). Flanders was particularly critical of this form of productivity bargaining, claiming that such agreements would cause more problems than they would solve. Flanders claimed, for example, that the use of partial agreements risked setting off a series of wage-claim chain reactions and that the ultimate consequence would be one of '. . . sacrificing long-term strategy to short-term tactics' (1975: 71).

The 'open-ended' type of productivity agreement

The open-ended or enabling type of productivity agreement represents yet another variation on productivity bargaining practice. Under this type of agreement, proposals about changes to work are not specified in detail; rather, they rely on management function clauses. Open-ended agreements are based on the doctrine of reserved management rights, that is management has complete freedom of action except as specifically limited by the agreement.

Open-ended agreements are based upon a general statement of intent to work in more efficient ways, utilizing such phrases as 'time, tools and ability permitting'. As Daniel notes, '... the chief goal would be to create more flexible working, informally, in day-to-day activities, within the framework of an open agreement (one not specifying particular changes) accepting that goal' (1970a: 21). Open-ended agreements typically consist of no more than one or two pages, which outline some general statement of intent to work more productively.

McKersie and Hunter (1973) have associated open-ended bargaining with the notion of 'integrative or cooperative bargaining'. They have suggested that, while this approach '... makes it less likely that "hard" results will be realized (in the short run) ... it is more likely to involve the complex subject of flexibility, where the payoffs to management may be quite high' (1973: 302). McKersie and Hunter also note that this type of productivity agreement prevents new rigidities when future changes in the production process are made, as was often thought to be the case with the item-by-item approach of the classic comprehensive-detailed agreements (1973: 303).

Open-ended agreements can be applied to both large groups of workers (for example, all workers in a multi-plant company) or to a smaller group of workers (for example, a section of plant). Management may prefer to install a 'partial-open-ended' agreement which applies to only one section of the work-force, if this particular section is considered to be the only group that management would trust to live up to the spirit of the agreement.

The 'framework' type of productivity agreement

The last type of productivity agreement is known as the 'framework' agreement. This type of agreement was formed to accommodate those firms which negotiated on an industry-wide or multi-plant basis. As Towers notes, the general purpose of framework agreements

> ... is to establish a 'framework' or series of general guidelines on pay and productivity which apply to the industry as a whole but allowing individual companies and plants freedom to nego-

tiate their own agreements in accordance with their own special circumstances. (1969: 25)

Although framework agreements are similar to the open-ended agreements in that they are non-detailed, they do differ from the open-ended agreements described above in that framework agreements represent only the first stage of the productivity bargaining process; after a framework agreement is negotiated, individual plants or units would negotiate a second set of agreements. The open-ended agreements referred to in the previous section exist in their own right.

As productivity bargaining evolved over the past twenty-five years, other mutations or forms developed. Some of these fit the general definition of productivity bargaining while others are simply disguised as productivity bargaining. The multiplicity of types of productivity bargaining is revealing in itself and is suggestive of the difficulties and tensions associated with productivity bargaining.

To understand the different types of productivity bargaining more fully we need to turn to the history of the process.

The evolution of productivity bargaining: 1960–1985

It has been commonplace (McKersie and Hunter, 1973; Nightingale, 1980) to refer to two rather distinct phases of productivity bargaining: the initial pioneering period, extending from 1960 to 1966, and the 'incomes policy' period, extending from 1967 to 1970. The literature on productivity bargaining has, however, been amazingly silent with respect to any developments in productivity bargaining following these two phases, as if the process had completely withered away or had been relegated to a marginal role in British industrial relations.

This section argues, however, that productivity bargaining never completely disappeared and in fact resurfaced with renewed vigour in two further distinct phases: first, under the impetus of incomes policies in the late 1970s and secondly (spontaneously) in the 1980s as a managerial response to the ongoing recession. Productivity bargaining has not been a mere artefact of the 1960s, but has remained central to British industrial relations through to the mid-1980s.

It could be put forth that industrial-relations academics, like fashion designers, have tended to interpret and understand developments within industrial relations in a 'fadist' manner and, resultingly, have not been able to see the productivity bargaining strategy as a *continuous* one. Industrial life cannot simply be defined around a series of discrete 'here-today-gone-tomorrow' initiatives where, for instance, productivity bargaining is replaced by industrial democracy which, in turn, is replaced by quality circles, and so on, but rather needs to be interpreted in a more continuous manner.

A hint of the 'trendy' nature of industrial-relations research is revealed in Marsh's (1985) *Employee Relations Bibliography and Abstracts.* Of the thirty-nine references listed on productivity bargaining there is not a single academic publication that is devoted to an analysis of productivity bargaining in the post-1970 period. There are, however, ten non-academic publications listed (in various trade and professional journals) which review productivity bargaining in the post-1970 period. This, in itself, appears to suggest that, while academics have more or less dropped productivity bargaining as an important agenda item for research, practitioners are demonstrating its continued importance.

The first phase: 1960–1966

The very first phase of productivity bargaining is considered to have started with the signing of the Fawley productivity agreements in 1960 and to have ended in the latter half of 1966 with the Labour government's prices and incomes standstill (McKersie and Hunter, 1973; Nightingale, 1980). McKersie and Hunter (1973: 45) found that some 73 productivity type agreements were struck during this period. In 1966, the National Board for Prices and Incomes estimated that 'over the last six years, productivity agreements ... have probably affected no more than half a million workers' (1966: 8).

It is important to note that the agreements made during this early period were struck, for the most part, on a voluntary basis, that is to say with no hard inducement from the state or for that matter from employers' organizations.

McKersie and Hunter (1973: 47) note that patterns are difficult to define for this initial period and that by the end of the period, productivity bargaining had taken on many different forms and had extended to a wide variety of industrial situations in both capital- and labour-intensive industries, operating under different market, technical and manpower conditions. McKersie's and Hunter's survey of the seventy-three agreements struck in the period does, however, reveal common design features, which tend for the most part to be patterned on the Fawley Blue Book agreement. The three most important management objectives during this classical period were, in order of importance, the restructuring of the nature of the work, the rearrangement of working hours and, finally, the reduction of manning levels (McKersie and Hunter, 1973: 32–3). A total of fifty-eight out of those seventy-three agreements included clauses on the nature of work 'involving greater flexibility between crafts and job enlargement' (McKersie and Hunter, 1973: 75).

It is generally recognized that those firms which negotiated productivity deals in this period tended to have better developed and more mature personnel functions and to be in a better position to adopt a costly and time-consuming approach to industrial relations than firms in the 'secondary sector' of the labour market. Productivity bargaining, at least in the context of the comprehensive agreements, appeared to require a prior level of sophistication in human resources management and both the time and money to sustain such an approach.

The second phase: 1967–1970

The second wave of productivity bargaining, from 1967 to 1970, was characterized by such a surge in productivity bargaining that it prompted Marxist critics like Cliff (1970) to suggest that a major new 'employers' offensive' had been lodged by capital. The rapid acceleration in the use of productivity bargaining was the direct result of the introduction of incomes policies by the Labour government. The prices and incomes standstill in 1966 permitted employers to grant wage increases above the 'norm', if corresponding improvements in productivity were agreed by the workers concerned. The productivity criterion to be used in the first half of 1967 was patterned upon a clause in the earlier 1965 voluntary White Paper on Prices and Incomes (Cmnd. 2639) whereby exceptional rises above the norm were allowed:

> Where the employees concerned, for example, by accepting
> more exacting work or a major change in working practices,
> make a direct contribution towards increasing productivity in
> the particular firm or industry. Even in such cases some of the
> benefit should accrue to the community as a whole in the form
> of lower prices. (1965: paragraph 15:1)

Marsh notes:

> It was left to the N.B.P.I. (National Board for Prices and
> Incomes), as the handmaiden of the Incomes Policy, to spell
> out the direct connection between pay, productivity and pro-
> ductivity bargaining, and to expand the concept to emphasize
> its applicability and practicability on differing circumstances.
> (1972: 95)

The N.B.P.I. did so in a fairly broad manner and made provisions both for comprehensive agreements covering either a whole plant or several plants, and for partial agreements confined to single departments or even to small groups of workers. Importantly, the N.B.P.I. stipulated that 'direct contributions towards increasing productivity' could also be made by payment by results as well as by productivity agreements (Marsh, 1972: 95).

The opportunity to secure above the norm or exceptional pay increases through 'productivity' criteria soon resulted in an overwhelming increase in the number of productivity agreements being struck throughout Britain. Over the period from 1967 to 1969 the Department of Employment recorded some 4,091 productivity agreements. From this data McKersie and Hunter have calculated that

> ... a realistic estimate of the total workers covered at least
> once during the period might be in the order of 6 million,
> including those under framework agreements, or less than 3
> million if the framework agreements are excluded. (1973: 65
> and 68)

The primary management objective or aim of the agreements struck during this second phase was seen to have shifted from an earlier emphasis upon restructuring the nature of work towards a greater interest in raising effort standards within pre-existing tasks. McKersie's and Hunter's (1973: 74–5) analysis of these agreements reveals that the 'quantity of work' objective (defined as speeding up machinery, eliminating breaks and overcoming restrictions in output) figured in over thirty per cent of the cases. The second and third most important objectives were seen to be method changes and manning improvements. According to McKersie and Hunter, changes to the 'nature of work' had slipped from the top spot in the first phase to fourth in the second phase, with only seventeen per cent of agreements dealing with the nature of work (1973: 76). On the whole, the overall shift in the second period was towards direct changes in the intensity of labour.

During this incomes policy period a shift was also seen toward agreements of the 'partial' type which consisted either of simple effort bargains or of buying out one or more restrictive practices of particular groups (see Flanders, 1972: 12). Flanders, harking back to the good old days of the classic period, was especially critical of this shift, suggesting that partial productivity agreements '... were just another way, the latest fashionable way, of permitting management to do what it had done before, namely yield to group pressures when they became too threatening with no overall policy in mind' (1972: 12). Flanders also developed this argument further, in a highly critical attack on partial agreements in *The Times* article 'The case for the package deal' (9 July 1968). Similarly

Nightingale, in contrasting the second phase of productivity bargaining to the first, has suggested that '. . . the battle for men's minds, for a new co-operative, jointly regulated system of plant bargaining, no longer took pride of place' (1976: 21).

The extent to which the second period actually represented a shift toward the partial type of agreement may have, however, been somewhat exaggerated. In the case of Flanders' allegations about the existence of such agreements, for example, these may have been driven more by a need to justify his own personal philosophy than by reality. Daniel and McIntosh (1973: 24), for instance, reported in their survey of a random sample of sixty-two productivity agreements of the same period, that just over half of the agreements were designed in a 'comprehensive' fashion and in about a further fifth of the cases 'all manual workers' were eventually covered by the agreements.

There are obvious difficulties in tracing the actual fate of productivity bargaining as we turn into the 1970s. First, the industrial-relations literature is, for the most part, silent with respect to post-1970 developments. With the demise of incomes policies, less and less attention was paid by the Department of Employment to the recording of productivity bargains. Also, by this time, as the process had become publicly discredited by the flagrant negotiation of 'bogus' agreements, it may be that, even though some companies actually were operating from some form of productivity bargain, they may have preferred to couch the process in different terms.

The Incomes Data Services describe the incidence of productivity bargaining between 1971 and 1977 in terms of a '. . . long and virtually complete absence from the collective bargaining scene' (December 1979: 31). The demise of the process is generally attributed to a management perception that the deals that were struck during the previous incomes policy period had been merely 'bogus' and used simply to evade incomes policy. Hawkins has added to this speculation by observing that '. . . what killed productivity bargaining in the end from a trade union point of view was not a growing resistance to the idea itself but rather the high and rising level of redundancy and unemployment which accompanied the economic recession of 1969 to 1972' (1978: 89).

Recognizing the administrative constraints involved in calculating the extent to which the process is used, it is suggested here that the decline of productivity bargaining into the 1970s may have been exaggerated and that the process had by no means come to a halt. In fact, it is argued that some important developments and extensions occurred within productivity bargaining from the early to mid-1970s.

First, it is worth noting that the actual number of 'bogus' agreements in

46

the 1967–1970 incomes policy period appears to have been exaggerated. Daniel's and McIntosh's (1973: 30) survey of productivity agreements struck during the same period revealed that nearly two-thirds of the agreements did in fact have real substance (i.e. they were not simply agreements which were struck to circumvent incomes policy); they reported that '... management respondents had not generally become disillusioned with the concept of productivity bargaining, nor did they feel that they had exploited all of its potential' (1973: 52). Just over one third of their respondents reported that they saw some 'limited scope' for further similar agreements in their plants and a third felt that there was 'some considerable scope' for such agreements in their plants. My own case study of industrial–relations strategy at Esso's Fawley Refinery over a 25-year period shows that two major productivity deals were struck in the early 1970s.

Secondly, it appears that the arrival of productivity bargaining may have been slow or 'lagged' in those organizations where it may have been considered difficult to apply. Referring to the early 1970s, Towers has noted that those '... sectors in which productivity bargaining still seems to have some momentum are those in which it is apparently more difficult to apply, such as local government occupations, postal services and at certain Ministry of Defence establishments, especially workshops' (1972: 31).

The third phase: 1977–1979

It is possible to identify a surge in productivity bargaining in the latter part of the 1970s, this time linked with the introduction of incomes policies by the Labour government in August 1977. Once again, like the incomes policies of the latter part of the 1960s, a productivity rider had been injected into the criteria for obtaining above the norm pay increases; this time, the rider was labelled 'self-financing' productivity agreements. Such schemes were not to lead to any increase in unit costs but rather, in ideal terms, to a decrease in unit costs. Negotiators had to be able to demonstrate that the scheme was indeed self-financing and, according to the terms of the incomes policy, it would have to be 'checked' at regular intervals to ensure that it remained so. The Department of Employment came to define a 'self-financing productivity scheme' as

> ... a scheme whereby the savings achieved in unit costs out-
> weigh the costs of the scheme such as the extra payments to
> those directly or indirectly involved, and any extra capital or
> running costs. Such schemes do not raise prices. The scheme

47

must be demonstrated to be self-financing and be subject to regular checking that it remains so. (I.D.S. Report 263, August 1977: 2)

One of the results of this particular incomes policy period was the widespread introduction of group-based bonuses which were meant to be linked to either production targets, increases in profitability, or value of goods per employee. The association of these group-based bonus schemes with productivity bargaining served to dilute the distinctiveness of productivity bargaining during this period. Many of these group bonus schemes did not involve any changes to working practices and therefore could not strictly be defined as productivity agreements.

What then was the extent to which productivity bargaining was actually used within the period? Clearly, the broader the definition, the greater the usage, while a narrower, more restrictive, definition of productivity bargaining suggests a more limited use. This problem relates to sorting out the relationship between traditional productivity bargaining schemes, newly evolved productivity schemes and more traditional forms of collective bonuses.

White's (1981) survey of 401 manufacturing firms at the end of the 1970s probably provides the best picture of the trend in the use of productivity bargaining, mostly because he comes to terms, at least partly, with the relationship between productivity bargaining and various payment systems. White provides for both 'self-financing' productivity deals in general, and what he refers to as 'negotiated productivity rates', a term he uses to '... suggest schemes that have the general character of productivity bargaining, but may be less formal, less elaborate, and on a smaller scale' (1981: 78 and 80).

White's data reveal that by 1978 just over half of his firms' sample had 'some type of self-financing productivity scheme' (1981: 81). Furthermore, he notes, that if one takes '... into account the overlap between plant bonus schemes, negotiated productivity and self-financing productivity schemes, it is possible to conclude that about seventy-five per cent of the manufacturing plants had one or more of these approaches in operation' (1981: 88).

With regard to the agreements which White termed 'negotiated productivity rates' he found that almost forty-five per cent of manufacturing plants in the sample had struck productivity deals of this type (1981: 80). Table 1 (from White, 1981: 82–3) lists the productivity factors associated with these agreements and shows that by far the most widely pursued improvement in work practices was increased flexibility (over one-third of all plants identified this as a factor in the negotiation of higher wage rates).

Table 1. *Productivity provisions negotiated in the late 1970s − U.K.*

		All	Food, drink and tobacco	Chemicals and coal and petroleum products	Mechanical engineering	Electrical engineering	Clothing and footwear
Base	N	401	95	67	118	71	50
	(%)	(100)	(100)	(100)	(100)	(100)	(100)
Productivity factors:							
working flexibly/ covering more than one job/ agreeing to do a wider range of work	N	139	32	25	37	22	23
	(%)	(35)	(34)	(37)	(31)	(31)	(46)
accepting reduced manning levels for the work	N	34	10	10	2	5	7
	(%)	(9)	(11)	(15)	(2)	(7)	(14)
working with new technology	N	48	10	10	12	6	10
	(%)	(12)	(11)	(15)	(10)	(9)	(20)
agreeing to work at a higher standard rate	N	20	2	6	2	7	3
	(%)	(5)	(2)	(9)	(2)	(10)	(6)
agreeing to handle a wider range of products	N	24	3	9	5	1	6
	(%)	(6)	(3)	(13)	(4)	(1)	(12)
agreeing to reduce overtime working	N	10	3	3	1	1	2
	(%)	(3)	(3)	(5)	(1)	(1)	(4)
agreeing that overtime, if worked, will be paid at ordinary not premium rate	N	4	0	0	2	2	0
	(%)	(1)	(0)	(0)	(2)	(3)	(0)
accepting increased assembly line or process speeds	N	16	2	3	0	5	6
	(%)	(4)	(2)	(5)	(0)	(7)	(12)
any of above productivity factors	N	171	38	29	42	33	29
	(%)	(43)	(40)	(43)	(36)	(46)	(58)
No productivity factors used/ not applicable	N	230	57	38	76	38	21
	(%)	(57)	(60)	(57)	(64)	(54)	(42)

The factor next most frequently mentioned was 'working with new technology', the proportion being twelve per cent of all plants (1981: 82–3).

It would appear, therefore, that a significant amount of real productivity deals (whereby working practices were being exchanged for higher wages) did in fact take place in this period and that it was not just a period in which various forms of customary collective incentives had been ushered in under the guise and language of productivity bargaining (with no real accompanying changes to the organization of work).

The high volume of productivity dealing that went on in this period leads White to suggest that many productivity agreements had been '. . . absorbed into collective bargaining'. In other words, White points out that many firms no longer regarded bargaining about work practices '. . .

49

as a separate exercise or method, but merely as an aspect of how wage rates are normally determined' (1981: 134).

The continued emphasis on negotiations around the nature of work demonstrates management's sustained faith in the time-honoured and laborious practice of negotiating changes to workplace organization. The continued significance of productivity bargaining was revealed by White in the telephone follow-up procedure part of his survey where it was shown that managers '... referred not only to recent government influence, but to much earlier phases of incomes policy which had started their payment systems down the track of productivity bargaining' (1981: 134). Clearly productivity bargaining had a continued and long-lasting impression on the minds of British management.

The fourth phase: 1981–1985

It becomes increasingly difficult to talk in terms of phases or waves of productivity bargaining when we begin to understand the extent to which it has become integrated into conventional collective bargaining. Still, it is possible to suggest that a fourth phase of productivity bargaining has followed the incomes policy period of the latter part of the 1970s. This phase, like the first phase from 1960 to 1966, has been wholly voluntary on the part of British management. The precise time at which the third phase ends and this fourth commences is difficult to pinpoint, partly due to a lack of data, but it is suggested here that it commences in 1981, at around the time of the recession, and continues to 1985.

Within this fourth period, productivity bargaining can perhaps best be viewed as a management response to coping with the recession. Many firms have been confronted with a need to reduce manning levels to fit decreased product demand and have often couched these demannings within the logic of productivity bargaining. The high cost of labour plus pressure to introduce new technologically advanced production processes has also been seen to force negotiators to discuss more fundamental changes in working methods rather than indulging in piecemeal negotiation of revised performance standards (I.R.R.R., 332, November 1984: 8). Thus, in recent years, many British managers returned, quite voluntarily, to the technique with which they had become familiar – productivity bargaining.

Writing in the early 1970s, McKersie and Hunter suggest that '... a renewed vigour in the use of productivity bargaining will require a reduction in unemployment as an essential starting agreement' (1973: 376). It was only once this goal was achieved that McKersie and Hunter saw trade unions as likely to give their general support to productivity

50

bargaining. The fourth phase of productivity bargaining is characterized by precisely the opposite conditions, that is high unemployment and recessionary economic conditions. In other words, productivity bargaining has not proved to be incompatible, therefore, with high unemployment.

During this current fourth phase of productivity bargaining, it should be noted that the Confederation of British Industry (C.B.I.) has repeatedly called on its members to focus their attention on the pay–productivity nexus (see, for example, the C.B.I. pay reports and in particular the 1982–3 report). Most recently, on 18 November 1985, Sir Terence Beckett, the director general of the C.B.I., publicly called for a 'revolution in our thinking' to produce a new industrial culture which would say 'no' to unearned pay increases. Under the banner that 'you should pay nowt for nowt' Sir Terence made a plea for the 'complete elimination of pay increases that are not related to the achieved increases in the output of goods or services' ('Achieved increases not ill defined aspirations', *The Financial Times*, 19 November 1985).

In the 1980s, Sir Terence has not been alone in extolling the virtues of productivity initiatives. The personnel and industrial-relations trade journals have increasingly turned to productivity bargaining as a new *cause célèbre* (see for instance I.R.R.R. 316 and 317, March and April 1984). Brewster and Connock have gone so far as to suggest that 'future industrial-relations historians may characterize the 1980s as the decade of "dissolving demarcations"' (1985: 42). They note, in fact:

> Managements in the vanguard organizations are attempting to develop pay structures which encourage task flexibility – or at least do not hinder it ... progress in increasing task flexibility in the 1980s has been real enough. (1985: 58)

What is most striking about these pieces (including Sir Terence's own remarks) is that they often give the impression that productivity bargaining is surfacing for the first time, as a new feature of British industrial relations. The language and rhetoric used to peddle the productivity bargaining gospel is particularly revealing. Note, for instance, the words used by the I.R.R.R. to describe the Mobil Oil Coryton deal, which is said to evoke '. . . a number of concepts in such a radical fashion as to result in joint cooperation and workforce exploration of new frontiers of work organization, control and union organization' (323, July 1984: 7). *The Financial Times* itself was to run an article entitled 'Enter the jack-of-all-trades' which pointed to a '. . . human drama in which ossified working practices and demarcation lines are being wrenched into a new era of flexibility' (article by B. Groom and D. Goodhart: 17 August 1983).

There is, of course, nothing 'radical' about these proposals; the language used to describe productivity bargaining could not be closer to the language used in the early 1960s. What is happening is that productivity bargaining is simply being repackaged and resold as the latest technique in the management arsenal. This resurgence of interest in demarcations and flexibility makes one wonder what happened to the 1960s managerial assault on these very same practices.

There is evidence enough to suggest that productivity bargaining has remained a significant industrial-relations strategy in the 1980s. The I.R.R.R.'s (288, January 1983: 2) review of 600 collective agreements in 1982 reveals that just over 100 of these had formal productivity provisions. Although it is not clear to what extent the changes were 'bargained', P. Edwards' survey of senior managers at 229 manufacturing sites found that some eighty-four per cent of respondents reported that at least one change in working arrangements had been made during the past two years (1984: 7). Edwards reports that '. . . of those introducing changes, more than half had introduced at least three, and one sixth introduced more than four' (1984: 7).

Batstone's survey of 133 manufacturing plants in the summer of 1983 confirms that there '. . . has been a major drive by management to achieve new working arrangements . . . in the changed economic environment of the 1980s' (1984: 242). Batstone reports that 'in all but 14 per cent of the plants "major" changes in working practices have been introduced in the last five years' (1984: 242). Interestingly, Batstone was also able to report that 'in all but 11 per cent of plants which introduced changes in working practices these were the subject of bargaining with the unions' (1984: 243). These agreements were, therefore, in keeping with the aspect of the traditional definition of productivity bargaining, that the change be 'negotiated' and not simply imposed. Batstone's more recent survey (1985) of 1,024 shop stewards, conducted in 1984, revealed that nearly two-thirds of the shop stewards had negotiated workplace changes within the context of a formal agreement.

Finally, and most recently, Atkinson's and Meager's survey of seventy-two big British firms in 1985 (in four contrasting sectors) revealed that 'nine out of every ten manufacturing respondents had been seeking to increase the functional flexibility of their workforces since 1980' (1986: 27). The survey also confirmed that '. . . most of the changes observed had been achieved through collective bargaining rather than imposed by diktat' (1986: 26).

It is difficult to define the actual types of productivity deals used in the 1980s. In 1982, the I.R.R.R., however, reviewed just under 100 agreements which had productivity provisions and '. . . all but a handful were in the form of a revision of working practices, increased job flexibility, acceptance of new technology or working methods, revised manning levels and other cost cutting measures' (I.R.R.R. 288, January 1983: 2). Craft flexibility was found, further, to be of particular importance. Edwards' survey of 229 manufacturing establishments, each employing at least 250 workers, revealed that '... the most popular changes were introducing new technologies, increasing efficiency with existing equipment and introducing more flexible forms of working' (1984: 7). Batstone (1984) suggests that the nature of changes to working practices in this recent period are likely to be of two interrelated kinds: 'The first is simply the need to reorganize work in the face of redundancies and new capital equipment; the second is attempts to improve the effective utilization of labour time more generally, by increasing levels of effort and by greater flexibility' (1984: 242).

Doubtless it is best to characterize this recent period as one of considerable variety. Specific bonus schemes, however, may actually be of less relevance to employers in this period as they '... are most likely to be effective when the economy is moving out of a recession and companies need increased output to meet increased demand' (I.R.R.R. 239, January 1981: 5).

The history of productivity bargaining in Britain is summarized in table 2.

Conclusions

This chapter has sought to demonstrate the importance of productivity bargaining for the notion of strategy in industrial relations. The emergence of productivity bargaining has been equated with the birth of strategic thinking in industrial relations. Productivity bargaining was distinguished from traditional collective bargaining, from payment by results and from unilaterally imposed change. The various generic types of productivity bargaining were also reviewed. Finally, the evolution of productivity bargaining was traced from 1960 to 1985, and we have seen that productivity bargaining extended beyond the two well-known phases and never completely withered away in the post-1970 period. A third and fourth phase were identified, the third being associated with incomes policy in the latter part of the 1970s and the fourth being a voluntary initiative on the part of British management to cope with the recession. The identification of these two later phases has helped demonstrate that productivity bargaining has remained a central industrial-relations strategy in Britain. Time and time again, in moments of crisis and uncertainty in the business environment, both the British government and employers have constantly turned to productivity bargaining.

Table 2. *History of productivity bargaining in the U.K., 1960–1985*

Phase	Impetus	Coverage	Productivity bargaining type	Key management objective
1960-6	Spontaneous	73 agreements – $\frac{1}{2}$ million workers	Mixed first agreements: comprehensive	Nature of work
1967-70	Incomes policy induced	4,091 agreements – 6 million workers (including framework agreements)	Partial	Raising of effort standards
1977-9	Incomes policy induced	Survey evidence indicates $\frac{1}{2}$ of manufacturing firms (White, 1981)	Self-financing productivity deals	Nature of work flexibility
1981-5	Spontaneous	Survey evidence indicates majority of firms	Mixed	Nature of work but considerable variety

4

The control implications of productivity bargaining

Introduction

The Esso Fawley Blue Book productivity deal was to set off a thorough and long-lasting debate about the ways in which British industrial relations were managed. This chapter reviews three fundamental claims about the way in which productivity bargaining would affect industrial relations in Britain. The first of these relates to the hope that Britain would be transformed from a 'half-pay and half-effort' society to a 'full-pay and full-effort' society; the second relates to the hope that productivity bargaining would lead British management to abandon unitarist management techniques for a new 'higher order' pluralist based strategy of joint control; the third relates to the claim that the increased formalization and bureaucratization brought on by productivity bargaining would restore order at the workplace.

Increased management control by shifting from a 'half-pay and half-effort' strategy to a 'full-pay and full-effort' strategy

Different commentators were to stress different aspects of the impact that productivity bargaining would have on management's control over labour. Bill Allen, the American consultant who was the architect of the Blue Book deal, focussed, for instance, upon the 'labour market' aspects of productivity bargaining. His evaluation of the Blue Book was concerned with an understanding of various approaches to managing unit labour costs.

Bill Allen, who, in the aftermath of the Blue Book deal took on somewhat heroic proportions in the British media, was to provide the strategic or philosophical basis of the Blue Book. He produced two highly influential memoranda for Esso management in 1958 which were to set the tone for the creation of the Blue Book. The first memorandum highlighted the need for management to take the initiative in managing industrial relations. The most important point that Allen argued was that 'management reacted rather than acted' (Flanders, 1964: 77). The second memorandum (November 1958) was to foreshadow the Blue Book and is reproduced in full in appendix 'A' in Flanders' (1964) study of the Blue Book.

The central argument of Allen's second memorandum 'was built up around a single theme: the need for a low-overtime – high-wage policy' (Flanders, 1964: 79). In this memorandum, Allen argued that Fawley's wages policy was wholly inadequate. Base rates for maintenance workers were considered to be set at a mere subsistence level. Allen believed that Fawley's industrial-relations strategy was based on the erroneous assumptions:

> ... (a) that wages policy should be roughly equivalent to those paid by other employers in the local community, with good fringe benefits and no redundancy strengthening the recruitment appeal on income and job security grounds and (b) that overtime was inevitable in running a refinery both for technical reasons and to satisfy workers. There was, in addition, a general assumption that the principal way of getting more work done was to employ more workers. (Flanders, 1964: 79)

The earnings of craftsmen employed by the main contractors on the site were, in fact, substantially greater than those of refinery employees (£21.5.0 as compared with £15.14.6 average gross weekly pay for the six months ending 30 April 1958). It was not unusual at this time for full-time Esso Fawley workers to terminate their Esso employment contracts to assume employment with local contractor firms (interview with Fawley manager). Esso Fawley could be characterized, in the pre-Blue Book period, by minimal labour market segmentation and the relative lack of an 'internal labour market'.

According to Allen, an indulgency pattern had set in at Fawley whereby management had come to accept over-manning, unnecessary overtime and restrictive working practices as normal and natural. The situation was seen to benefit neither workers nor management. Workers were considered to be both underemployed and to be living on a subsistence wage, while management was plagued with all the problems of working with a 'half-effort' work-force. As basic wages were kept at a low or subsistence level it was, however, not costing management that much to live with these inefficiencies; accordingly, Fawley management assumed a tolerant view towards low levels of labour efficiency.

Bill Allen's view of low levels of labour productivity was much less tolerant; he was to make a call for a major shift in the way British managers approached the handling of its unit labour costs. His formula was revolutionary and novel, and one which would still shock much of British management today. As Flanders proclaimed, 'the consultant threw a big stone into a rather stagnant pool' (1964: 79). In short, Allen, as a management consultant, was to make a call for British management to raise or 'bump up' the wages of workers. Allen's approach to the management of unit labour costs was that a low-wages strategy was not the only way to keep unit labour costs down.

Prior to productivity bargaining, British management had, for the most part, taken a defensive approach to matters of unit labour costs, accepting the existing low level of effort as an uncontrollable datum and paying the level of wages which could be afforded in the light of this low productivity (McKersie and Hunter, 1973: 320). The strategy employed appeared very much to be one of 'low-effort/low-wages'. What Allen was suggesting was that British management move to a 'high-wage/high-effort' strategy. The formal title of the Blue Book, 'High productivity and high wages', reflected this strategic shift. An increase in wages was to be offset by an increase in effort on the workers' part, so that overall unit costs would not rise, and would possibly even be lower than during the low-wages and low-effort era. McKersie and Hunter have isolated the importance of this strategy for productivity bargaining and have suggested that

> In a very important sense, then, productivity bargaining is intimately concerned to bring about a shift from a low-wage/ low-effort strategy to a high-wage/high-effort strategy. (1973: 321)

The movement to a high-wages strategy was not to be an easy one. Managers first needed to be convinced of its efficacy. A low-wages strategy had, after all, its own intrinsic appeal to managers as a low-pay strategy provided management with a convenient excuse not to exert itself in drawing maximum efficiency from the work-force. To pay workers a high basic wage meant that management must be capable of extracting its pound of flesh from workers, that is, management *itself* must be organized and efficient. Those managements pursuing a high-wage approach would need to be confident, therefore, that they had sufficient control over their work-force to win the extra increments of effort that would justify higher wages. A fear that managers commonly expressed was that they had insufficient control and that workers would take their high wages but would not respond in turn by granting higher levels of effort. The result of this would potentially be a move to a 'high-wage/low-effort' syndrome (in a kind of a wage-drift).

While managers may have had some reservations about pursuing a 'high-wage' policy, workers themselves sometimes expressed suspicion about moving to such a policy (Cliff, 1970). This suspicion was based on a fear that wages would be increased in the short term only, and that management would subsequently let wages slide so that the workers would find themselves caught in a 'low-wage/high-effort' syndrome.

Allen's new proposed 'high-wages' strategy relied heavily (although not specifically stated) upon the reconstruction or 'internalization' of labour markets. A high-wages strategy involved what could be termed the 'balkanization' of labour markets – with Fawley Refinery moving towards the creation of its own 'internal labour market', one which would be isolated, at least from a pay perspective, from the external labour market. Under productivity bargaining, pay would no longer be related to the external 'going rate' but rather to 'internal' factors – such as labour productivity. Allen believed that those firms engaging in productivity bargaining would increase their own wages, which would bring the pay structure out of line with the local labour market. As Allen's second memorandum put it: 'The non-staff personnel of the M. and C. (Maintenance and Construction) Division should be paid substantially more for the work they perform than do other British workers of similar backgrounds' (appendix 'A', in Flanders, 1964: 262).

According to McKersie and Hunter, productivity bargaining would also help to create an internal labour market through programmes of 'decasualization' and through various fringe benefit schemes which encourage long-term career employment within the same company:

> Such 'fruits' of productivity bargaining as sick pay, improved holidays, and retirement schemes can be characterized as moving the labour market of the individual firm from an open to a closed system. Under an open system, workers flow in and out of employment with a particular firm and these flows take place for various skill areas. Under a closed system the port of entry is at the bottom and workers stay with one firm and gradually progress upwards. (1973: 295)

Productivity bargaining was also seen to 'internalize' labour markets through its effect on the restructuring of worker skills. As McKersie and Hunter note, 'the move to new skill groupings with an overriding emphasis on flexibility has meant that job duties reflect more the exigencies of the particular situation than the dictates of the external labour market' (1973: 293). In fact, McKersie and Hunter identified the change in plant-level relations resulting from productivity bargaining as a shift from a 'craft' system to an 'administrative' system for controlling manpower utilization:

> The term 'craft system' refers to an external labour market

approach to selecting, training, and allocating workers to employment opportunities. By contrast, the 'administrative system' relies upon procedures and rules that have their origin in the particular firm – hence, the characteristics of an internal labour market. (1973: 345)

McKersie and Hunter point out that under a 'craft' system, job definitions are determined by the occupational definitions found in the local labour market. Each particular craft maintains a considerable degree of autonomy in regulating the standards and conditions of a particular task. The craft system is organized in such a way that work is managed on an *ad hoc* basis on the shop floor; management authority is abdicated to the worker and to craft traditions. An 'administrative' system on the other hand involves the training and placement of workers according to the particular needs of the employer. Job design and duties are based on the particular technology, scale of operation and other considerations *internal* to the firm.

McKersie and Hunter suggest, furthermore, that the 'craft' system had increasingly become a much less appropriate way of organizing work, because of changes in technology and changes in production processes. New specialized equipment made it desirable for companies to hire workers at the bottom, train them and move them to higher positions during their careers. According to McKersie and Hunter, it became '. . . the special function of productivity bargaining, therefore, to bring the design of shop floor relations more into line with the requirements of the work system' (1973: 350). Moreover, the growth in the size of product markets and the movement to larger-scale production was seen by McKersie and Hunter as making it possible for employers to hire workers for extended periods of time and to take advantage of the economies of scale that generally resulted from a high division of labour.

In summary, then, productivity bargaining was seen to increase management control over labour by shifting from a 'low-wage/low-effort' strategy to a 'high-wage/high-effort' strategy. Allen's was an inspired and *visionary* piece of consultancy. He was, in a way, calling for a 'Japanized' industrial-relations strategy, that is for the deployment of a micro-'corporatist' strategy for internal company workers. Seen in this light, productivity bargaining needs to be linked to much of the so-called 'dual labour market theory'.

Increased management control by shifting to a pluralist strategy for joint control

Productivity bargaining was seen to do more than alter labour costs and markets; it was also seen as a means by which to usher in a new pluralist based strategy for control. Productivity bargaining came, in fact, to be seen as the very embodiment of pluralist industrial relations. For those with a pluralist frame of reference, productivity bargaining arrived like some kind of 'godsend', as a technique that would be able to translate the pluralist dream into reality. While Bill Allen was to interpret productivity bargaining within the context of labour markets, later on others like Flanders were to reinterpret the significance of productivity bargaining within the context of the institution of collective bargaining and worker participation.

One of the major lessons that Flanders was to extract from the Fawley experiment was that neither 'coercion' nor 'manipulation' would improve productivity. In order for management to make any inroads in the area of productivity improvement, they would need to cast aside 'outworn ideologies' (Flanders, 1975: 269). As Flanders asserted: 'Co-operation in the workplace cannot be fostered by propaganda and exhortation, by preaching its benefits' (1975: 172–3). Both of these methods fail because they '... involve no commitment to act'.

Flanders was a kind of 'Hegelian' in that he saw management as constantly progressing from one approach to another, arriving ultimately at an industrial-relations *Weltgeist*. This higher order approach or system was to be a 'pluralist' one which would attempt the greater integration of work-force and company purposes:

> The business enterprise does not have a unitary structure of authority; in some degree it is always a pluralistic society composed of groups with divergent interests and values. Whether management appreciates this or not, it is invariably confronted with the problem of reconciling the impersonal aims of the enterprise with the personal aims of its many constituent groups. (1975: 150)

In the post-war period, British management was seen by Flanders as operating from a 'traditional' or 'authoritarian' style of management which rejected '... any division of or sharing of authority within the firm ... it was held that there should be no collective bargaining with shop stewards, but only joint consultation with workers' representatives, who having expressed their opinion must leave management to decide' (1975: 172). Flanders was dismissive of this approach, not only from an effectiveness point of view but also and importantly from a *moral* point of view. For Flanders the industrial-relations system needed to be reconstructed to accommodate not only more planning from above but also and crucially '... more democracy from below' (1975: 113).

Control implications of productivity bargaining

Just as democracy was seen as essential for the polity so was it essential for the workplace. Power relations in the workplace, just like in society in general, could not be ignored. For Flanders, productivity bargaining marked a significant and important attempt at coming to terms with the competing interest groups within industry:

> ... bargaining of this sort represents an approach to industrial democracy which promises to have most meaning for industry's rank and file. It enables them to participate in influencing managerial decisions where they have the greatest impact on their lives and, while it may set in train events that will modify their traditional values, they are not being forced or tricked into relinquishing the principle of self-determination which protects their dignity as human beings. (1975: 153)

Flanders himself came to interpret the Blue Book experiment directly within these terms:

> If the word has any meaning when applied to the processes of labour relations, Fawley management acted democratically. The politics of the workplace, it has been argued, cannot be ignored; political considerations influenced the behaviour on both sides, but they were the stuff of democratic politics. Regarded in this light, the new trends in labour relations were a function of a more energetic participation of the work groups in the determination of their own destiny. (1964: 208–9)

Thus, increased worker participation was not to be valued merely as a device for improved productivity or as an end in itself but rather as a route to the goal of democracy at the workplace:

> Such bargaining is not only creative in the sense that it contributes to higher productivity. It also serves to create new social relations in industry in which it is possible for the participants to act responsibly. Managements and worker representatives are not called upon to abandon their own proper functions and the different responsibilities entailed, but they are placed in a position to fulfil them in ways that pay regard to the wider social consequences of their actions. (Flanders, 1975: 153)

In this way, productivity bargaining was seen as having a 'higher order' role or function:

> To see it simply as a device for raising labour productivity – by

which employers insist on an economic return for their wage concessions – is to underestimate both its long term contribution to the reconstruction of workplace relations and the exacting demands which it places on management and unions if it is to be undertaken seriously. (Flanders, 1975: 203–4)

Productivity bargaining was, therefore, considered by many to be ideologically sound in itself. Economic growth and more effective industrial democracy were considered the twin pillars of productivity bargaining.

Central to Flanders' interpretation of productivity bargaining, therefore, was the notion of 'joint regulation': 'The distinguishing, common feature of all the major, genuine productivity agreements is that they are attempts to strengthen managerial control over pay and work through joint regulation' (Flanders, 1975: 204). Joint regulation was not only seen, however, as good in itself, in terms of the enshrinement of democratic principles within the workplace; it was also seen as a *necessary* step for managers to take if they were to regain control at the shop floor. This belief was based upon the idea that worker control was so tightly entrenched that managers could not '. . . re-establish control unilaterally' (Flanders, 1966: 6). Workers and union officials would only give up 'custom and practice' control, provided that they were given some other form of control, i.e. *joint* control of rules and procedures. If control was to be regained, an entirely different approach needed to be embraced. According to Flanders' now well-known saying:

> The paradox, whose truth managements have found it so difficult to accept, is that they (management) can only regain control by sharing it . . . Co-operation demands first and foremost the progressive fusing of two systems of unilateral control – which now exist in conjunction and frequently in conflict with each other – into a common system of joint control based on agreed objectives. Such agreement can only be reached through compromise. (Flanders, 1975: 172–3)

Under productivity bargaining, subjects which were traditionally excluded from the scope of collective bargaining and normally considered to be the sole prerogative of management, were to be brought to the bargaining table. Moreover, the unilateral 'custom and practice' control held by unions and shop stewards was to be replaced by 'joint control'. As Flanders put it, comprehensive agreements were

> . . . a means of diminishing the informality, autonomy and fragmentation of local bargaining, and of contracting areas of

unilateral regulation by management and workers in favour of
joint control by collective agreement. (Flanders, 1975: 70–1)

It was believed, furthermore, that the extension of plant democracy would
lead to increased levels of union cooperation and consensus; the more
workers and unions became involved in the decision-making process, the
more they would come to identify with the firm. Referring to productivity
bargaining, the National Board for Prices and Incomes concluded, for
instance, that

> ... increased management control was generally achieved
> through the consent and co-operation of workers and through
> greater participation by trade unions in decision-making either
> through shop stewards or full time officials (N.B.P.I. Report
> no. 123, 1969: 92)

Rather than attempting to keep the union at arm's length and restricting
the scope of joint regulation, management was to embrace a different
strategy: 'The new modes of bargaining, with their "joint problem-
solving" approach along with appropriate frames of reference, may also
increasingly come to be seen by management as the best strategy ...' (Fox,
1971: 176).

There was, therefore, a widespread belief in the 'normative' or 'ideological' control dimension associated with productivity bargaining. Nightingale notes that integral to the classic productivity bargaining phase was
'... the commitment to "cultural" changes aimed at eliciting a better spirit
of cooperation among workers' (Nightingale, 1980: 325). In this way,
productivity bargaining can be seen as an 'integration' based strategy. The
object of the exercise was to bring the union directly into the management
decision-making apparatus. Unions were to be raised to a partnership
level with management.

Like Flanders and other reformists, the Marxians were to associate
productivity bargaining with both 'pluralist' based control and 'incorporation'. They take as given that management is both interested in and
intent on *shifting* its industrial-relations strategy in this direction.

The fundamental difference in the approach between the reformist
school and the Marxian school lies in the degree to which each one
believes that a 'consensus' of interests is possible within the context of a
capitalist employment relationship. In the Marxian perspective, conflict is
seen to be so fundamental to the employment relationship that it cannot
be accommodated through the productivity bargaining process. The
reformist position, on the other hand, while recognizing the existence of
conflict, does not see it as so fundamental that it cannot be reconciled. In
the language of Marxism, productivity bargaining is seen to lead to

worker 'subordination' and 'incorporation', whilst in the language of reformism, productivity bargaining leads to 'consensus' and 'cooperation'.

The Marxian school, as we have suggested above, shares with the reformist school the belief that productivity bargaining is an 'integration' or 'incorporation' based strategy. As Cliff states:

> The real aim of Donovan, of In Place of Strife, etc., is basically not to smash the unions, or even to weaken them as organizations, but to integrate them with management. This 'partnership' is to be embodied in Productivity Deals and formalized procedures in the plants. (1970: 139)

The widening of the collective bargaining agenda embodied in the notion of joint regulation, is therefore seen by the Marxian school as a means of incorporating trade unions into the capitalist enterprise. Topham has described this 'incorporation' as follows:

> A more subtle undermining of the steward's position takes the form of an attempt to incorporate him into management activity . . . some (stewards) undoubtedly (must) be swayed by the whole solemn aura of the process, and become totally absorbed in the pure process of rationalization, ending up with a high degree of commitment to the success of the scheme on which they have lavished so much time and care. (1969: 88)

While the Marxians easily accept the reformist view that the advent of productivity bargaining resulted in a shift from a unitarist based control strategy to a pluralist based strategy, they do not share the reformist belief that the 'joint regulation' aspect of productivity bargaining will, in itself, be in the interests of the worker. The call for 'joint control' is seen to be little more than empty rhetoric, a means by which to incorporate workers and unions into the logic of the firm through a sophisticated con game. As Cliff puts it:

> There is a very real danger that the less politically sophisticated workers (and even stewards) will swallow this eyewash; that they will accept that formal plant bargaining has replaced the old relationship of conflict by a 'fair' system of joint control. Believing this, they will feel it wrong to act 'unconstitutionally', outside the formally agreed procedure; and in this way they emasculate themselves, destroying the basis of their existing strength. (1970: 142)

From the Marxian perspective, trade unions were also seen to be drawn into the role of policemen of these very agreements, which in turn could mean the policing of shop stewards by the union hierarchy itself. As Cliff suggests:

> The aim of the employers' strategy is to split the workers one from another, to destroy work-place organization by either muscling the shop stewards or integrating them into the union machine and to use the union leadership as a disciplinary agent against those who fight back. In other words, the strategy is aimed at finding a *permanent* solution to employers' problems. (1970: 11, emphasis in original)

Both the reformist and the Marxian schools assume, in practical terms, that managers did, in fact, deign to shift their unitarist industrial-relations strategy to a pluralist one of joint control, even though for Marxians, this 'joint control' was more one of appearance than of substance.

Increased management control through greater formalization

It was also believed that productivity bargaining, at least productivity bargaining of the comprehensive type, would usher in a new era of 'bureaucratic' control. The formalization and codification of workplace rules was seen as essential to the process. As Flanders put it,

> ... the reconstruction of workplace relations implies a much greater formalisation of plant bargaining in its procedural and substantive aspects. Written agreements are needed in the first place to reduce uncertainty and ambiguity in the relations between the parties. Oral understandings can genuinely be forgotten and when this happens misunderstandings and mistrust may easily result. Formal agreements will also help to dispel the cloud of pretence and subterfuge which has surrounded all kinds of additional payments made within the plant. Negotiators have to be more careful about the consequences of their decisions when they can be called to account for them, and their relations are placed on a more open and honest footing. Moreover, the object is to create a more controlled situation, and specification in agreement is one important means of control. (1975: 205)

The Donovan Report, in fact, strongly implied that 'informal workshop understandings' were, by their very nature, a source of contention and inefficiency and recommended that wherever possible collective agreements should be 'written down and precise' (Hawkins, 1971: 16–17).

Productivity bargaining was seen to be capable of replacing a system of shop-floor fractional bargaining with a set of rational rules which would provide a more orderly structure of workplace relations. McKersie and Hunter note, for instance:

> Prior to productivity bargaining, decisions were made in terms of precedent, customary practice, or the dictates of stewards and foremen. Such a control system could be characterized as haphazard and personal. By contrast, under productivity bargaining, the control process becomes more deliberate, rational and professional. It remains just as much a product of joint influence, but the process of joint regulation has been placed on a more systematic and impersonal basis. (1973: 287)

Nightingale, commenting on the control implications of productivity bargaining, also describes the process as fundamentally bureaucratic. He states that productivity bargaining '... involved the displacement of control through economic incentives by control through the supervised application of closely defined rules and standards' (1980: 320).

Like the reformists, Marxian scholars also saw formalization as an important control device. Cliff argues, for instance, that the growing formality implied by productivity bargaining would necessarily mean the removal of unwritten rights and the imposition of formal agreements that would be inflexible and not subject to trade union erosion. The Marxians feared that '... by introducing greater formality into the shop-floor situation, productivity bargaining would undermine workers' day-to-day control over their jobs and their ability to bargain over line speeds, the rate for the job, conditions of work, and so on' (Nightingale, 1980: 321). Marxians also believed that '... union officials and shop stewards, in particular, would become increasingly bureaucratized and remote from their members and that this would have the serious effect of weakening shop-floor organization' (Nightingale, 1980: 321).

For both reformists like Flanders and for the Marxian school, it was believed that the formalization to be brought on by productivity bargaining would have clear management advantages in the area of control over labour.

Conclusions

It has been seen that productivity bargaining is, or has in the past been, associated with increased employee effort by means of shifting the industrial-relations strategy (1) from one of 'low wages' to one of 'high wages' (this represented a move towards labour market internalization), (2) from one of unitarism to one of pluralist based 'joint control' and (3) from one of informality to one of formal rules. Such beliefs about the control implications of productivity bargaining tend, however, to treat the subject at an abstract level, simply assuming that there is a perfect correspondence between the theory of productivity bargaining and what actually occurs at the workplace. As Hawkins says of the 'Oxford' approach it '. . . betrays a rather uncritical faith in the long-term benefits of these agreements, which has yet to be justified by empirical evidence' (1971: 31).

A major reservation on the reformist and Marxian views on the control implications of productivity bargaining relates to the actual, as opposed to the predicted, results of the agreements. It is clearly a mistake to confuse intentions with reality. To do so usually means giving management too much credit for its ability to implement and sustain a strategy based on productivity bargaining. Not only does it assume a perfect rationality on the part of management, but it also ignores the disturbances of a wide variety of external factors and, more importantly, the power of labour in subverting or defusing the content of a particular agreement.

Questions need to be raised about how productivity bargaining actually operated in the workplace and how effective a strategy it actually proved to be. For instance, did the process of labour market 'internalization' pan out as Allen would have hoped? Did management really embrace productivity bargaining within the context of a pluralist philosophy or did it do so while remaining well within the context of a unitarist philosophy? Did formalization actually prove to be an advantage to management in controlling labour? Furthermore, was management capable of operating a strategy based on productivity bargaining in an effective and unproblematic manner, or was such a strategy deflected off course, distorted by its own internal contradictions and pressure from workers and trade unions? This last question is one, of course, which relates to the ability of management to design, implement and effectively operate a long-term, strategic approach to human resources management.

In order to test management's ability to sustain a strategic approach to industrial relations, direct reference must be made to empirical reality and not to mere abstraction. Because part of the definition of a strategic approach is the long-term planning dimension, it is important, further, that the empirical data itself be historical. Not only does an historical context allow us to test management's ability to sustain an industrial-relations strategy, but it also enables us to uncover the various meanings of that strategy within the complexities and tensions of everyday organizational life.

The clock is now turned back some 25 years to the striking of the first historic Blue Book productivity agreement. It is here that the industrial-relations strategy based on productivity bargaining at Fawley Refinery will be evaluated from 1960 to 1985. It will be seen that the aims, objectives and meanings of such a strategy will depart, sometimes quite dramatically, from its stated objectives.

5

Case study background

Introduction

This chapter provides background information to the following case study. It discusses the particular research methods employed, describes the state of the business environment both in the oil industry in general and as it has affected the Esso U.K. refining operation between 1960 and 1985, and provides a general description of refining operations at Fawley, as well as an overview of Fawley's organizational structure. Finally, a list of each of the 21 productivity agreements struck at Fawley Refinery between 1960 and 1985 is provided.

Research methodology

The research method employed here is known more precisely as the 'extended case study' approach, because

> ... it deals with a sequence of events over quite a long period of time, where the actors are involved in a series of situations in which their structural positions must continually be re-specified and the flow of actors through different social positions specified. (Mitchell, 1983: 194)

The particular value of the extended case study is that it '... enables the analyst to trace how events chain on to one another and how therefore events are necessarily linked to one another through time' (Mitchell, 1983: 194). The processual dimension is thus highlighted. The case study method appeared to provide the best approach to the analysis of strategy in industrial relations as this method permits research entry into the industrial subculture or subterranean aspects of organizational life. Much of what is interesting about workplace control often, as we will see, lies 'below the waterline of organizational visibility', and it is a powerful feature of the case study method that it enables one to dip below this critical waterline.

The particular case study site selected by a researcher can '... have a major impact on the empirical patterns which are identifiable ... and the nature of the theoretical developments and policy implications which follow' (Pettigrew, 1985: 39). Clearly there were research advantages in selecting Esso's Fawley Refinery as my case study site. First, the individual case study is interesting *in its own right* as it explores industrial-relations strategy at the landmark site of the very first productivity agreement. As a result, the case study site possessed a naturally bounded time-frame for research, from 1960 to 1985.

The Fawley site could be considered the extreme case in that Fawley has been associated with the purest form of productivity bargaining (and has been pointed to as the exemplar case). Fawley was seen, moreover, as the first British firm to engage in the process of strategic industrial-relations management (Lupton, 1966). The Fawley site provided, therefore, an opportunity to test arguments where one is most likely to find industrial-relations strategy in its most efficacious form. Fawley stood, therefore, as an ideal laboratory case for the evaluation of the nature and meaning of strategy in industrial relations.

Secondly, there existed the attraction of knowing that comparatively rich research materials and data could be obtained, thanks not only to prior scholarly work on this particular site (Flanders' own analysis of the Blue Book productivity deal), but also to government publications about the site (for example by The National Board for Prices and Incomes and the Donovan Commission) and to a continuing set of newspaper articles which have invariably made reference to Fawley when addressing the productivity bargaining issue. These references proved to be of considerable value in this historical analysis.

The actual field work undertaken at Fawley took place over a nine-month period from July 1983 to April 1984. On site, field work was conducted on average about two to three days a week (with intermittent periods of off-site analysis of company documentation). A number of visits were also made to Esso's head office in London, reviewing company documents and magazines stored in the corporate library. The importance of the Blue Book to the Esso culture is reflected in the fact that the original Blue Book agreement is now housed in this library, much like a relic in a museum.

Three principal techniques were used in conducting the research: (1) a study of written documentation, (2) a series of semi-structured and in-depth interviews with designated key actors from both union and management ranks and finally, (3) simple observation. There was an attempt to compare the data collected by these different methods in order to validate relevant and critical bits of information. To the extent that there was a conscious attempt to compare data from a variety of sources, it could be said that a strategy of 'triangulation' was pursued (Cicourel, 1964 and 1973).

Research access was granted through management, not through the union. The access provided could only be described as fully open. All the company industrial-relations files and documents were open to me for inspection. Fortunately, Esso Fawley had not discarded old files, and a continuous set of documentation existed from 1960 onwards. All old files were housed in a large storage room and I had access to all of these. The good retention and organization of records may have had something to do with management's awareness of the historical significance of the Blue Book and other industrial-relations initiatives and the need to ensure their place in the 'history of Fawley'. The difficulty associated with the review of management documentation was not the lack of information, but rather its over-abundance. The problem was one of separating the 'wheat from the chaff' of literally thousands upon thousands of pages of industrial-relations minutes, notes, letters and plans (which represented the total written output of both management and unions over a period of twenty-five years).

Once a trust relationship had been established with the unions (after about two months in the field), all of the union files and documents were also made available to me. I considered the development of a trust relationship with the unions to be critical to the project for a variety of reasons, not least of which was to provide a valuable check on the validity of data derived from management. The development of a trust relationship with the unions proved to be a longer process than originally anticipated. Perhaps predictably, the pivotal moment in the establishment of trust took place not in the workplace but 'over a few drinks' (and to be precise, at 3.00 a.m. at a casino in Bournemouth, on the last night of a three-day shop steward conference).

Formal documents, however, do not tell the whole story. As with any industrial-relations initiative some of the more important observations that can be made never reach the point of formal recording in either trade union or management documents. Personal interviews were conducted to go beyond the limitations of formal documentation. My interviews covered a wide cross-section of refinery personnel including all members of the employee relations department, key members of line management, a sample of front-line supervisors, each of the branch officers, senior shop stewards and a sample of the domestic shop stewards. Ex-Esso managers were also interviewed off the site. Apart from that, I made much of listening and informal discussion in offices, canteens and frequently after working hours in pubs with managers, shop stewards and workers.

I was also invited to a number of special conferences, including shop steward training programmes and special 'organizational development' activities concerning wage personnel. When not involved in such activities or in semi-structured interviews, I always had the freedom to drop into a manager's office or the shop stewards' central office, for an informal chat over a cup of coffee. As the distance from Oxford required overnight stays, many an evening, furthermore, was spent with Esso personnel discussing the research. The value of these more informal meetings cannot be overestimated.

Business environment: the oil industry in general

In the early 1960s Blauner (1964) and other 'white heat' enthusiasts, had a deep faith in the business prospects of continuous process industry. The industry was generally seen to be characterized by capital expansion, relatively high levels of profitability and stable product demand. Blauner's own argument, that workers in this industry were under less pressure and had a greater sense of security than in other industries, rested in part on the assumption of a relatively stable business environment (Eldridge, 1971: 189).

The link between business stability and continuous process industries can, however, be questioned. For example, the rapid growth in demand for petrochemicals in the post-war years was, itself, halted as a result of the mid-1950s recession. The continuous process industry and especially oil and chemical refining operations have, since the 1950s, been caught in a vicious 'boom-and-bust' business cycle. If there was a period of real growth and expansion in refining capacity it occurred from the mid-1960s to 1973. Due to the severe impact of the crude oil price explosion of 1973–4, world-wide demand for petroleum products declined dramatically, especially in the heavy fuel oil market. The fall in U.K. inland demand for petroleum is well documented (Williams, 1982: 26). The market peaked in 1973 with inland deliveries of 99 million tonnes; falling to 81 million tonnes in 1975; reviving to 84.5 million tonnes in 1979, before falling to 71 million tonnes in 1980 and 66 million tonnes in 1981 (Williams, 1982: 26).

The O.P.E.C. induced oil shock of the mid- and late 1970s resulted in a general decline in demand for fuel oil products. For oil refining, this post-1973 period can in fact be described as a situation of massive world-wide over-supply of refining capacity. Moreover, over-capacity in the 1980s has reduced oil refining to an activity of very little relative profit.

The second oil price surge in 1979 and the onslaught of the recession in

1980 were to have a further devastating effect on the U.K. refining business. Consumption of petroleum products declined in the U.K. by sixteen per cent in 1980 (*The Petroleum Economist*, August 1981: 326). Despite fourteen refineries being closed down in Europe in 1982, European capacity continued to outstrip demand by six to seven million barrels a day (*The Petroleum Times*, March 1984: 30).

In addition to an overall market decline, oil refiners also had to face simultaneously a major swing in the product market or 'composition of the sales barrel'. The overall trend has been a decline in demand for heavy fuel oil products and a rising demand for the 'lighter' products such as gases, motor spirits, and naphthas for chemical feedstocks. This change, known in the business as 'barrel whitening', marked a shift in the market away from the low-value 'bottom end' of the barrel products to high-value products. In addition to the need to 'whiten' the product barrel, the refiners were also faced with a much less predictable mix of 'crude slates' and, as a result, required as much processing flexibility as possible (*The Petroleum Times*, February 1982: 15). Most European refineries were caught without such flexibility, as they were designed and built to give optimum yields on a single or small number of crudes (*The Petroleum Times*, February 1982: 15).

The rapid change in the composition of the sales barrel since the mid-1970s presented a major dilemma to refiners. To meet the changing pattern of demand for oil products, refineries were forced to make substantial investments in refinery processing equipment. The falling profits, however, reduced the financial resources available for the costly investment needed to adjust the refinery yield to the changing pattern of demand. Refineries got caught in a bind of needing to introduce new equipment, while being constrained from doing so due to reduced profit levels. The funding of this new equipment depended, furthermore, on addressing the problems of surplus capacity in the old 'bread-and-butter' heavy fuel oil area.

In this situation of declining demand and the intensification of competition, refineries in Britain and Europe were forced into major rationalization of operations which focussed on all costs, including labour costs. Because they represented variable rather than fixed costs, labour costs came under particular scrutiny. Refineries attempted to cut manpower to the bone in order to reduce costs. Job security was replaced with a spectre of job loss and redundancy. The move to reduce manning levels was also associated with attempts to utilize existing labour more effectively. The main thrust of the attempt to maximize labour utilization was to try to create more flexible working practices. This meant that the complex job grading schemes and institutionalized mobility routes that Blauner associated with continuous process industry were often to be broken up and replaced by shorter and more open-ended job grades.

The general effect of these changing business conditions was the evolution of different refineries, ones with smaller throughput, producing a greater proportion of the 'lighter' products.

Business environment: the Exxon parent company and the Esso U.K. refining operation

The business conditions surrounding Esso U.K. Ltd, and its U.S. parent company, Exxon, have, for the most part, mirrored those which surrounded the oil industry as a whole. As the largest oil company in the world, Exxon felt the brunt of the decline in demand for oil products. The 1950s downturn in the business environment was, as Flanders has shown, the main impetus for Exxon's (then known as Standard Oil of New Jersey) emphasis upon productivity improvements at Esso's Fawley Refinery in Britain. According to Flanders, the immediate cause of the Blue Book '. . . appears to have been an intensification of competition in the American markets following the 1953–4 recession' (1964: 65).

In the recent past, Exxon has gone through similar buffeting. Its 'downstream' operations, that is refining and marketing, have been significantly restructured. Since 1978 Exxon has shed 15,100 jobs in downstream operations, which represents a twenty-two per cent reduction (*The Financial Times*, 25 July 1984). Further, the group has reduced its refining capacity by 1.3 million barrels a day, or twenty-two per cent and, since 1978, has closed or sold thirteen refineries (*The Financial Times*, 25 July 1984).

Like the parent company, the Esso U.K. refining operation itself has been caught in a turbulent business environment. Of Esso's two refineries in the U.K. (Fawley Refinery and Milford Haven Refinery) one, Milford Haven, was closed down in March 1983. In contrast to Fawley, Milford Haven was caught with much more limited 'up-grading' facilities and was not considered capable of responding to the swing in the product market towards the 'light end' of the barrel.

While there was a substantial growth in the Esso U.K. refining business from the early 1960s to 1970, the growth rate began to dip as early as 1970 as a result of general business uncertainty. In the early 1970s, demand was still expected to grow, and many oil companies, including Esso U.K., had been busy expanding existing facilities. A big surge in new capacity, including some at Milford Haven, had come into operation just as demand sagged. The result was that Esso and the U.K. refining industry were caught wrong-footed. There has not, for instance, been a requirement for crude expansion within Esso U.K. since 1971. Fawley Refinery's production itself has shown a consistent downward trend since 1974.

The 'white heat' enthusiasts could not, then, have been further from the mark in their high optimism for the continuous process industry. Instead, the refining industry has been characterized by a general decline.

Refinery operations and industrial relations at Fawley

Esso Petroleum U.K. Ltd. is the oldest affiliate of the American based Exxon Corporation (known as Standard Oil of New Jersey in Flanders' era). Fawley Refinery is now Esso's only refinery within the United Kingdom (after the closure of the Milford Haven Refinery in 1983). It is a large refinery, as refineries go; it is the largest refinery in the United Kingdom and one of the largest within Europe. The refinery has a design capacity of 15.6 million tonnes per year which represents about twelve per cent of the U.K. capacity.

The Fawley site is shared by both the Esso Petroleum Company and Esso Chemicals Ltd. The Esso Petroleum side is devoted to 'oil refining', while the Chemical side manufactures various petro-chemical products. The first chemical manufacturing plants were installed at Fawley in 1958 and Esso Chemicals Ltd. became a separate company in 1966. Both Esso Petroleum and Esso Chemicals operate with their own separate management teams, each having, for instance, their own employee relations departments. This particular research has focussed exclusively on Esso Petroleum Company Ltd., i.e. the refining side of the business. However, my analysis of Fawley from 1960 to 1966 includes both the petroleum and chemical operations, as both were formally integrated into the same business during that period.

While the oil refining business is technologically complex, the basic process can be described fairly simply. As one 'old hand' at Fawley put it to me: 'Oil refining is about boiling oil.' The first link in the long chain of refinery operations is the 'distilling' of crude oil into fractions, i.e. the natural proportions of light and heavy molecules that make up the crude oil. Further transformations can take place, depending on the product desired. This can be done by 'cracking' (breaking down), 'polymerizing' (building up) or 'reforming' (changing the structure) of molecules. Finally, there is 'treating' which includes the removal of impurities and unwanted substances from the oil.

As of July 1983, there were 530 salaried staff employees at Fawley Refinery. There is no recognized collective bargaining or negotiations for any of these staff employees. The balance of the employee population at Fawley is classified as either 'process' or 'maintenance' workers. There were 480 process workers and 420 maintenance workers employed at Fawley as of July 1983.

The process workers are divided into two categories: (1) operating 'shift' workers and (2) non-operating day workers. Operating shift workers are responsible for the actual processing of the crude oil. This group works either in centralized control rooms, monitoring the 'process' – through computer or analogue controls – or out in the field, adjusting valves, looking after pumps and doing similar jobs in accordance with central control-room instructions. Non-operating process workers are charged principally with oil movement and storage – oil of both the crude and refined variety. These jobs vary from the receiving of the crude oil from tanker ships to the storing of refined oil products in various tank fields.

The maintenance workers themselves are also divided into two categories: (1) craft and (2) non-craft workers. Craft workers include mechanical fitters, electricians, pipefitters, bricklayers, carpenters, boilermakers, welders and instrument fitters. Some craft workers belong to mobile teams which cover maintenance work for process units in various zones within the refinery, while other craft workers do maintenance work in a centralized workshop. Non-craft workers are semi- and low-skilled workers performing such work as rigging, scaffolding, insulation, crane driving and general labouring.

All of the process workers are represented by Branch 2/328 of the Transport and General Workers' Union (a refinery based branch). There is a total of five branch officers for the Fawley site, three of whom are representatives on the refining side and two on the chemicals side. There is also a full-time official (located off-site) and a network of some thirty-two shop stewards which represent various 'blocks' within a process unit. Collective bargaining is totally plant based, that is, there are no national or company-wide agreements. Formal negotiations take place yearly through the 'full negotiating committee' – consisting of the five branch officers, the full-time official and various management representatives, including the Refinery and Esso Chemicals senior managers. There is also a second-level 'negotiation and consultation' committee which meets bi-monthly (and has the power to change the terms and conditions of employment as set in the annual agreements). Finally, there is also a 'joint consultative committee' structure whose main function is to provide a forum for management to discuss business plans with shop stewards.

Various groups of maintenance workers, on the other hand, are represented by the following unions:

1 Mechanical fitters and welders: the Amalgamated Union of Engineering Workers (A.U.E.W.).

2 Electricians and pipefitters: the electrical, electronic, telecommunications and the plumbing union. The E.T.U. and P.T.U. are separated out locally at Fawley.
3 Bricklayers and carpenters: the Union of Construction, Allied Trades and Technicians (U.C.A.T.T.).
4 Non-craft maintenance workers (riggers, scaffolders etc.): Transport and General Workers' Union 2/22 Branch.

A similar negotiating and consultation structure exists for the maintenance workers as for the process workers.

In addition to the above hourly paid maintenance workers Fawley also has maintenance workers who cannot be included in the above categories. The instrument fitters, boilermakers and some welders are currently on individual 'staff status' contracts. This particular maintenance group does not have collective bargaining rights on the site. There are approximately ninety-seven Esso Petroleum Company maintenance workers who are covered by these contracts.

Fawley's maintenance (as well as construction activity) is supported by a contractor labour force. Agreements affecting the contractors are negotiated between the contractors and Area No. 5 of the Confederation of Shipbuilding and Engineering Unions.

The Esso Fawley productivity agreements: 1960–1985

Productivity bargaining at Fawley was not to begin and end with the Blue Book. From 1960 to 1985, Fawley management negotiated a total of twenty-one productivity agreements as well as two proposed agreements that broke down during the negotiation stage. Of these concluded agreements, fifteen were thought to be more substantial than the others, that is they were considered to have had a greater impact on working practices. A list of the twenty-one productivity agreements (and two proposed agreements) is given below, with the 15 more substantial agreements marked by asterisks.

The Fawley productivity agreements: 1960–1984

The 'craft' Blue Book	1960 *
The 'Transport and General Workers' Union' (T.G.W.U.) Blue Book	1960 *

The T.G.W.U. Orange Book	1962 *
The 'craft' Orange Book	1962/3 *
The T.G.W.U. process workers' interim deal	1967 *

The T.G.W.U. process workers' productivity '68 agreement	1968	*
The T.G.W.U. non-craft maintenance productivity agreement	1968	*
The craft '68 deal	1968	*
The craft and non-craft maintenance productivity agreement	1969	*
T.G.W.U. process '70 deal	1970	
Process 'Day Workers Mini Deal'	1971	
Maintenance progressive approach	1972	*
Pink Book – proposal only (process and maintenance)	1974	
Maintenance agreement: 'Individuals working within related groups'	1975	*
Process efficiency agreement (P.E.A. '75)	1975	*
Process 'improved shift operation control system agreement'	1978	
Process 'qualified operator training period reduction agreement'	1978	
Process plan '80 – proposal only	1978	
Maintenance target approach	1978/9	*
Process payment by results (addendum to 1975 P.E.A.)	1979	
Process productivity agreement	1981	*
Maintenance enabling agreement	1982	*
Personal increments payment system	1984	

It is clear, then, that Fawley management fully embraced productivity bargaining as its industrial-relations strategy. Looking at the above list it can be seen that there are intervening years without active productivity 'dealing' between them. Productivity agreements were, however, still in force, and it is possible to argue that the entire 25-year period was one of sustained commitment to the notion of productivity bargaining. The significance of productivity bargaining to Fawley and the relationship of the technique to traditional collective bargaining was put in this way by one Fawley manager:

> Sometimes we go into our annual negotiations as productivity bargainers, other times as collective bargainers, and still other times we go in as collective bargainers and leave as productivity bargainers. (Interview with Fawley manager)

How close did Fawley Refinery come to achieving the objectives stated in this string of productivity deals? Chapters 6, 7, 8 and 9 evaluate the effectiveness of these deals at the level of their rational or stated objectives. It is hoped that, by examining the extent to which the Fawley productivity agreements actually achieved their objectives I will be able to shed some light on the value of the rational approach to strategy in industrial relations. As the case study unfolds and it becomes clear that productivity bargaining is not the success that may have been anticipated, the relevance of the political approach and particularly the (as yet undeveloped) symbolic approach becomes more apparent for the notion of industrial-relations strategy.

6

The Fawley Blue Book revisited

Productivity agreements can conceivably change attitudes to make British industry more receptive to change. Equally they can generate general increases in incomes out of all keeping with the changes in practices they actually effect. None of us can tell what the net result will really be. All we know is that something deeply significant is in motion which cannot be stopped and that we must try hard if we are to extract from it the good rather than the ill. He who would do this must, however, first go back to Genesis, to Fawley where it all began ... (Aubrey Jones' foreword to the paperback edition of A. Flanders, *The Fawley Productivity Agreements*, 1964: 11)

Introduction

The highly celebrated status of the Blue Book has meant that the first productivity agreement took on almost mythical proportions. Over time, it has become increasingly difficult to determine what is fact and what is fiction. Various individuals, groups and coalitions have sought to 'tell the story', often as will be seen, to suit particular goals and needs. This chapter returns to the Blue Book era in an attempt to re-evaluate the significance and meaning of the Blue Book productivity deals for Fawley Refinery.

This chapter reviews the historical rationale for the introduction of the Blue Book productivity agreements, describes the actual content of the agreements and evaluates the extent to which these agreements attained or realized their stated objectives. My own evaluation of the Blue Book is compared to other evaluations that have been made in the past such as those of the National Board for Prices and Incomes, Report No. 36, Royal Commission on Trade Unions and Employers' Associations, Research Papers 4, Esso Fawley Refinery's internal self-evaluations and, finally, Flanders' own seminal evaluation of the Blue Book. As Flanders' evaluation of the Blue Book remains the only detailed published study of the agreements, my own findings are compared directly and principally with his.

An attempt is made to evaluate the Blue Book productivity agreements, not only within the context of the time frame covered by Flanders' analysis, from 1960 to 1962, but also from an extended time frame, covering the period up to 1967 which is the point in time that marked the striking of Fawley's second generation agreements. It is argued that the two-year time frame employed in Flanders' analysis was not long enough for the full effects of the agreements to become manifested. Furthermore, it is commonly argued by organizational theorists (Bennis et al., 1961) that most major organizational changes are associated with an early 'honeymoon' phase characterized by euphoria and associated with the design and early implementation stages of the change. Such euphoria can often serve to distort the evaluation of change projects. The high celebrity status of the Blue Book may have extended the honeymoon phase and, as a result, extended the period of time required to evaluate the implications of the Blue Book. It must be noted that Flanders himself expressed doubts about too early an assessment:

> The objection might well be raised that it is still too soon to venture any judgments on the value of the agreements. That applies to all contemporary studies, and my justification is that the agreements are of sufficient current interest to warrant the publication of provisional conclusions. (1964: 18)

My assessment of the Blue Book also seeks to answer three penetrating questions raised by Aubrey Jones in his foreword to the paperback edition of Flanders' study, the *Fawley Productivity Agreements*:

> 1. Did it score a lasting success in its aims? Or did it roll back for a little the waters of custom which subsequently flooded in again more strongly than before?
> 2. Alternatively, even if success was lasting, was it paid for in other directions, and did it conceivably set in train a series of disadvantages even greater than those which it may have removed?
> 3. ... When weekly earnings are increased by something like 20 per cent are expectations created which cannot indefinitely be met? It is understandable that a change of practice may initially be worth a great deal. But as time goes on expectations in pay will continue, while the value of the change in practice may

conceivably exhaust itself. Is it possible that there is trouble in store here? (in Flanders, 1964: 9–10)

Before embarking upon a re-evaluation of the Blue Book, this chapter first addresses the historical origins of the Blue Book agreements.

The historical origins of the Blue Book

According to Flanders, 'the Blue Book story begins with the blowing of a keen wind of change across the Atlantic in 1956, when Standard Oil (New Jersey) displayed a heightened and probing interest in the topic of manpower' (1964: 65). Flanders suggests that the parent company's interest in manpower utilization stemmed from both an intensification of competition in the American markets following the 1953–4 recession and, at a deeper level, from the company's need to adjust the size of its manual labour force relative to its productive capacity (ibid.: 65).

At around this time, Standard Oil had introduced statistical comparisons of manpower utilization in all its refineries across the world and, according to these, it was found that 'the Fawley Refinery made comparatively poor showing' (Flanders, 1964: 65). These international comparisons were made on the basis of numbers of men employed per unit of production, the results of which were set out in world-wide Standard Oil 'league tables'. With the advent of these 'league tables' Fawley Refinery, along with the other Standard Oil Refineries, became locked into a 'numbers game'. D.A.C. Dewdney, a director of Esso U.K. Ltd., described the origins of the Blue Book directly within the logic of this 'numbers game': '... the honest fact is that the true origins of the Blue Book lay simply in the fact that payroll costs at the refinery were higher than those in other refineries' (*Esso Magazine*, Autumn 1967).

While Fawley management's account of the origins of the Blue Book accords, for the most part, with Flanders' account, management made it clear to the Donovan Commission that there was a certain independence of action on its part, an internal 'will of management' which served to propel the process of change:

> Flanders has described how at Fawley the pressure from Standard Oil Company (New Jersey) was an important part of starting the process ... But these were not the continuing impulses which kept the negotiators going. What these pressures did was to accentuate the need and intensify the will of managements to perform more effectively. The initial pressures were important, but lost their significance relatively quickly.
> (Minutes of evidence, Royal Commission on Trade Unions and

82

Employers' Association, 7 June 1966, written memorandum of
evidence submitted by the Esso Petroleum Company in advance of the oral hearing: Commission's reference WE/143;
page 1645)

As a result of the general profit squeeze and Fawley's unfavourable
position at the very bottom of the world-wide league table, a small
committee was formed at Fawley in 1957 to investigate working methods,
with a view to improving efficiency and improving Fawley's position in the
league table. One of the first decisions that this committee took was to
turn for help to an external, American-based consulting firm by the name
of Emersons. One of the consultants to be brought over was a man by the
name of Bill Allen – a man who was to be held in high regard by Fawley
management. Members of Fawley management commented that Allen
was a 'deep thinker' who was 'very good at getting other people to think'
(Flanders, 1964: 72–3). According to Flanders a positive synergistic
working relationship was struck between the American way and the
British way of working: 'The American tenets "that every problem can be
solved" and "there is no virtue in delay" were combined with the British
emphasis on proceeding by conciliation, tolerance and humanity' (1964:
73).

Allen was to act as the key catalyst for change. He argued that
managements need not be passive, simply accepting organizational structures and working arrangements as given. Instead, Allen saw a need for
management to question these arrangements, to seek out new and more
efficient ways of working. Management's role was not merely to be one of
maintaining systems, it was also to be one of actively intervening and
changing systems where necessary: 'Erroneous beliefs can be changed!
That epitomizes the consultant's outlook and surely represents its most
daring premise' (Flanders, 1964: 81). Allen had served, in other words, to
compel '. . . a re-examination of some of management's fixed ideas and in
so doing propelled it into action that it had not seriously contemplated
before' (Flanders, 1964: 79).

In the past, Fawley management had operated from a '. . . general
assumption that the principal way of getting more work done was to
employ more workers' (Flanders, 1964: 79). High levels of systematic
overtime and rigid work demarcations were accepted as natural and
normal. One by one each of these firmly established traditions came to be
questioned by Allen and by Fawley management – the most important of
which was considered to be the high levels of overtime being worked. By
the beginning of 1960 Fawley management had drawn up a detailed and
closely interrelated catalogue of proposals – the Blue Book. The basic idea

of this set of proposals was that overtime should be cut dramatically. A number of changes were proposed to permit this reduction. For example, craft demarcations were to be relaxed where craft skills overlapped and process workers were to be permitted to perform some craft jobs. The Blue Book was premised around a single theme: the need for a 'low-overtime–high-wage policy'.

The actual timetable for the production of the Blue Book is shown below:

> **Timetable for Blue Book at Fawley**
> *Mid-1957* Work started at the refinery on identifying areas of inefficiency
> *November 1958* Memorandum from the consultant
> *November 1958–December 1959* Development period: discussion at plant and shop-floor level, involving stewards, supervisors, management and men
> *February 1960–May 1960* Formal negotiations
> *July 1960* Agreement
> Source: Memorandum of evidence submitted by Esso Petroleum Company Ltd to the Royal Commission on Trade Unions, pp. 4–5.

The content of the Blue Book

In July 1960, the first productivity agreements were signed; one with the Transport and General Workers' Union, which organizes all the non-craft hourly-paid employees in the refinery, and the other with a body known as the Craft Union Committee, consisting of seven unions representing Fawley craftsmen. These two agreements are usually taken or considered together as one productivity deal, the Blue Book.

Flanders has described the Blue Book agreements as having two prominent features: (1) '. . . a quite specific productivity package deal' and (2) '. . . a radical attack on systematic overtime' (Flanders, 1964: 81). With respect to these two areas, the key improvements sought by the Blue Book agreements can be summarized as follows:

Feature I: 'The productivity package'
From the angle of productivity improvement, the Blue Book provisions sought:
(1) to eliminate the occupation of craftsmen's 'mates', and to transfer and train mates for alternative useful work. 280 'mates' were to be redeployed;

(2) to achieve greater flexibility of working by a relaxation of existing demarcation practices. Flexible working was to occur both within departments and between departments. 'This meant a relaxation of craft demarcations at the fringes – an item which went under the title of inter-craft flexibility. Another proposal was the transfer of minor maintenance work from the craftsmen to process workers. A further one – the carrying out of a certain amount of slinging work by the craftsmen themselves' (Flanders, 1975: 53);

(3) to ensure that every craft group was prepared to take administrative orders from any staff supervisor regardless of the supervisor's or the worker's particular craft;

(4) to alter working time arrangements through the abolition of 'unproductive' time allowances such as walking time, washing time, and set tea breaks. In the maintenance and construction areas 'temporary' shifts were to be introduced when deemed necessary;

(5) to eliminate special payments such as heat and dirt money;

(6) to abandon a points rating scheme which was used for fixing wages. 'The old point rating scheme which applied to all non-staff, non-craft employees had produced 154 different jobs with 22 different pay rates in Process alone ...' (Flanders, 1964: 89). There was to be '... less promotional mobility ...' and '... greater job versatility ...' accomplished through the '... consolidation of pay rates to five main shift grades (and two day grades) ...' (Flanders, 1964: 90);

(7) to introduce a system of 'substitute' working on the process side. Substitutes were to be highly flexible trained operators who could move from one unit to another.

Feature II: The systematic attack on overtime

The second major aspect of the agreements '... was that they embodied a radical attack on systematic overtime' (Flanders, 1975: 53). In 1959, prior to the 'Blue Book', overtime at Fawley, as a percentage of actual hours worked, was running at a refinery-wide average of eighteen per cent among the day workers in the maintenance and construction area and at fifteen per cent among the shift workers in process (Flanders, 1975: 53–4). The Blue Book sought to cut overtime down to a stated maximum of two per cent in maintenance and construction and, while no specific target figure was mentioned for process (it merely referred to a low minimum), management expected to cut overtime by two-thirds (Flanders, 1975: 54).

In order to obtain worker agreement to overtime reduction and the 'productivity package', the company offered all workers large increases in wage rates to the order of forty per cent. This wage increase was to be paid in instalments. One third was paid immediately as an initial instalment and one sixth of the total at six-monthly intervals over a two-year period. As Flanders notes, 'these phased increases were designed to correspond *pari passu* with the targets for overtime reduction so that they compensated for the dwindling overtime element in the worker's weekly pay packets' (1975: 54). While basic rates were to be increased very considerably at Fawley, cuts in overtime pay meant that take-home pay was not to increase by anything like the same proportion. Between 1960 and 1962, for instance, average *hourly* earnings of weekly-paid employees at Fawley went up by about thirty-five per cent; the average working week, including overtime, however, was reduced by five and a quarter hours, resulting in an average *weekly* earnings increase of about twenty-one per cent (The Royal Commission on Trade Unions and Employers' Associations, Research Papers 4, 1967).

Wage increases were to be accompanied by the introduction of a 40-hour week in place of the previous 42 or 42.5 hours. There was also a pledge of 'no redundancy' as a result of the Blue Book provisions. This 'no-redundancy' pledge was significant for management as it '... puts considerable onus on the accuracy of manpower forecasting and budgeting ...' (McKersie and Hunter, 1973: 38).

This, then, was the content of the first historic productivity agreement.

Past evaluations of the Blue Book agreements in practice

In addition to Flanders' detailed evaluation of the Blue Book agreements which will be discussed in the following section, various agencies and individuals have attempted to evaluate these same agreements, virtually all of which have made favourable final judgments. Perhaps, not surprisingly, Fawley management's own overall assessments remained favourable – even over the extended time frame to 1967. Esso's own evidence to the Donovan Commission five years after the striking of the Blue Book deal was to confirm that restrictive practices had not re-emerged (Daniel, 1970a: 18). In an article in *Personnel magazine*, Jones reported the following on Fawley's evaluation of its productivity bargaining, seven years on:

> ... there has been no serious collapse in any of the major implementations, and some six years after the Fawley 'Blue Book', Tom Batho, Employee Relations Superintendent at the Refinery, was able to answer the question 'Is your company still pleased that it undertook productivity bargaining?' with an unequivocal 'Very. We have made money out of it and so have our employees.' (1967: 22)

Another press report, one year later, carried an equally positive account. The title of this article relates to Bill Allen's hopes and dreams for a 'full-pay/full-effort' work-force: 'Jack's pay packet is bigger – and that's good news for Britain'. This article reported that

> ... at Fawley, where productivity agreements were first estab-
> lished eight years ago, the transition has been painless. Old
> union lines of demarcation have become blurred. You won't
> find a carpenter doing an engineer's job but they do help one
> another more than before. Nobody blows the strike whistle for
> a minor infringement of old rules. They get the job done and
> share the profits ... Esso's refinery manager Archie Foster said:
> 'People in other parts of the world are no better at their jobs
> but do have the ability to get stuck into making the necessary
> change without dancing around. To those on the brink I would
> say: Come on in, the water's fine.' The men at Fawley have set
> an example. They work harder but they make more money and
> have more leisure. Their affluence is confirmed by a problem of
> the near future. They are going to need more spaces in the
> workers' car parks. (*The Daily Express*, 17 May 1968; article by
> A. Fyall)

Academic doyens have for the most part remained faithful to the Blue Book and have proffered positive assessments. Clegg, for instance, in discussing the fate of the Blue Book has noted that 'generally all these (Blue Book) aims were achieved after the agreement came into force, although subsequently overtime rose well above the new target' (1976: 307). Similarly, Towers notes that

> the (Fawley) management were clearly happy with the outcome
> of the first agreement since they followed it up by further
> agreements and a general attempt to link all future *substantial*
> pay increases to productivity improvements. From the union's
> point of view, a substantial pay increase and cuts in the work-
> ing week were important gains which must have more than
> compensated for the changes in working practices. (1972: 28)

On Towers' assertion, it is interesting to note, however, that the opposite could just as easily be argued: that the reason Fawley followed the Blue Book with further agreements was precisely because management was not happy with the outcome of the first agreement and that it was not able to achieve what it had set out to achieve.

Within academia, Fox (1974) has been somewhat of a lone wolf in criticizing the Blue Book. Fox has reinterpreted Flanders' own data on the Blue Book in terms of a theory of 'trust'. He suggests that the management proposals to reduce worker discretion through increased bureaucratization were perceived by workers '... as a low trust initiative to which they (the workers) countered with low-trust responses, handling the negotiations and the implementation of the resulting agreement as an exercise in economic rather than social exchange' (1974: 129). The importance of Fox's evaluation of the Blue Book rests not with any new data, but rather with the reinterpretation of old data in the context of a new theory. Fox's theory of 'trust dynamics' is developed further in chapter 11, which reconsiders the control implications of productivity bargaining.

An evaluation of productivity bargaining at five principal companies, including Esso Oil Company Ltd., by the National Board for Prices and Incomes (N.B.P.I.) came out with an overall favourable assessment of the technique as follows:

> The first and firmest (conclusion) is that there is little evidence that the gains of productivity bargaining will slip away through failures of management control or through workers slipping back into old habits or inventing new restrictions. The only instance we have discovered is a rise in overtime levels at Fawley. But this was due to a conscious choice of management and did not seriously offset the considerable savings due to the agreements. (N.B.P.I. Report No. 36, 1967: 29)

The N.B.P.I.'s evaluation does report, however, that

> the response of the shop stewards has not been so uniformly favourable. We have come across a number of stewards in Alcan and Esso and particularly in Electricity Supply, who have expressed vigorous criticism. (N.B.P.I. Report No. 36, 1967: 27)

Unfortunately, however, the N.B.P.I. does not fully elaborate on the reasons for such 'vigorous criticism' but only reports that '... some craftsmen shop stewards feel that too many concessions have been made on flexibility, but most criticism is heard where groups of workers have experienced a drop in earnings' (N.B.P.I. Report No. 36, 1967: 27).

An evaluation of productivity bargaining in over twenty undertakings, including Esso, by the Royal Commission on Trade Unions and Employers' Associations (Research Papers 4) also reported favourably on Esso's experience with productivity bargaining:

> Esso have not supplied detailed calculations, but they have said: 'Esso is satisfied that the agreements it has been able to reach so far were well worth making in financial terms.' If this

were not so, it would certainly be odd that Esso having made one productivity agreement have gone on to make two others. (R.C.T.U., Research Papers 4, 1967: 36)

Flanders' own study of the 'Blue Book' remains '. . . the only detailed study of a productivity agreement in depth, i.e. that puts the formal agreement, its negotiations and effects into any institutional, organizational and cultural context' (Daniel, 1970a: 3). Flanders' evaluation is far from a simple management 'white-wash'. It is a careful and well balanced account of the history of the Blue Book which does not simply serve to applaud Fawley management nor blindly to extol the virtues of productivity bargaining as a kind of a panacea. Flanders after all did suggest that '. . . the Blue Book did not inaugurate an era of "sweetness and light" expressed in trouble-free relations' (1964: 207).

On balance, however, Flanders' evaluation of the Blue Book is favourable and concludes that, to a considerable measure, the economic, institutional and cultural aims of the agreements were, in fact, achieved. As a concluding sentence by Flanders had it: 'The Fawley experiment stands as a practical demonstration that management can evolve and act upon higher standards' (1964: 255–6).

Blue Book evaluation: case study findings, 1960–1967

This section evaluates the effectiveness of the Blue Book productivity agreements over an extended time frame from 1960 up to the striking of Fawley's second generation productivity agreements in 1967. Flanders' evaluation format is employed and the agreements are assessed in terms of their stated objectives and in terms of their 'economic', 'institutional' and 'cultural' results. It will be seen that, over this extended time frame, the Blue Book fails quite dramatically with a 'creep back' to old working practices occurring in most areas. In fact, this 'creep back' became most significant after the final Blue Book wage instalment was paid to Fawley workers in August 1962 (it is interesting to note that Flanders' own analysis of the Blue Book covered that period when wage instalments were still being paid out to workers). It will also be seen that Fawley management, faced with the realization that it could not win higher effort levels in return for higher wages, abandoned its 'high-wage and high-productivity' based strategy and gradually slipped back to its former 'low-wage and low-productivity' mode.

In 1961, after some dispute about its compatibility with the Blue Book, a small 'supplementary' wage increase was negotiated across the board at Fawley (Flanders, 1964: 149–53). Fawley management was forced to modify its principle of only granting productivity linked pay increases. A second productivity agreement was struck in 1962, known as the 'Orange Book'. Best seen as an 'addendum' agreement to the Blue Book, the 'Orange Book' sought

> ... to clear up difficulties which had confronted management in applying certain clauses in the 1960 agreements, as for example the different wording of the Maintenance and Construction and Process sections on the transfer of minor maintenance work, or in regard to the working of overtime alongside temporary shifts. (Flanders, 1964: 183)

Negotiations over the 'Orange Book' were complex and protracted. Fawley management felt that '... workers became quite concerned about the value of restrictive practices and entered into the negotiations with a very calculating attitude' (McKersie and Hunter, 1973: 353). In November 1962 the non-craft group, members of the Transport and General Workers' Union, agreed on further flexibility of working but the Craft Union Committee resisted further intercraft flexibility. Finally, in January 1963, the craft group agreed to increased flexibility only in the event of plant maintenance 'shut-downs' or overhauls. Between 1963 and 1967 there were no new productivity agreements struck at Fawley and the terms and conditions of the Blue Book (and the Orange Book) remained the same, although pay increases came from conventional bargaining. What, then, was the fate of the Blue Book between 1960 and 1967?

Reduction of overtime

Flanders felt strongly about wage drift in the form of high levels of continuous overtime, declaring that 'systematic overtime is symptomatic of managerial irresponsibility' (1975: 56). The reduction of high levels of unnecessary overtime demanded, according to Flanders, '... a conscious effort and planning. Until the Blue Book little of this was forthcoming' (1964: 59). The effective management of overtime levels was seen to require long-term planning and a more systematic approach to the utilization of labour. Supervisors needed to improve their planning and coordination of work on a continuing basis. It required, in effect, strategic planning.

The high level of overtime at Fawley was seen not only as the prime cause of inefficiency and high labour costs but also as the primary means to a solution of other problems (McKersie and Hunter, 1973: 6). The overtime objectives stated in the Blue Book were tied into other Blue Book provisions, most importantly to the flexibility initiatives. As Flanders

The Fawley Blue Book revisited

notes, 'greater flexibility throughout the refinery was a condition for reducing overtime ...' (1964: 176). The extent to which management was successful in reducing overtime can, therefore, give us some indication of the success of other Blue Book provisions. The Blue Book overtime reduction provisions were also important in their own right as the second most important area of cost savings (next to those savings associated with manpower reductions).

Flanders points to the phased overtime reduction targets as the '... one precise measuring rod embodied in the 1960 agreements of management's progress in fulfilling its objectives on the work as opposed to the wage side of the bargain' (1964: 153). The overtime objectives were critical to the overall evaluation of the success of the Blue Book agreements precisely because overtime levels are 'quantifiable'. In this sense Flanders was quite willing to use the overtime objectives as an indicator or test of the success of the agreements. Flanders suggested, further, that if Fawley management was unable to keep overtime levels down it could '... scarcely expect to sustain much confidence either in its judgment or its executive capacity ... management's morale and reputation were at stake, reason enough to accord the task a high priority' (1964: 153).

According to Flanders, Fawley management was, for the most part, successful in reaching its overtime objectives. Flanders notes that, by the end of the fourth phase of the agreement in July 1962, refinery-wide overtime had been brought down from 18 per cent to 7.5 per cent. Flanders notes, however, that there was a marked difference in overtime reduction between the maintenance and construction department and the process department. Table 3 gives the six-monthly averages for all the principal groups of wage earners, together with a detailed breakdown for the crafts in the five scheduled phases of the agreement (table as provided by Flanders, 1964: 155).

As the table shows, the process shift workers were only able to bring down overtime to 10.7 per cent in the last phase while the maintenance and construction day workers (the bulk of the maintenance and construction work-force) were able to reduce overtime from 18 per cent in 1959 to 1.6 per cent in the last phase. Of the eleven principal day craft groups, six worked less than 1.0 per cent overtime in the July 1962–January 1963 period, and none of the craft groups worked in excess of 3 per cent in this period.

Flanders explains that the reason for differential departmental success lies in terms of the extent to which goals and targets were made explicit in the agreement. The reason that the process department was not as successful as the maintenance and construction department is attributed largely to technical considerations and to '... the realms of managerial

91

Table 3. *Reduction of overtime under the 1960 agreements**

	1959	July 1960– Jan. 1961	Jan. 1961– July 1961	July 1961– Jan. 1962	Jan. 1962– July 1962	July 1962– Jan. 1963
A. PRINCIPAL DEPARTMENTAL GROUPS						
Departments						
Maintenance and construction						
Day	18	12·7	9·5	4·8	5·8	1·6
Shift	13	13·2	9·8	6·2	5·8	7·8
Process						
Day	25	16·3	10·5	9·7	6·1	6·2
Shift	15	13·8	12·1	12·9	10·7	10·7
Technical						
Day	16	13·3	12·9	10·3	8·3	5·4
Shift	15	13·0	9·5	4·5	5·8	1·7
Security guards	15	13·0	3·5	6·0	3·3	2·3
B. PRINCIPAL DAY CRAFT GROUPS						
Crafts						
Welders	26	18·7	10·0	5·2	10·2	0·2
Boilermakers	24	16·5	11·5	8·3	11·7	1·0
Pipefitters	21	13·7	9·0	4·2	7·9	2·5
Bricklayers	21	17·0	18·7	7·0	5·2	1·2
Auto mechanics	20	12·0	7·0	3·7	3·4	0
Mechanical fitters	16	10·2	8·0	4·5	5·6	0·6
Instrument fitters	13	6·7	3·2	1·2	4·4	2·1
Turner-fitters	13	11·2	7·2	5·2	5·3	0·7
Carpenters	11	8·5	4·2	1·7	2·8	1·2
Electricians	10	8·2	4·2	1·5	3·6	0·2
Painters	9	7·7	2·0	1·0	0	0

* Hours of overtime worked by weekly-paid employees expressed as a percentage of the normal working week after 1960 and previously of actual hours worked.

planning, for example by a more selective application of double manning' (Flanders, 1964: 162). As Flanders notes:

> It was not so much the intrinsic difficulties of conducting in Process the same kind of concerted, week by week, strategic attack on overtime as took place in Maintenance and Construction, although different planning problems had to be solved. It was rather that it had been impossible to prepare for this by careful calculation over a period like the year or so that Maintenance and Construction devoted to the purpose. (1964: 163)

For Flanders, therefore, overtime could be successfully managed, provided it were put to some form of strategic attack. The maintenance and construction department was a vivid testimony to this ability, with

The Fawley Blue Book revisited

much of the success of overtime reduction attributed to better management planning and organization. As Flanders notes, 'management was forced to reduce the time spent on certain jobs, to alter the ways of doing them, to try to make technical improvements or where necessary, to increase the labour available' (1964: 157). Fawley management, at least in the maintenance and construction area, had come to accept its 'managerial responsibility' and through judicious and well-planned management activity had come effectively to control overtime levels. Looking to the future, Flanders felt confident that Fawley management would be able to sustain such control. As Flanders noted,

> ... there are currently no signs of any organized pressure on the workers' side to increase it. On the contrary most of the stewards are pleased to have contributed towards what is after all a union objective, and at least the majority of their members are not noticeably dissatisfied with having done so. (1964: 165)

It is, however, really only when we use an extended time frame that we can put a strategic planning process to a true test. If we extend the evaluation period beyond 1962, was Fawley management able to sustain its strategic attack on overtime levels?

The National Board for Prices and Incomes (N.B.P.I.) report (Number 36) notes that '... during the 1965 and 1966 period overtime at Fawley rose to levels not far below those experienced before the agreement' (1967: 26). The N.B.P.I. report notes that, in 1966, overtime averaged around 15 per cent for the process department and 10 per cent for the maintenance and construction department. The N.B.P.I.'s report of this resurgence appears to be apologetic and suggests that the increase in overtime levels '... has not been caused by pressure from workers ...' (Report No. 36: 26–7). The N.B.P.I. report also states:

> On the maintenance side it (high overtime) was partly due to an unpredictable rise in the number of fires and breakdowns. On the process side, it was primarily due to the number of workers leaving under the Voluntary Separation Scheme of 1964 ... (Report No. 36, 1967: 27)

The N.B.P.I. report nevertheless insists that there was a '... great difference between overtime working before the Blue Book and overtime working now':

> In the first case the object was to sustain earnings, and control of overtime was weak. Now the object is to get work done, and managers believe that, as conditions change, they will be able to reduce overtime once more. (Report No. 36, 1967: 27)

93

The N.B.P.I. appears to defend the overtime creep-back, explaining it away in terms of specific structural contingencies (such as fires and breakdowns) and not to management's planning capability or to pressure from workers. The N.B.P.I.'s logic appears to have been that, if certain structural contingencies could be eliminated, overtime would drop once again.

My data collected at Fawley do not square with the optimism of either Flanders or the N.B.P.I. Both Fawley managers and trade union officials admitted that the overtime problem was never brought under control. Fawley overtime charts showed that the creep back on overtime levels began as early as 1962 in the maintenance craft areas for all crafts with the exception of carpenters, instrument fitters and electricians. Overtime rates began to accelerate for all craft groups, reaching a peak of 10.5 per cent in 1966. Although overtime levels dropped in 1967, hitting an average low of 6 per cent for all trades, they never came close to reaching the original Blue Book target of 2 per cent. With respect to the N.B.P.I.'s belief that overtime levels would indeed fall off after 1966 once various operating contingencies had been sorted out, precisely the opposite actually occurred. Overtime levels invidiously crept back in the craft area from 1968. In 1969, overtime levels for the pipefitters and boilermakers reached levels in excess of 20 per cent, which was even higher than the pre-Blue Book overtime rates.

The overtime pattern worked by non-craft maintenance workers is similar to the craft pattern, i.e. a general trend upwards from 1962 to 1965, followed by a drop in 1967 and a further rise thereafter. Interestingly, in 1966, overtime levels for both rigger-scaffolders and crane drivers reached levels in excess of pre-Blue Book overtime levels. Average overtime for all non-craft trades in 1966 reached a peak at 10.5 per cent. While average overtime levels for all non-craft trades dipped to 6.0 per cent in 1967, Fawley management was still beset with severe problems in the management of overtime for rigger-scaffolders, crane drivers and transport drivers.

What is interesting and perhaps more than coincidental is that, in July 1962, average overtime for both craft and non-craft maintenance work started to creep back up at about the same time as the last of the six-monthly instalments was to be paid out to workers. Once the 'carrot' or inducement of a wage instalment was gone, workers seem to have returned to overtime working as a means of increasing wages.

Overtime in the process department itself remained consistently high. The N.B.P.I. reported process overtime at 15 per cent in 1966 with the expectation of some decline, although this did not actually take place. Process department overtime rose to an average of 17 per cent in 1967 and dropped only to 16.5 per cent in 1968. Furthermore, process department manning levels (whether increased or decreased) through the period from 1966 to 1968 were to have no effect on the high overtime levels.

Clearly, then, overtime levels were rising for reasons other than 'fires' and 'breakdowns' in the case of the maintenance department, and manning reductions in the case of the process department. It is far more likely that overtime levels remained high due to problems of management control and worker and trade union pressure.

Overtime statistics do not on their own, however, tell the whole story. It is possible that overtime working can be disguised or masked in different forms, for instance, in the form of contractor labour or temporary shift working. As will be seen below in my 'economic' evaluation of the Blue Book, it does appear to be the case, for instance, that contractor labour was being used as a kind of substitute for overtime working. Any analysis of the success of the overtime objectives needs to take account of such processes of simple labour substitution.

Flanders himself noted how the temporary shift working arrangement (an arrangement which had been included in the Blue Book in order to facilitate the completion of urgent maintenance work and to help to bring overtime levels down) began to be interpreted by Fawley maintenance workers as a form of '... compulsory cut-price overtime' (Flanders, 1964: 158). The resistance that Fawley management first encountered to temporary shift working immediately after the signing of the Blue Book, first by the boilermakers and then by the welders, never waned. Moreover, the reduction in manning levels brought on by a subsequent voluntary redundancy programme made the temporary shift working arrangement increasingly worthless and, in turn, adversely affected management's overtime objectives. As the Fawley case demonstrates, changing circumstances may serve to devalue or minimize the operational effectiveness of a particular provision within an agreement.

There is evidence, further, that overtime levels may have been pushed up in both the maintenance and process departments as a result of trade union and worker pressure to keep total wages or earnings up in the form of 'wage drift'. It would appear that overtime payments were increasingly seen by workers as a means by which to 'renegotiate' the terms of the original Blue Book agreement. As one senior shop steward put it:

> We had a number of years (from 1962 to 1968) when we didn't get much in our bargaining. The men began to feel that maybe they weren't getting enough for the Blue Book. We started to use overtime to get what was owed. (Interview with senior shop steward)

These sentiments were echoed in the Craft Union Committee's 1964 wage negotiations strategy:

> The Blue Book principle was to create a base rate which would not need the support of overtime working to maintain its value. This principle has been forgotten. We now have to try and achieve a decent take home pay by working overtime which is limited. (Union document)

Pressure also appears to have been placed by workers on front line supervision to keep overtime levels up. As one supervisor put it:

> Some of the supervisors kept a clamp on overtime but they sometimes found it difficult to get the men to do other things for them. Some of us started to use overtime as a way of getting other parts of the agreement going. (Interview with front line supervisor)

The creep back of overtime levels suggests that Fawley management had, in effect, made few advances within the realm of strategic planning. Trade unions were able to exert pressure to ensure that overtime levels were kept high, first by restricting temporary shift working and secondly by applying shop floor pressure on front line supervision to keep overtime levels up.

The failure of Fawley management to hold down overtime levels has, of course, negative implications for the other Blue Book provisions as many of the other proposed changes (like the introduction of flexible working) were intended for the express purpose of bringing overtime levels down. The fact that overtime was not held in abeyance would suggest that the other Blue Book provisions were themselves not working according to plan.

Elimination of mates

At Fawley Refinery there were 275 mates serving 494 craftsmen before the implementation of the Blue Book. After the agreement there was only one mate and 559 craftsmen. The withdrawal of 274 mates resulted in a net increase of 65 craftsmen, with the rest of the mates being redeployed elsewhere. Flanders describes the redeployment of mates as '... one of the easier provisions of the agreements to apply ...' and says that 'apart from the craft unions' disappointment about the numbers of additional craftsmen, the redeployment objective was accomplished without serious union resistance or prolonged criticism ...' (1964: 175).

My case study findings do confirm that there was no reintroduction of mates over the entire life of the Blue Book period, whose provisions still apply to this day. Unlike the overtime and flexibility provisions, which involved a long-term strategy, the abolition of mates could be managed on a 'one-off' basis. Once the mates had been removed from their jobs, redeployed and retrained for other employment, it was unlikely that subversive 'creep back' would occur. There is an important lesson here for management in the striking of a productivity deal. Certain provisions, like redeployment or job redundancy, require less of a long-term effort or ongoing management process than other provisions, while certain other objectives may have a greater potential for creep back.

It needs to be pointed out, however, that the redeployment of mates was not problem- or cost-free. First, the withdrawal of 274 mates resulted in a net increase in craft strength of 65 (Flanders, 1964: 168). In the non-craft group it was estimated that approximately 25 non-craft employees were engaged for new auxiliary jobs to replace certain of the mates' functions, such as safety and heavy carrying (Flanders, 1964: 168). Only 18 of the original 275 mates actually left the company and most were redeployed in maintenance and construction. While the position of mates had theoretically been eliminated it was eliminated at the cost of increasing total manning levels.

It is important to note, as well, that a good number of the mates who were to be redeployed were to find themselves still assisting craftsmen while not formally being defined as mates. This is evidenced by the fact that when, in 1964, Esso introduced a voluntary redundancy programme, it was reported that some of the workers who left on the redundancy scheme, '. . . were craftsmen's mates, whose jobs were eliminated under the Blue Book agreement but not all of whom had been satisfactorily absorbed' (E. Wigham, 'Fawley–Stage III', *The Times*, 19 July 1967). The bulk of the workers who were to leave on the redundancy programme were to be 'semi-skilled' (N.B.P.I. Report No. 36, 1967: 50) or, in other words, the old mates who had been unsuccessfully redeployed. The redeployment was really, therefore, one of labelling or 'name changing' rather than one of substance.

Progress in job flexibility

The Blue Book provision to obtain greater flexibility in its use of labour through the relaxation of job demarcations '. . . was envisaged as a long-term task . . .' (Flanders, 1964: 176). The flexibility initiatives were seen to require a sustained managerial effort and could not be managed in a once-and-for-all manner.

Flanders divided the progress in job flexibility into main union groupings: those internal to the craft union committee (i.e. inter-craft), those internal to the Transport and General Workers' Union (both operating process shift workers and day non-craft maintenance workers) and finally between the craft unions and the Transport and General Workers' Union.

Flanders' assessment of progress in inter-craft flexibility is not entirely optimistic but this conclusion apparently is based on a single interview with a department head. This department head suggested that possibly five per cent of craftsmen's time was spent on work outside their craft after the agreement and that '... probably no more than half of the possible flexibility formally granted to management under the agreement had actually been used' (Flanders, 1964: 177). Flanders also notes that while shop stewards and union delegates honoured their stated commitments, they refused to go beyond them and that '... management's hopes that the spirit rather than the letter of agreements would prevail in inter-craft flexibility were almost wholly shattered' (1964: 177).

Within the context of job flexibility between craft workers and the Transport and General Workers' Union, Flanders reports a number of set-backs. Flexibility between craft workers and process shift workers was impeded through a 'loophole' in the agreement which permitted process workers to argue about when an individual was 'available' for a job or not.

Finally, flexibility between workers in the Transport and General Workers' Union is reported to have been smoother and more rewarding for management. In some cases Flanders states that flexibility '... brought about very big productivity increases; e.g. among the bitumen fillers by 100 per cent and the road and rail fillers by 43 per cent ...' (Flanders, 1964: 180–1). Flanders does not, however, advise us of the source of such figures nor of how such improvements in productivity were actually monitored and measured. Doubtless these were Fawley management's own estimates.

Flanders' assessment of flexibility progress is not, as we have seen, entirely favourable. My own case study findings over the extended time frame to 1967 reveal considerably greater failure. By the end of the Blue Book evaluation period, Fawley management actually concluded that '... detailed items of flexibility have no lasting value'. This dismal view of flexibility progress was corroborated by trade union documents and interviews. One of the maintenance shop stewards, speaking about progress on Blue Book inter-craft flexibility, voiced the opinion that '... The Blue Book flexibility items weren't worth the paper they were written on. That Book was collecting dust faster than it took to write it' (Interview with senior shop steward). Much the same story was told about flexibility associated with process department workers. As one steward put it:

> We never extended any flexibility ... while some was extended in the beginning, it was never significant. As far as I can remember, the Blue Book hardly changed our jobs at all. (Interview with T.G.W.U. steward)

There may, in fact, have been a *net loss* in total flexibility, as a result of the withdrawal of prior 'informally' granted flexibility. One front line supervisor explained the loss of flexibility in this way:

> Not only were we not getting the flexibility we were paying for but some workers started to withhold the flexibility that we had already achieved on an informal basis before we introduced the Blue Book. They (the workers) began to withdraw this flexibility whenever we began to push for our Blue Book flexibility. (Interview with front-line supervisor)

Supervisors referred to this informal flexibility as 'goodwill' flexibility and the extent of its use depended directly on the supervisor's relationship with his crew. For many of the supervisors, then, winning flexibility was not based on formal productivity provisions; rather it flowed from a special relationship that had been built up over the years between supervisor and worker. This point was reinforced by a number of stewards in the refinery. As one steward put it: 'There were some good supervisors and some bad ones. The men knew who the good ones were. If they (the supervisors) asked you to do something ... well, you'd do it ... even if it wasn't right' (Interview with shop steward). Flexibility, therefore, wasn't something that was merely granted on a contractual basis but rather something that was linked to a more complex set of workplace relations and directly associated with the nature and quality of supervisor–worker relationships.

It appears, in fact, that the formalization of working practices was to result in precisely the *opposite* of what was planned. The bureaucratic process of specifying formally and in detail all changes to working practices served ironically to *heighten* worker demarcation awareness. This strange reversal of the intentions of the flexibility initiatives occurred as a result of the need first to write down or 'code' past demarcations before they could be negotiated away. Once such demarcations had been written down, they began to be used as critical reference points by workers and stewards. The record of demarcations, even though written down only for the purpose of being altered, served to give them new life via a formal 'stamp of approval'. The Blue Book, in other words, helped to emphasize custom and practice rules, thereby making them more difficult to overcome.

The Blue Book deal appeared to create a growing web of restrictive rules. For example, based on interviews with Fawley's Refinery manager (I. Upson) and with the chairman of the shop stewards (C. Foxley), *The Sunday Times* reported:

> With the benefit of hindsight, however, we can now see that failure over demarcation was written into the (Blue Book) deal. One sentence is especially revealing. While both sides agreed to encourage flexible working, it said 'in the case of certain specified jobs, particular agreements will apply'. A nine page appendix spelled out in detail what these would be. But that was precisely the trouble. New working practices were so well defined that they became new restrictive practices. The result according to Upson, was that 'we had merely altered the place of the demarcation barriers'. The chairman of the shop stewards committee, Charlie Foxley, agrees: 'The Blue Book invented demarcations because it defined specific things' ... (Jacobs, *The Sunday Times*: 20 July 1975)

It would appear, therefore, that the Blue Book resulted in a proliferation of rules which served in the end to increase rather than reduce job demarcations. This proliferation of rules resulted from constant debates on the shop floor about precisely how a demarcation relaxation was to operate. The Blue Book demarcation rules were not wide enough to take into account all of the various operating contingencies, so that rules were constantly being generated in order to fit such contingencies. According to one Fawley manager, in fact, 'it was calculated that for every demarcation relaxation gained three rules were developed relating to the usage of the changed work practice'. This rule proliferation process was explained as follows:

> For example, whilst it was agreed that a pipefitter might carry out door removal in tanks and towers, etc. although this had previously been the province solely of the boilermaker, rules were developed which permitted this efficiency provided it happened 'on an occasional basis only', 'no more than two doors were involved and provided that there were no pipefitter contractors on site'.

With this experience, it is not surprising that Fawley management was to conclude that a more fundamental change in attitude of the labour force was required if real and ongoing improvements in efficiency were to be realized. Fawley workers came, in fact, to cite selectively either old 'custom and practice' rules or new formal rules in accordance with their particular needs.

Interestingly, Hawkins has reported a somewhat similar situation in one of his own case studies:

> ... the most significant aspect of these negotiations is that *all* the proposals for increased flexibility had *already been operative* to a considerable degree on an informal, *ad hoc* basis ... In other words this productivity deal was attempting to formalize practices which already existed informally. The rejection of the deal by the men, however, marked the beginning of a period of 'work to rule' under which a fitter, for example, would call an electrician merely to turn off the power switch of his machine. (1971: 18)

The Blue Book flexibility provisions apparently also ran aground due to the vast technical training of workers that was required before the flexibility items could be implemented in the first place. Fawley management came to conclude by the end of the 1960s that productivity 'deals involving vast retraining exercises have an inbuilt failure mechanism, i.e. "I am not trained therefore I cannot, etc." ...'. Much of the actual failure of the flexibility provisions related to management's inability and/or lack of desire to organize the training requirements for the proposed flexibility. According to one Fawley manager, the flexibility training programme 'never really got off the ground', thereby eliminating any hope of realizing flexibility progress.

In order for the flexibility initiatives to be successfully implemented, a major training programme first needed to be mounted and sustained over time. The training department was, however, ill-prepared to take on such a task. According to one manager, the training department, at the time of the Blue Book, had a 'relatively low status' and was 'undermanned and underresourced' (interview with Fawley manager). The expectation that such a department could launch a major training programme was seen to be a mere 'pipe dream'. This was a classic situation where the designers of a change programme were the 'power brokers' in the organization, while the implementors were a relatively powerless group.

It needs to be noted, finally, that changes in technology and operating methods over time at Fawley served to undermine the value of the agreements. Even the most minor change in operating methods could make a flexibility provision redundant. As one manager put it,

> stewards can always jump on a change, no matter how big and tell us that the provision no longer applies. To get a provision to apply again could take endless negotiation. In most cases these provisions just had a quiet death. (Interview with Fawley manager)

Management's indifference to training requirements and to the problems associated with the proliferation of rules and with increased 'formalization' all contributed to the demise of the flexibility provisions by the end of the 1960s.

Other Blue Book objectives

The remaining key Blue Book objectives related to the change in the supervisory structure, working time arrangements and special payments. Flanders notes that those changes

> ... that were intended to give management greater freedom in its use of supervision appear to have had no more than a small effect. There was only a very limited amount of multi-craft supervision, and the union membership of first-line supervisors continued, much as before, to make them reluctant to act in any way that could incur strong union disapproval. (1964: 181)

With respect to working time arrangements and, in particular, to the change from a set tea break to one taken during a natural break in the work, Flanders found that, while '... the majority of supervisors disliked the change ...', it was not possible to determine whether more or less time was lost (1964: 182). Finally, Flanders states that there was no renewed bargaining over special payments money such as heat, dust and restricted space payments (1964: 182).

One test of the effectiveness of these provisions is the extent to which they reappear in future productivity deals. The elimination of the set tea break is instructive here. Fawley management found that the new system of taking tea breaks 'within the natural sequence of work' had actually resulted in a loss of management control and that time spent on tea breaks had actually increased. As one manager put it, 'although some of us thought we might have control problems in this area, we felt we could handle them'. As a result of this loss of control, Fawley management was forced to 'buy back' the old tea break arrangements in a later, 1968 productivity deal with the craft unions and Transport and General Workers' Union. The Blue Book deal provided for a 'high trust' tea break; the later 1968 agreements, however, re-introduced fixed tea breaks for the morning in which a '... hooter will sound at ... (tea) times to denote when to start and stop work' (1968 Craft Maintenance productivity deal).

The tea break issue was to be the first of a series of 'buy backs' by Fawley management, whereby management sought to buy back an old working practice in either its original form or in a slightly modified form. One of the central themes of productivity bargaining at Fawley is the extent to which the same items appear and reappear in subsequent generations of productivity deals. This was to be the case, for instance, with 'special' or 'abnormal' conditions money. The Blue Book sought to get rid of such payments, but they were to creep back slowly but surely. The constancy of the creep back can be seen some 22 years after the signing of the Blue Book, when, in 1982, the Maintenance Enabling agreement sought as one of its few provisions to buy out all 'abnormal conditions money'.

The Blue Book – workers' objectives: higher pay, no redundancy, fewer working hours

The principal rewards that Fawley workers received for striking the Blue Book deal were (1) increased pay to the order of forty per cent, (2) a reduction in the working week (from 42 or 42.5 to 40 hours) and (3) a 'no redundancy' policy. Payment trends are of particular interest because they themselves are linked back to the philosophical basis of productivity bargaining at Fawley, i.e. to the need to move towards a balkanized labour market characterized by a 'low overtime–high wage policy'. According to the Blue Book, high levels of effort were to be rewarded by high levels of pay. Flanders describes the effect of the Blue Book on workers' pay as follows,

> Thus whereas the refinery ranked less favourably than the generality of industry in 1960 – offering only another 6s. 2d. in earnings for an extra two hours work – it was well in the van by 1962, when its weekly-paid employees received £2 2s. 2d. more for a working week that was $2\frac{1}{4}$ hours shorter ... Fawley management had declared in its Introduction to the Blue Book that one of the aims was 'to place our employees among the highest paid in the country'. This had been achieved. (1964: 197)

While it was true that the wage increases associated with the Blue Book allowed Fawley workers to jump ahead in the local labour market, this was only to be a temporary phenomenon. After the Blue Book and Orange Book wage increases had been passed on to Fawley maintenance craftworkers (from 1960 through to 1962) there was a dramatic drop in percentage wage increases from 1963 until 1968 when the next maintenance productivity deal was struck. Two of the five years between 1963 and 1968 saw a complete standstill in wage rates. The wage increases agreed to during this period came from 'conventional' bargaining and, in each year, fell below the national average for all manual workers.

The quest for productivity

The extent to which Fawley's wage rates had slipped in its own local labour market was revealed in Esso evidence to the Donovan Commission as follows:

> We did a recent survey in the Southampton area in the oil industry, chemicals, shipbuilding, heavy electrical, light engineering, a nationalized industry and a contracting industry. We found in these eight industries (that) . . . on hours worked in the week it was lowest; and on total weekly earnings it (Fawley) came sixth out of eight. (Donovan Commission, Report No. 39, Esso Petroleum Co. Ltd. evidence, 1966: 1676).

This erosion of differentials stood as a constant theme in trade union documents over the period, one of which declared that 'we have been underpaid since the Blue Book days, and we never gained much since these days' (Transport and General Workers' Union minutes, June 1971). In October 1967, 400 craftsmen at Fawley were to go on a 'work to rule' and an overtime ban. The dispute arose directly over a concern that craft

> . . . rates of pay have fallen behind compared with other similar workers and it seems that Esso management has taken a long time to come to the bargaining table for wage negotiations . . . the craftsmen suspect that management are dragging their feet. (B.B.C. Television, Transcription, 10 October 1967, 5:55 p.m. Short title: 'Esso work to rule')

This wage slippage had a number of interesting implications for Fawley management. First, as workers from other firms caught up with and even passed Fawley workers, Fawley workers came increasingly to question the fairness of the Blue Book deal. This invariably meant that Fawley workers looked for opportunities to 'revalue' the terms of the original agreement. This renegotiation of the agreement took place, for the most part, on an 'informal' basis, through a slow creep back to old working practices. As one shop steward put it, 'if we weren't getting the pay, then they weren't getting the work' (interview with shop steward). McKersie and Hunter have themselves pointed to a downward slide in the earnings of Fawley workers in the post-Blue Book period:

> . . . pressures emanating from the labour market affected the enthusiasm with which workers implemented the various agreements. The first agreement, the Blue Book, was implemented quite successfully because the wage increases and other benefits afforded under the agreement allowed the workers to spurt ahead in the 'local-league tables'. However, as other groups

caught up and even passed the Fawley workers, the enthusiasm for productivity waned. (1973: 264)

The drop in the relative positioning of Fawley workers' wages in the labour market meant, in effect, that Fawley management had abandoned the philosophical and strategic basis of the Blue Book that had been touted by Bill Allen, that of a 'low overtime–high wage' policy. By 1963 Fawley management had really lost the desire to pursue a high wages policy.

It is interesting to note that Marxian scholars such as Cliff have interpreted the drop in wage rates as '... *evidence of the loss of shop floor control*' (1970: 28). It is possible and perhaps more probable to advance an opposite argument: that the reason that Fawley management abandoned a high wages policy was because they were not able to win or realize the extra effort from Fawley workers to warrant higher wage increases. The fact that Fawley management did not continue with a high wages strategy may itself be evidence of the strength and power of workers to devalue at the outset the content of the Blue Book agreement. In order for managements to pursue a high wages policy they must first be capable of extracting the extra surplus value from workers.

Another worker objective, the 'no-redundancy' pledge, was offered to workers to allay fears about possible reductions in manning levels due to the proposed changes to working practices. From Fawley management's perspective, a no-redundancy pledge put considerable onus on the accuracy of manpower forecasting and budgeting, linking changes in product demand and production technology with manpower plans. In other words, it required a strategy. The 'advances' in manpower planning which were introduced during and after the Blue Book proved, however, to be inadequate. As the National Board for Prices and Incomes noted,

> by the beginning of 1964 ... it was evident that the refinery was heavily overmanned. Demand had not increased as rapidly as expected so that Management had to lower its estimate of future labour requirements. Further, the potential efficiency of manning as a result of automation and reorganization (both of which had been assisted by the productivity agreements) was higher than had earlier been expected. The problem of manpower was more than one of simple arithmetic – it was evident that the composition of the labour force was unsatisfactory ... Many semi-skilled men – especially those who had been mates before the 1960 Agreement – had found difficulty in coping with the change involved in moving from heavy outdoor jobs to responsible process jobs. (Report No. 36, 1967: 50)

The quest for productivity

As a result of manpower planning difficulties, Fawley had to amend its original 'no-redundancy' pledge and, in 1964, introduced a 'voluntary separation scheme'. Under this, 400 workers left the company, 320 from the maintenance and construction department and 80 from the process department (the bulk of the maintenance workers to leave were the old 'mates' who had been 'successfully' redeployed to other jobs).

According to the National Board for Prices and Incomes, the voluntary separation scheme at Fawley, '... at least in the short run, added considerably to feelings of insecurity ... which now run much higher than they did before the process of productivity bargaining began' (Report No. 36, 1967: 26). Undoubtedly the programme also contributed to some further 'devaluing' of the Blue Book agreement by Fawley workers. The non-craft maintenance workers, a group hit particularly hard by redundancy, were to become increasingly embittered and suspicious about the productivity programmes at Fawley. A letter to Fawley's industrial relations superintendent from the Transport and General Workers' Union states, for instance:

> Our membership at the Refinery for December 1959 was 680, in December 1967 the membership was 373. I appreciate that in all of the Productivity Agreements that have been agreed at the Refinery it has stipulated no redundancy clauses, but by a normal wastage and voluntary separation scheme we have reached the position where we need to examine in close detail whether or not the Blue Book ... and the proposed Productivity Agreement has in fact any value for our membership. We would therefore like to discuss with you at your earliest opportunity this question of contractors working at the Refinery, with the object of agreeing to a suitable labour force as far as our maintenance activity is concerned. Secondly, better consultation with our Day work Branch shop stewards before contractors are engaged in maintenance work on the Refinery, and finally long term prospects in relation to Productivity Agreements covering this membership of the Refinery. (Transport and General Workers' Union letter: November 1968)

With regard to the Fawley redundancy programme, Klein claims that, 'the company (Esso) was aware that it had become a different kind of employer, and a good deal of heart-searching was going on about this' (1976: 24). The need to reduce manpower was basically in direct conflict with management's need to win the high levels of commitment and consent required to realize other Blue Book objectives.

Assessment of results: economic, institutional and cultural

Flanders concludes his evaluation of the Blue Book productivity agreement by assessing its economic, institutional and cultural results. He concludes that, to a considerable extent, these three aims were achieved, but argues that preserving and consolidating the situation requires continual care, attention and hard work, a better understanding of the industrial plant as a social system, and a capacity to learn this by experience (Lupton, 1966: 49). These claims are now reassessed in turn.

Economic results

In economic terms, the agreements were intended to raise labour productivity and to distribute the gains to the company and its employees without causing an inflationary rise in costs (Flanders, 1964: 191). While Flanders is somewhat reluctant to make an economic evaluation of the Blue Book, he nevertheless makes some attempt based on '. . . calculations made by Fawley management' (1964: 195). The productivity of maintenance workers was seen to rise by '. . . about 50 per cent over the two years following 1st August 1960' (1964: 192). Process shift workers' productivity was seen to rise by forty-five per cent (1964: 195).

There are obvious difficulties associated with the attempt to measure improvements in 'labour' productivity (see Smith, 1973 for a comprehensive treatment of this problem). Such problems stem from the fact that both production inputs and outputs are invariably changing over time. Fawley did attempt, however, in 1966 to conduct an economic evaluation which included an assessment of productivity improvements. Some of this evaluation material was used apparently in preparation for the evidence to be submitted by Esso Petroleum Company Ltd. to the Royal Commission on Trade Unions and Employers' Associations in June of 1966. Much of the evaluation is based on hypothetical calculations (such as what would have happened if no Blue Book deal had been struck), and some of the background calculations are not always made clear. But management's evaluation of the Blue Book, covering the period from 1960 to 1965 does raise some interesting questions about the value of the Blue Book productivity agreement.

The overall conclusion of this internal evaluation reveals either a break-even or slight deficit position by the end of 1964. If benefits and particularly the separation plan gratuities are included, then by the end of 1964 the Blue Book was operating in the red. In 1965, owing to manpower reductions, Fawley moved into a credit position and was, reportedly, saving at the rate of about £500,000 per annum on wages and £80,000 per annum on benefits. These savings, however, related principally to the 1964 voluntary redundancy programme and could not be directly attributable to the Blue Book deal itself. Moreover, Fawley was not able to absorb the contracted construction work as hoped. This was running at about £200,000 per annum. As the audit was not able to uncover any direct financial cost savings deriving from the Blue Book, Fawley management came, in the Blue Book aftermath, to define Blue Book benefits in 'soft' or qualitative terms; in terms of such things as 'improved worker commitment and morale'.

This conclusion contrasts rather sharply with evidence supplied to the Royal Commission on Trade Unions (Research Papers 4, 1967). The commission reported that 'Esso have not supplied detailed calculations, but they have said: "Esso is satisfied that the agreements it has been able to reach so far were well worth making in financial terms"' (Research Papers 4, 1967: 36).

One needs, of course, to take the claims of the less tangible benefits of productivity bargaining (like a change in worker attitudes) with a 'pinch of salt'. As Daniel (1970b) has noted:

> it is far too easy for a management which did not succeed in achieving any hard savings to justify their efforts to themselves and to others in terms of indirect benefits; like the production manager who could not show any evidence that productivity had risen after a fairly major exercise, in which consultants had also been involved, but who felt that it had all been justified by the effect on 'the moral fibre of the workforce'. (*The Times*, 28 September 1970)

Esso did, however, provide some more general calculations to the Royal Commission on Trade Unions on 'labour and equipment costs before and after the deal' and this is presented in table 4 below (Memorandum of evidence submitted by Esso Petroleum Company Ltd. to the Royal Commission on Trade Unions and Employers' Associations, June 1966: 1655).

While highlighting such savings as those related to manpower reductions, this table does not include those losses associated with the general rise in overtime levels and contractor labour usage. The increased use of contractor labour is interesting in itself as the Blue Book was supposed to have '... enabled the Company to reduce its emphasis on contractors' (National Board for Prices and Incomes, Report No. 36, 1967: 50). Fawley management felt that if work could be restructured through the flexibility initiatives, then manning reductions would not necessarily be followed by either increased overtime or contractor use. The fact that

Table 4. *Labour and equipment costs before and after the Blue Book*

	Before deal	After deal
Men	1000	815
Units	500	312
Wages cost per year	£1,065,000	£1,021,000
Total cost per year	£2,017,000	£1,670,000
Average hours worked per week	$54\frac{1}{2}$	42
Average earnings per year	£1,065	£1,255
Capital committed in units	£5,000,000	£3,120,000
Reduction in men		18·5%
Reduction in units		37·6%
Reduction in capital committed		37·6%
Reduction in hours worked		23·0%
Reduction in total cost		17·2%
Increase in average earnings		17·8%

overtime and contractor labour costs did not fall would, in itself, suggest that the flexibility initiatives were not working as intended.

Fawley's productivity improvement over the period from 1960 to 1966 came principally through manpower reductions, most of which resulted from the 1964 voluntary separation programme. It was directly through this programme that Fawley was able to make some improvements on the Standard Oil of New Jersey 'mechanical index' (an index which relates the number of men employed to investment as a means of comparison between different refineries throughout the world). Such advances, however, occurred directly as a result of the voluntary redundancy programme as opposed to contributions made through the productivity bargaining process. If there was a lesson for Fawley management in this period, therefore, it was that 'labour shedding' provided a more certain and irreversible step towards increased productivity.

While Fawley was able to improve its own 'mechanical index' it was not, however, able to improve its position within the American parent Exxon league table which makes efficiency comparisons between Exxon refineries all over the world. Ian Upson, Fawley's refinery manager, claimed, in fact, that one of the reasons that Fawley embarked on a 'second generation' of productivity dealing was because it was still '... within one or two of the bottom of the league' (*The Sunday Times*, 20 July 1975, article by E. Jacobs, 'The great productivity myth'). Fawley Refinery found itself, therefore, dealing with a 'moving target'.

The quest for productivity

Institutional results

Flanders' analysis of 'institutional' changes in labour relations revealed a situation that was far from 'sweetness and light'. For Flanders '. . . labour relations acquired a greater formality in that they (labour relations) were governed by more explicit and less flexible rules' (1964: 199). Flanders notes that, while the unions were fully prepared to honour any specific commitments which they had accepted in signing the agreements,

> . . . they adopted a measured attitude towards their obligations under the agreements and refused to give anything away they had not signed for. At the same time they were not averse to exploiting any loopholes in the wording of the agreements, and began to query customary practices accepted without demur before. (1964: 199)

According to Flanders,

> Fawley management considered this trend to be an expression of opportunistic calculation on the unions' part; a sign that they knew the value of their concessions to the company and were going to see that they got a good price for every one of them in the future. (1964: 199–200)

It was with regard to the institutional results that Flanders begins to discuss some of the problems associated with greater formality and rule based control. He notes, for instance:

> Growing formality made for less give-and-take and ease of accommodation in daily relations. The stewards' augmented influence tended to make union negotiations more protracted and complex . . . The conclusion is inescapable that the immediate effect of the Blue Book and its successor was to make labour relations more conflict-prone – in the sense of rendering them more liable to the confrontation of opposed interests or viewpoints. (1964: 206–7)

Flanders also suggests that, in some cases, workers were able to turn the new 'rules' back on their makers. He notes, for instance, that, 'by sticking to the letter of the agreements, or rather to the most favourable interpretation, they could contain management and reassert the significance of their own role' (1964: 201).

According to Flanders, however, these institutional problems needed to be balanced against the higher and more important imperative of a '. . . more energetic participation of the work groups in the determination of their own destiny' (1964: 209). The resistances and rivalries thrown up by

The Fawley Blue Book revisited

the Blue Book were seen by Flanders to have 'a social value' (1964: 209). For Flanders 'they must be understood and appreciated as a necessary accompaniment of a growing industrial democracy raising the status of the workforce' (1964: 209). Thus, the greater turbulence in the labour-relations environment needed to be balanced off against the positive aspects of increased worker participation: 'If the word has any meaning when applied to the processes of labour relations, Fawley management acted democratically' (1964: 208).

Some of the problems Flanders saw in the short term in the institutional area appear to have endured over a longer time span. In 1967, when Fawley management was approaching its next round of productivity bargaining, Eric Wigham of *The Times* noted, for instance:

> It has been discovered that trade unionists who have been
> through such an experience (of productivity bargaining) once
> are much more sophisticated in later negotiations ... There is
> also a weariness with constant change and some sense of being
> cheated. (*The Times*, 19 July 1967, 'Fawley – stage three', by
> Eric Wigham)

Furthermore, referring to his own company's history of productivity bargaining, Mr N. Biggs of Esso observed that

> ... when employees have seen their future wage progression
> linked not to productivity as such but to changed working
> practices, the price of change and the resistance to change will
> certainly increase as the scope for future changes in working
> practices declines. (Norman Biggs, University of Manchester
> Institute of Science and Technology Foundation Lecture, deli-
> vered January 1970)

One Fawley manager claimed that workers did, in fact, come to put 'prices' on changes to working practices and that this psychology of pricing partly served to devalue the content of the Blue Book agreement: 'The Blue Book hadn't left an awful lot of space in terms of traditional productivity bargaining. The workers, sensing that there wasn't much space left simply clawed back the agreements to get some' (interview with Fawley manager).

Finally, with regard to Flanders' claim that the Blue Book was '... the stuff of democratic politics' (1964: 209), it is important to note that productivity bargaining at Fawley did not appear to fit the classical 'pluralist' model. Flanders' ideal industrial-relations model, based on the notion of the extension of collective bargaining and worker participation,

111

appears infinitely more 'ideal' than 'real' in terms of the Fawley experience. Fawley managers rarely, if ever, associated the Blue Book with a new 'pluralism'. Certainly the origins of the Blue Book were not based on any high altruism. Fawley managers were more concerned with 'reducing costs' than with the creation of '... new social relations in industry in which it is possible for participants to act responsibly' (Flanders, 1975: 153). As one of Esso's managers put it:

> It is tempting to describe productivity bargaining as a philanthropic innovation ... leading vaguely to a new relationship between management and employees or, at best, as being responsible for a revival in joint consultation at the factory level. But it will be dangerous if it is forgotten that the essential purpose of a productivity bargain is to reduce costs. (Bamforth, 1966: 208)

This same message was provided by Esso in their written memorandum of evidence submitted to the Royal Commission on Trade Unions and Employers' Associations as follows:

> But the main drive in recent years to improve the quality of the labour contribution has derived from economic pressures rather than social motives. It would be incorrect to suggest that the reason why Esso embarked on the work at Fawley (or later in marketing) was to create new patterns of industrial relations; to give a lead in these things; or purely to improve the lot of its employees. (Written memorandum of evidence submitted by the Esso Petroleum Company in advance of the oral hearing commission's reference WE/143, June 1966: 1645)

It would also seem to be the case that, as it became apparent that the Blue Book was not working as it should, Fawley management began, in the mid-1960s, to think in terms of moving towards a 'union-free' environment. In 1964 Fawley management initiated a dialogue with external consultants about '... possibilities of operating without unions' (interview with external consultant).

The idea that productivity bargaining somehow represented a *deliberate and conscious* shift towards a new strategy of pluralism did not hold true for Fawley. As one manager put it:

> When we struck the Blue Book deal our intention was to free ourselves from union control. We didn't want to replace custom and practice control by a new set of restrictive practices. We were hardly thinking at the time of bringing unions into a

new partnership with management. It was, after all, the unions
who had created all the restrictive practices in the first place.
(Interview with Fawley manager)

The intentions of Fawley management at the time of striking the Blue
Book were clear: management wanted to reassert its control but not at the
expense of buttressing the unions' role in management decision-making.
Fawley management's intentions were directed at that of which Flanders
himself was so adamantly critical, the simple one-off 'buy-out' of informal
custom and practice rule. It is difficult to detect any altruism on the part of
Fawley management in introducing productivity bargaining in terms of a
desire to democratize workplace relations. It would appear that a shift to
an integration- or incorporation-based strategy was the last thing on the
mind of Fawley managers.

While Fawley management never intended to be tied to a new set of
jointly determined formal workplace rules, the actual objectives did not
correspond with reality. Fawley management found itself tied not only to
the new, jointly determined rules but also to the legacy of past 'custom and
practice'. In this sense, the new era of 'joint control' needs to be seen not in
terms of a deliberate management objective, but rather as an unintended
(and according to some Fawley managers a negative) consequence of
productivity bargaining. Part of the failure of the Blue Book deal can
possibly be explained by exploring management's intentions in introducing the Blue Book in the first place. From the case study it would appear
that Fawley management introduced the Blue Book with the intention of
restoring 'unilateral' control and that there was little desire to operate
through a process of joint control. When confronted with the reality of
'joint control' Fawley management responded not in terms of welcoming
a new era of union participation but rather recoiled from this experience.
By responding to this new joint control in a hostile (or 'unitarist') manner,
Fawley management ensured that the notion of 'joint control' would not
prosper at Fawley.

Cultural results: changing attitudes towards change

Flanders notes that 'both the long-term economic and deeper social
justification for the (Blue Book) experiment were seen in its objective of
changing attitudes towards change' (1964: 209). It was seen above that the
economics of the Blue Book did not suggest anything more than a break-
even position and that, therefore, Fawley managers increasingly came to
justify the Blue Book in terms of more subtle 'cultural' changes. My own
case study results, however, suggest that, rather than making workers

more open and receptive to change, the Blue Book actually served to create a climate of resistance to change.

The Fawley Waterside Labour and Trade Union Liaison Committee noted, for instance, in an internal communique:

> The Blue Book after five years is nothing more than a series of broken promises. None of the aims were kept. Wage increases have not been maintained over the years, nor have we been able to get any increased leisure time. (April 1965)

A Transport and General Workers' Union minute expressed union sentiment in this way: 'Esso has lived on its good name of the past. Once you could trust them now you could not' (Transport and General Workers' Union Minutes, June 1971).

The growing hostility by Fawley workers toward the Blue Book was echoed just as strongly in a Fawley union newsletter (May 1964). This letter is worth quoting at length as it contrasts quite vividly to Fawley management claims about changes in worker attitudes:

> Once again the Blue Book is in the news, once again the people who had little to do with either its negotiations or its working effect have been interviewed to say what a gift from the high heavens it has been, and express surprise that other industries are not queuing up to get on the bandwagon. But is the Blue Book so great a masterpiece, has it improved both the company's coffers and the conditions of its employees?
>
> Well in the first place it has never been completed in Process, and already is being overtaken by the following White Paper agreement. Where is the extra leisure, the management have mishandled so badly the recruitment into the Process Department that it is so undermanned that higher overtime than pre Blue Book has to be worked to keep the refinery going. Merit steps, what a joke, maintenance of equipment, when? No redundancy, well ask the staff.
>
> One thing we can tell the company's directors, that whereas at one time not so very long ago the Company's name stood for security and pride amongst its employees, it now stands for uncertainty and suspicion, the cooperation that used to be there is beginning to get tarnished. I wonder which is more attractive, being rich but hated, or being well off but respected, and finally don't let us forget that all those other industries who did not jump on the Blue Book bandwagon, have quietly caught up with the Esso rates of pay and conditions, and may I say, have on some subjects overtaken Esso.

How about profits well we don't know, we are still being continually told that to survive the Company has to change its habits, we do notice that it has done so in creating more airy fairy departments which for some reason suddenly are very important, only to be changed again back to mediocrity soon after.

This type of sharp indictment of the Blue Book would seem to be more easily translated into resistance than acceptance.

Conclusions

It has been seen that, over an extended time frame, the stated objectives of the Blue Book (both on the management 'achievement' side and worker 'reward' side) have failed quite dramatically. Over this period, the philosophical and strategic basis of the Blue Book agreement, that of a 'low overtime and high wages' policy, was abandoned in favour of the old 'high overtime and low wages' policy. Fawley management, faced with an inability to achieve higher levels of effort from its work-force, moved back to its low pay 'indulgency' strategy.

From a purely economic perspective the Blue Book was seen to have resulted in a break-even position, if not one of deficit. Moreover, productivity bargaining at Fawley did not appear to be directed at the creation of a new 'higher'-order pluralism. Rather, it was more closely aligned with 'unitarist' ideas or objectives. Finally, from a cultural perspective it was seen that there was a growing worker hostility to the Blue Book and no sign of a new positive or receptive attitude to change.

Certain Marxian scholars like Cliff (1970) have argued that through productivity bargaining, management has been able to achieve its control objective. As evidence of this, Cliff offers the fact that 'Esso was able to negotiate a new deal in 1968 with extensions of flexibility and reduction in manning' (1970: 28). Case study findings have demonstrated precisely the opposite. The reason that Fawley turned, once again, to productivity bargaining in 1968 was very much because management had not been able to achieve the original Blue Book objectives, although inducements from the late 1960s incomes policies cannot be ignored.

7

Fawley's second generation productivity agreements: 1967–1971

Introduction

In chapter 6 it was seen that the Blue Book productivity agreements failed to achieve their overt or stated objectives. One might expect that such dramatic lack of success would have relegated the productivity bargaining process at Fawley to mere historical curiosity. Rather than diminishing in importance, however, productivity bargaining remained entrenched in Fawley's industrial relations. This chapter reviews Fawley's experience with its second generation productivity agreements, extending from 1967 to 1971. This period encompasses the first of the Labour government's late 1960s incomes policies, the terms of which provided that productivity bargaining could be used as a means of winning pay awards above and beyond the norm established by government. Productivity bargaining did not reappear at Fawley, however, as a means of evading incomes policies. It will be seen that each of the productivity agreements struck during this period was a substantial agreement in its own right.

This chapter evaluates the extent to which three process productivity deals and three maintenance productivity deals actually met their stated objectives. On the process side the agreements focussed upon the introduction of new technology while the maintenance deals sought to build on the objectives of the Blue Book, especially in terms of flexible working arrangements, tea breaks and so on. Compared to the Blue Book, these agreements were far less comprehensive and each will be only briefly discussed and evaluated. The profusion of agreements and the unevenness of the data means that each productivity agreement cannot be systematically evaluated.

The process workers' productivity deals: 1967, 1968 and 1970

The interim process shift agreement: October 1967

From the late 1960s onwards, Fawley Refinery was to experience rapid technological change in the form of computerized control systems. The

116

technological changes occurring during this period were to alter the very face of process work at Fawley. In Flanders' era, there existed what was referred to as a 'dispersed control room structure'. The fuel processing plants at Fawley (the largest refining units) were operated from eight local control rooms. Process work involved 'inside' control room duties (monitoring dials and pen-recorders through conventional analogue control techniques) and 'outside' duties (checking pumps and furnaces in accordance with operating requirements). The demarcation between 'inside' and 'outside' jobs was not, however, very rigid and workers typically rotated between them. The notion of the work team had particular significance within this structure as both inside and outside workers cooperated closely. Even in those plants where less flexibility had been realized between inside and outside work, outside workers typically spent a great deal of time within the control room, either assisting in the monitoring activity or alternatively keeping up with the current state of the process.

The advent of 'direct digital computer control' in the mid-1960s was, however, to revolutionize process operations. The first 'direct digital control' system was introduced at Fawley in 1967 and, at the time, represented the most advanced use of computer control in the refining industry. It was to win for Fawley, in 1969, the distinction of being the first oil company to receive the Queen's Award to Industry for technological innovation. It was the purpose of the 1967 process productivity agreement to gain employee acceptance of this new computer technology.

After a lapse of five continuous years without striking a new productivity agreement, Fawley management returned to the technique in 1967 with the development of a deal made with the process shift workers. This agreement, signed on 2 October 1967 by the Transport and General Workers' Union and Esso Fawley management, was a stepping stone to a later, 1968 agreement and was therefore considered to be an 'interim' agreement. Quite apart from securing the union's agreement to the introduction of new technology, this agreement also served to gain union acceptance of new working arrangements which would alter skill levels. This agreement marked the first time that Fawley management was to utilize the productivity bargaining process as a device to assist in the introduction of new process technology.

More specifically, this agreement sought to achieve employee acceptance of the consolidation and computerization of all of the refinery's Zone I units (the key process operations areas). Such consolidation and computerization was to have a dramatic impact on the skill levels of many process jobs, increasing the skill of some while 'de-skilling' others. Other process units in the refinery continued to rely upon conventional analogue control methods so that there was, and still is, a mix in old and new process control methods at the refinery.

The advances in computerization that took place allowed management actually to make a choice as to whether the key production control activities would be distributed more evenly amongst process workers or whether these control activities were to be concentrated in the hands of a select few. Fawley management chose to organize production in such a way that fewer and fewer workers were in a position to intervene in the production process.

The nature of process work at Fawley was to change dramatically as a result of the advent of computerization and it is important to describe these changes briefly. Under 'direct digital control', a computer replaces conventional analogue control. The computer checks all measured values against stored normal values and informs the process operator of abnormal conditions via a typewriter or visual display unit. The advent of direct digital control was, for the first time, to open up choices to management about how process work was to be organized. Under the 1967 deal, Fawley management put forward a proposal to 'consolidate' the eight previous local control rooms in the fuel processing area into one large 'consolidated' control facility. The effect of this reorganization was to create two quite distinct and separate segments of workers within the 'operating' process department: (1) a few inside computer control room operators and (2) a large pool of outside manual workers. This reorganization was to eliminate entirely the existing flexibility between inside and outside jobs.

Under the centralized control room structure, the new central control room was to be manned by a small team of approximately three control room operators per shift. All of the key operating decisions were to be restricted to this small team of operators. This reorganization was to have particularly devastating effects on the nature of the outside workers' jobs as it removed any possibility of them sharing in the process control activities – although the full implications of these changes were not immediately noticed by workers. Outside workers were no longer to have access to the control room and were to have contact with central control only through radios. The outside workers' tasks would now be restricted to 'responding' to radio requests from central control to 'turn valves'. These outside workers were to be totally removed from the control processes and thus severed from a formerly 'integrated' work team.

Over the years since these changes, outside workers came to define themselves disparagingly as 'walking wheel keys'. Wheel keys are the outside operators' tool of the trade and are basically equivalent to the standard wrench. Most of the outside workers' job was now to be spent walking about the unit, wheel keys at hand, waiting for a radio dispatch to turn or rotate a valve. Outside operators were no longer to have an opportunity to manipulate the process, nor were they to be aware of the state of the process. One outside worker described his job in these terms: '... we're treated like idiots. We're just walking wheel keys. We wait for a radio call and then we tap a valve. We never even get to see the control room' (interview with process worker). Nichols' and Beynon's (1977: 11–47) rich ethnographic account of work life within the continuous process industry points to the existence of 'donkey' work (or low-skill work) within the industry – making the point that not all continuous process jobs are highly skilled with high levels of satisfaction (as Blauner, 1964, would suggest). My own findings reveal that recent technological changes may even have increased the number of low-skilled workers on site.

The 'inside' process control room jobs were also to be changed. On the one hand, their job was to be more complex in terms of monitoring more control 'loops' and larger segments of the plant while, on the other hand, increased computer control meant that the operator had to intervene less in the process. In effect, the inside control room operator's job became more one of a 'reviewer' than one of a 'doer' as computer control pushed the operator further away from the actual control process.

The overall effect of technological change, at least as Fawley management sought to organize it, served to segment labour groups, creating a greater division between inside and outside workers. Although outside workers' jobs became progressively deskilled, these workers continued to possess control at the tacit skill level. For example, outside workers would often rotate valves in a way that was 'contrary' to engineering specifications because of the operator's understanding of the 'quirks' of a particular valve. As a result, management needed to continue to win the active cooperation of these outside workers. Such cooperation and consent was, however, difficult to achieve within the context of a deskilled labour process, since management could not rely on the intrinsic qualities of the job to spawn the consent required.

The process of deskilling the outside workers' job at Fawley in fact appears to have resulted in a crisis of consent. This is evidenced further by Fawley management's recent plan, notably in 1983, to 're-skill' outside workers' jobs artificially through the placement of remote visual display units around the yard which would enable outside workers to observe the current state of the process, but not enabling them in any way to intervene in the process. The need to reskill jobs in this way highlights the problems and contradictions in pursuing a deskilling strategy.

The precise role of productivity bargaining in introducing technical change, at least for Fawley, is somewhat difficult to determine. There is no way of knowing whether Fawley's new computer equipment could have been introduced just as easily *without* the use of productivity bargaining. Many other U.K. refineries introduced the same technological changes without the use of productivity bargaining. In many cases new technology was simply accepted by workers as part of a 'natural' progression within the production process. Arguably much of the introduction of new technology needs to be seen in this way – as an issue that never reaches the bargaining table, simply because workers and unions often view the introduction of new technology as normal and inevitable. It would appear that this was precisely the case at Fawley. Much of Fawley management's communication to workers about the new computerized technology was couched within a logic of inevitability – that the new technology was simply a part of the 'forward march of progress'. Workers at Fawley appear to have accepted the introduction of new technology within these terms.

The link between productivity bargaining and technological change is, however, itself well established in the literature. McKersie and Hunter have noted in fact, that '. . . the main function of productivity bargaining has been to update the work organization to match the existing technology' (1973: 358). Referring to Fawley, McKersie and Hunter themselves note that '. . . management at Esso acknowledged that it would have been impossible prior to productivity bargaining to have introduced larger trucks or to have instituted computer control at the refinery' (1973: 282).

The claim that the introduction of computer control would have been impossible prior to productivity bargaining proved, in fact, to be entirely unfounded. An interview with a senior manager who was directly involved revealed that the new computer equipment was '. . . never a significant issue for workers or unions at Fawley'. As he put it,

> the new computer control equipment that we introduced and
> our planned reorganization of the control rooms never surfaced
> as a contentious issue. While I wasn't surprised, some other
> managers felt that we might get some resistance. In the end we
> got none. The whole idea was simply accepted from the outset
> . . . as something quite inevitable. What amazed me was that,
> for all the changes we were planning, the only issue of concern
> that was raised by the unions related to the quality of the
> radios we were going to give to the men. We spent the whole
> time talking about walkie-talkie radios, while in the meantime
> we were ripping down old process units and putting in millions
> of pounds of new computer equipment. The productivity deal
> became a joke because it got reduced to a discussion about

radios. The whole radio issue wasn't worth more than a couple of a hundred pounds to us. (Interview with Fawley manager)

This view was corroborated by a branch officer in the Transport and General Workers' Union, who, when asked to identify the key issues associated with the 1967 process productivity deal, said: 'Oh yes, that was the deal about radios.' The enormous technological changes that took place do not appear to have presented much of a problem, at least at the early stages of the agreement. Instead, the entire change was reduced to a trivial discussion about radios – hardly an issue worthy of the productivity bargaining process.

The process shift agreement: March 1968

The pay award associated with the 1967 deal was not solely a reward for the introduction of new technology, but it was also intended to pave the way for a further, broader productivity deal. This new deal was concluded in March 1968 and sought to increase productivity in a variety of ways: first, by improving performance within existing job descriptions, secondly, by extending the range of process operators' duties and responsibilities (including a series of maintenance flexibility items), thirdly, by reducing the number of process operator job grades (from six to three), fourthly by reducing process manning levels by approximately fifteen per cent (while at the same time proposing manning arrangements for new plants) and, finally, by clarifying provisions of the Blue Book and follow-up 1962 agreement (including an amplification of the 'job coverage' and 'substitute working' provisions as laid out in the Blue Book).

The 1968 agreement can be seen as an attempt to restructure work organization so that management could capture the full benefits of introducing new process technology. With this deal, productivity bargaining came to be defined principally as a means of reducing manning levels as a result of the ongoing introduction of new technology. For instance, the introductory preamble to the agreement asserted that 'one of the most significant opportunities for increasing productivity is to carry out the work requirements with fewer people'. As one Fawley manager put it:

We began to realize that our best chance at productivity improvement would come from shedding labour. This is something we could effectively control. Furthermore, the cost justification for the computer equipment we were installing in the late 1960s and early 1970s was based on an anticipated drop in manning levels. (Interview with Fawley manager)

The most innovative part of the 1968 agreement related, however, to the concept of 'ongoing change for ongoing reward'. This notion was to set the tone for what became known at Fawley, in the 1970s, as the 'open-ended' or 'indirect' agreements. In the 1968 agreement, a provision was included whereby additional equipment and new technology could be introduced without the need for further negotiation. It was agreed that all new equipment and technology would simply be recorded at the level of individual process units, in a log book, on an ongoing basis. This information was then to form the basis for the valuation of any increased efficiency payments which would normally be made at the same time as the annual negotiations.

A 'permanent productivity committee' consisting of two union and two management representatives was also established, meeting initially on a monthly basis for two consecutive days, to assist in the implementation of the agreement and to monitor the plant changes log book. The concept of a permanent productivity committee was in line with what would become the philosophy of the 'ongoing' or 'indirect' approach to productivity bargaining. The 1968 agreement placed greater emphasis on achieving general improvements in the use of manpower on an *ad hoc* basis, as distinct from stressing the attainment of specific productivity objectives through clearly spelled out changes in working practices. The 1968 agreement stated that

> productivity bargaining should be a continuing exercise ... and it is hoped that employees will continue to consider ways and means by which the refinery could be operated more efficiently. Ideas routed to the Committee via supervision and stewards could begin to establish a basis for the future.

In evaluating the content of the agreement it is first interesting to note that there is a fairly significant repetition of items from both the Blue Book and the 1962 Transport and General Workers' Union agreement. Substitute working practices, job coverage arrangements and the flexibility provisions appear in each of the 1960, 1962 and 1968 agreements. In the case of the job coverage provisions, the 1968 agreements sought to 'supplement and amplify' the relevant sections of the Blue Book. The real case appears, however, to have been more one of closing 'loopholes' found to exist in the Blue Book job coverage clauses (so that the movement of process operators between units would now apply during normal operation and not in exceptional circumstances only). Furthermore, the 1968 agreement sought to clarify the provisions associated with Blue Book flexibility objectives between process operators and maintenance workers. Difficulties had been encountered in securing a uniform application of these flexibility items across all areas of the process department. Some twenty-three areas of minor maintenance flexibility that were specified in the original Blue Book (section 5d) were now rewritten for the purposes of clarification. The original Blue Book agreement had been so complex and detailed that a multitude of competing interpretations over the wording had resulted, which in turn led management to renegotiate the phrasing of the agreement. With each subsequent agreement there is an attempt to correct the deficiencies of clauses in past agreements. The extent of the repetition of productivity items is revealing as it gives some indication, in itself, of the lack of success of past agreements.

The actual implementation and day-to-day operation of the 1968 process deal appears to have gone much the way of the Blue Book, that is, with little real success. There were, for instance, considerable delays in the demanning efforts and some demannings were not achieved at all (for example, in the poly, reforming units and the marine terminal). Furthermore, only limited success was attained with the extension of process operator duties, and flexibility between process and maintenance was hardly ever used. Moreover, the attempt to 'clarify' past productivity deals was 'not as good as hoped' (mostly due to 'problems with maintenance stewards'). With regard to the log books for introducing new equipment, major change was apparently still hard to implement without protracted negotiations. Finally, the 'permanent productivity committee had only a short life and was disbanded'.

The process operators did little to ensure the success of the 1968 deal and acted to subvert the agreement in a variety of ways. First, there was an outright refusal to accept parts of the deal that had been signed. An example of this can be found in the blocking of the 'job release' provision. The research that McKersie and Hunter conducted on the 1968 agreement reveals:

> The T.G.W.U. workers refused to implement the so-called 'job-release item' of the agreement. This provision enabled management to assign a worker of a certain team for a short time (a few hours) to other groups in case these groups could not meet their performance targets. The work teams, being very cohesive and having developed a spirit of group loyalty, refused for twelve months to comply with this rule. Because there was a degree of competition between the teams they were not willing to assist other groups in satisfying their targets. (1973: 275)

In addition to blocking the 'job release' provision, the manning arrangements for new plants were also apparently blocked outright. Refusal to accept parts of the deal was not restricted to the process operators who made up the principal party to the deal, but also to other groups who were directly affected by the agreement. In relation to the flexibility provisions between the process operators and the Transport and General Workers' Union maintenance groups, the maintenance groups simply, in many cases, did not allow process workers to proceed with the agreed mutual flexible working items. Furthermore, Fawley management had negotiated a number of provisions about possible craft–process flexibility, with the intention that the craft unions would come to agreement about these flexibility items after the 1968 agreement had been struck. This did not come to fruition. Thus, other individuals and groups who were not a main party to the 1968 productivity process deal, but who had an interface relationship with the main party, had the power to disturb the content of the agreement, and the case study findings suggest that this power was used.

The whole notion of paying for ongoing productivity (principally in the form of employee acceptance of minor and major equipment changes) appears to have backfired on management. Rather than being freely given, cooperation appears to have become more carefully measured out by workers. According to certain Fawley managers, workers were beginning, at this time, to become interested in and make demands for the benefits not only from improved labour productivity but also from the benefits or profits accruing to management as a result of new technology itself. There are many examples of the new rigid linkage between money and effort. In the early 1970s, for instance, when Fawley management was restricted by incomes policies (which did not have a productivity exception clause) from paying out wage increases, the process branch accordingly served notice to management that they would withdraw cooperation with respect to the introduction of new operating equipment. One manager claimed that '... before the log books were introduced, technological change was just taken for granted. Now we're having to negotiate these changes at some cost' (interview with Fawley manager).

The process agreement: May 1970

The limited success of the 1968 process deal is perhaps best seen in the content of the productivity deal struck with the process department following the 1968 agreement. This new deal was known as the 1970 process agreement. Patterned closely on the 1968 deal, this agreement served, more than anything, as an attempt to reaffirm the lost integrity of the 1968 agreement. Following the major productivity deals of the past – the 1960 Blue Book and the 1962 and 1968 agreements – the 1970 process agreement could be seen as a tidying operation (Income Data Services, Report 100, 13 October 1970: 6–7). Like the 1968 agreement it aimed to

achieve 'commitment of *continuing* support and cooperation in the following areas':
— the introduction and efficient operation of new plant
— the development of the full use of new methods and equipment
— the acceptance of and full use of new technology
— cooperation where applicable in cost reduction programmes and activities that may be developed within local areas.

The agreement did not, however, just deal in generalities. It specifically laid down a number of 'adjustments to current agreements and practices which are intended to improve refinery effectiveness'. Many of these were mere reaffirmations of provisions contained in past deals (such as a commitment to extend the responsibilities of chief operators and a commitment to take on additional flexibility between operators in certain areas). The very role of the 1968 Permanent Productivity Committee was questioned in the 1970 agreement where it was agreed that 'the existing structure of local committees set up in the 1968 productivity deal should be reviewed with a view to strengthening local discussions and consultation within the areas of their responsibility'.

Because it was a relatively minor 'tidying up' deal, little documentation existed on the 1970 agreement and it is, therefore, not possible to provide a detailed evaluation of this deal. One branch officer suggested, however, that the agreement was to go the way of previous deals: '. . . there was some noise made in the beginning but then we moved back to our old ways'. This kind of comment, however, should be taken lightly as many of the minor productivity deals were poorly remembered by Fawley employees.

One aspect of the 1970 agreement was that it made the subsequent pay increases for process workers effective from the same date as the pay increases of craftsmen. The two groups' negotiations had been separated since the beginning of 1969.

The maintenance productivity deals: 1968 and 1969

In 1968 and 1969 three productivity deals were struck that related to refinery maintenance workers. Two parallel agreements were struck in 1968, one of these with the Transport and General Workers' Union maintenance day workers, the other with the refinery craft workers. The third agreement, covering both these groups, was struck in 1969.

The Transport and General Workers' Union (T.G.W.U.) non-craft maintenance workers' deal: October 1968

The T.G.W.U. non-craft maintenance workers' agreement was an interim agreement and was to be followed by discussions concerning further

125

productivity proposals. The agreement included the following provisions:
— the widening use of basic skills (e.g. driving responsibilities to be shared rather than restricted to a separate function, the extension of slinging and scaffolding across the T.G.W.U. maintenance groups, increased responsibility for ordering of tools, safety equipment, materials etc.)
— reorganization of Blue Book tea break arrangements
— increased flexible working (in addition to experimental flexible working)
— changes in supervisory relationships in which workers would agree to be supervised, in special situations, by other than their own supervisor.

The principal features of the agreement related to flexibility in terms of both the agreed items and 'experimental' flexibility. On the agreed items, it would appear that little real flexibility had taken place, especially when it came to flexibility between T.G.W.U. maintenance workers and process shift workers. The T.G.W.U. maintenance workers managed to develop a rider about their flexibility with process shift workers, which prevented process shift workers from carrying out T.G.W.U. maintenance work unless the shift workers had been properly trained to carry out the maintenance work and unless this training had in fact been registered in a log book. According to one T.G.W.U. official, maintenance workers commonly evoked this rider to block process shift work flexibility.

Furthermore, Fawley management appears to have encountered some difficulty in scheduling and planning for flexible working, sometimes resulting in the temporary depletion and short supply of some maintenance groups. For example, it was found that workers from the transport department were being employed on cleaning out beehives at a time when manpower was being stretched to the limit trying to maintain the transport service.

The craft unions' productivity deal: October 1968

Like the 1968 T.G.W.U. maintenance workers' deal, the 1968 craft deal was an interim one and included the following provisions:
— the introduction of multi-craft supervision
— line supervisory promotion based on who is the 'most suitably qualified candidate'
— written down inter-craft flexibility
— revision of Blue Book tea break arrangement
— creation of 'standby call in'

The substance and content of the 1968 craft agreement was, for the most part, similar to that of the 1968 T.G.W.U. maintenance workers'

126

agreement. The provisions did, however, have a different effect on craft workers than they did on the T.G.W.U. maintenance workers. The introduction of multi-craft supervision was at first vigorously opposed by the craft unions and was, in fact, effectively blocked by the craft unions in the original Blue Book agreement. The movement to multi-craft supervision existed as part of a Fawley management strategy to break up or destroy craft based and craft controlled supervision and marked an attempt to strengthen the power of 'direct' forms of control. Furthermore, the promotion of craft workers into line supervisory positions was to be placed entirely within managerial hands based on the principle of the 'most suitably qualified candidate'. Promotion was to be linked to a '. . . system of individual merit with the best man getting the job'. Such a move was seen by Fawley management as the first step towards the establishment of an individual merit system for pay and promotion that was to be extended to the entire labour force. Fawley management's interest in tightening up front line supervision contradicts recent labour process theorists like Edwards (1979) who have suggested that there has been a transition away from direct forms of control (in the form of front line supervision) to bureaucratic and normative forms of control.

Apart from multi-craft supervision, a second area of importance for this productivity deal relates to the flexibility initiatives. Once again, Fawley craft workers did not appear to work the flexibility initiatives in the way that these were intended. In particular, the workers learned to use the 'language' of the agreement to their own ends. One word which was key to many of the flexibility provisions was the term 'augment' (to give an example of their usage: auto-mechanics will 'augment' mechanical fitters) and workers more often than not debated the meaning of 'augmentation'. As one steward put it:

> The word 'augment' was a powerful word for us. When we were asked to do a specific cross trade job we could always say that the job involved something more than simple augmentation. These arguments made some of our supervisors think twice about asking us to augment a job.

Like the Blue Book, the 1968 craft deal was to make little headway.

1969 agreement covering both T.G.W.U. non-craft and craft maintenance workers

The 1969 agreement with the T.G.W.U. and craft maintenance workers was significant in that it marked the first time that the craft unions had combined with T.G.W.U. maintenance workers to negotiate a joint productivity agreement. The key features of the agreement included the following:

— an extension of a multi-craft supervision (craft unions and the T.G.W.U. would participate jointly in this scheme and accept supervision from each other)

— reciprocal exchange of work between craft unions and the T.G.W.U. maintenance workers (e.g. extension of driving arrangements allowing craftsmen to transport men, tools, equipment at request of supervisor; T.G.W.U. workers permitted to carry out craft tasks as follows: relamping, servicing of mobile equipment etc.)

— union commitment to changes associated with the introduction and efficient maintenance of new technology, new maintenance methods and new organization.

This 1969 deal was essentially an orthodox flexibility deal and much of its substance related to the extension of flexibility between the craft and T.G.W.U. maintenance workers. In this respect it did not coincide with the dominant type of productivity bargaining of the time (i.e. those incomes policy related agreements that were concerned with the intensification of effort), but rather followed the classic style of seeking changes in the nature of work. This agreement came to be referred to by Fawley management as a '... major breakthrough in restrictive attitudes between the two groups'.

Given such a high level of optimism, how then did the agreement fare? Case data reveal that what was hoped to be a 'major breakthrough' in fact resulted in a 'major failure'. Few, in fact, of the flexibility items were carried through. For example, the extension of driving clause was not adhered to and was seen as a 'sore point' which has resulted in other flexibility items being blocked. Finally, by 1971 the craft unions made a formal declaration that no craft work was to be passed on to the T.G.W.U. non-craft maintenance workers.

Conclusions

In this chapter an attempt was made to evaluate Fawley's second generation productivity deals which extended over the period from 1967 to 1971. On the process side, it was seen that the deals were directed principally at the introduction of new technology. The precise role played by productivity bargaining in facilitating technological change, however, was not seen to be clear. In 1967, for instance, workers did not seem to object to the introduction of a computer control system, seeing it more as part of the inevitable march of progress. Moreover, Fawley management's pledge to pay, on an ongoing basis, for the introduction of any new capital equipment, only served to heighten the bargaining awareness of workers. Some workers began to demand money for productivity gains relating not only to improvements in labour productivity – but also more generally to improvements in the production system itself.

The maintenance productivity deals, on the other hand, attempted to build on the Blue Book agreement. These deals, rather than making major advances, sought to remedy old problems associated with the Blue Book agreement. These agreements, while less comprehensive than the Blue Book, were based, for the most part, on the Blue Book principle of 'listing' or 'detailing' changes in a formal manner. Like the Blue Book agreement itself, these agreements were to have little success. The problems associated with this listing type of agreement prompted management to seek out a new and different approach to productivity bargaining (to some extent patterned on the principles of 'ongoing' change introduced in the 1968 process deal). It is to this new form of productivity bargaining, known as the open-ended or indirect type, that Fawley turned.

8

The 1970s and the advent of the open-ended productivity agreements

Introduction

As pointed out in chapter 3 on the history of productivity bargaining, it has been fairly commonplace to suggest that productivity bargaining withered away with the collapse of the Labour government's incomes policy in 1969–70. The hysteria associated with 'bogus' productivity deals, that is, productivity deals believed to have been struck only to circumvent wage controls, had apparently served to discredit the productivity bargaining process. Esso's Fawley Refinery, however, did not lose faith in the technique, turning to productivity bargaining, in the early 1970s, with renewed vigour. In fact, compared with Fawley's second generation productivity deals struck in the late 1960s, the productivity deals that were to follow in the 1970s were considered by Fawley management, at the time, to be much more significant and substantial.

In the years prior to 1972, productivity bargaining at Fawley could largely have been defined as a 'shopping list' approach, whereby it was normal to bargain for specific and detailed productivity items. With the introduction of the 1968 process shift agreement, at which the concept of 'ongoing change for ongoing reward' was introduced, there was to be a marginal shift in this philosophy. In Fawley's third generation of productivity bargaining, emphasis was to be placed upon the need to improve productivity by changing worker attitudes and behaviour rather than focussing upon an exchange of concessions in the use of labour in return for improved rewards. This new period can be defined, for the most part, by the so-called open-ended or indirect approach to productivity bargaining. Apart from breaking away from the formal detailed listing of changes to an informal understanding or agreement on desired changes, the main innovation in productivity bargaining at Fawley during this period was the movement toward a general acceptance of change of a continuous nature rather than, as in the case of the Blue Book type of agreement, a once and for all trade-off. The move to open-ended or indirect agreements represented a shift in the underlying control apparatus from bureaucratic control to what Friedman (1977) refers to as a 'responsible autonomy' control strategy.

The 1972 progressive approach agreement, the 1975 maintenance deal, to a lesser extent the 1975 process efficiency agreement, and the 1977 target approach, were all, in fact, sold by Fawley management as representing a major new revolution in the use of the productivity bargaining technique. The authors of these four agreements went so far as to suggest that the changes to be brought about by these agreements were to be equal in magnitude to those (apparently) brought about by the Blue Book. While Fawley management was interested in presenting the 'on-going' technique as an innovation first initiated at Fawley, the technique had, in fact, already been developed and employed in other British companies. With the striking of these four agreements it becomes apparent that a third generation of Fawley managers had become caught up with the pursuit of a kind of Blue Book celebrity status.

Just as the earlier detailed comprehensive agreements were seen to be beset by their own problems and contradictions, so, too, were productivity agreements of the open-ended or indirect type. While the detailed provisions of previous agreements were found to be inflexible and at odds with the complex contingencies of the production process, it will be seen that the new open-ended agreements were so loose and informal as to be of little real value in increasing productivity. By the end of the open-ended period, just like at the end of previous periods, Fawley Refinery was still to be found at the bottom of the parent company's productivity 'league tables'.

The progressive approach agreement: April 1972

Part of Fawley management's rationale for introducing new productivity deals lay in trying to achieve, yet again, the objectives of past agreements that had not always been fulfilled. The philosophy and content of the 1972 agreement is itself born out of a critique of past productivity agreements, in particular the Blue Book.

The Blue Book productivity deal was criticized by the authors of the 1972 progressive approach as being altogether too bureaucratic. According to the then refinery manager, the act of detailing or specifying change was precisely the reason why the Blue Book agreement had failed: 'Deals concerning demarcation breakdown were self-defeating in that they almost gave a rationale and a cloak of respectability to an inefficiency which was no longer socially justifiable or in any way tolerable in the competitive economic climate of the seventies.'

According to the authors of the 1972 progressive approach agreement an entirely fresh approach to productivity bargaining was required, one which did not simply tie down both workers and management to another set of restrictive rules or foster a set of worker attitudes driven by the letter rather than the spirit of the agreement. What was seen to be required was the need to change worker attitudes, to reach a point where workers would naturally and spontaneously seek out the most productive way of working, without reference to any body of detailed workplace rules. According to Fawley management, this would require a revolution in the thinking of Fawley workers. This shift in approach was to represent yet another tactic to obtain worker commitment and consent.

The progressive approach agreement, struck in April 1972, applied to both craft and non-craft Fawley maintenance workers. A typical open-ended agreement, it contained very little specific detail, outlined in a few short pages. Despite its lack of detail, the design and negotiation of the agreement nevertheless extended over a nine-month period. The philosophical basis of this agreement was linked to the idea that attitude changes in the work-force would first need to be produced which, in turn, would cause changes in worker behaviour and productivity.

Rather than management 'buying out' a specific set of demarcations it would instead pay for efficiency changes on a continuous basis. One refinery manager described the progressive approach agreement in this way:

> There was no commitment that *A*, *B* or *C* had got to happen. The commitment was to sit down and examine work practices on an ongoing basis and the changes that could be agreed would be eliminated ... change would be based on the climate that surrounds us.

The most productive and efficient way of working was seen to be where '... an individual worked to his full potential commensurate with three vital factors (1) time available to complete the task (T), (2) the ability (A) to perform it, and (3) the necessity for the highest safety (S) standards to be observed'. Central to the change process was to be a steering committee, composed of managers and shop stewards, who would discuss and recommend workplace changes on an ongoing basis (within the 'Time, Ability and Safety' or T.A.S. parameters).

The main features of the 1972 progressive approach agreement are summarized below:
— a statement of principles
— a simple statement of intent to improve efficiency, to be followed up by

minutes and communications explaining the philosophy behind the document
— management commitment to improve wages and benefits in an ongoing manner
— individual safeguards against forced redundancy, group safeguards regarding the future of the maintenance work-force in the refinery, union safeguards relating to the existing trade union structure
— agreement that this agreement would not supersede other agreements
— establishment of a joint steering committee
— three-month termination clause to be exercised by both parties.

The progressive approach agreement was also seen by Fawley management to lead to a new payment systems philosophy which had its own trade union implications. In the long run Fawley management was hoping to move to a 'staff status' environment where there was to '... be an assurance of salary progression, and motivation to do the job was governed by the ability and desire of the individual'. As one Fawley manager put it:

> With the progressive approach we were laying the foundations for quite a new system of industrial relations at Fawley. A worker's pay would not be collectively determined but rather would be determined by individual effort. Merit would be the final determinant of pay, just like all other staff workers. (Interview with Fawley manager)

Fawley management was particularly keen not to have the progressive approach agreement meet the same fate as past agreements and identified a need for extra close follow-up, a full-time implementation team and a regular management progress review with senior management monitoring the results, in order to ensure the successful implementation of the agreement. What, then, were the results of the movement to this new form of productivity bargaining for Fawley Refinery? According to both Fawley management and unions, the progressive approach failed miserably. Senior management complained that the attitude of the work-force had not been the least bit amenable to change and that workers' attitudes had regressed to those typical of the 1960s.

Fawley management had initially assumed a decidedly defensive position in accounting for the fate of the agreement and argued that the progressive approach had been rendered ineffective by the government's incomes policy. This was the message picked up by the popular press: 'That first effort (the progressive approach) was effectively aborted by the Conservative government's pay controls ...' (E. Jacobs, 'The great productivity myth', *The Sunday Times*, 20 July 1975).

The official management position at the time, therefore, was that the progressive approach had been thwarted by external legislation, an influence outside the control of Fawley management. While government policy may indeed have restricted Fawley management's ability to realize its productivity objectives, the blame for this limited success cannot be laid solely at the door of incomes policy restrictions. In fact, the demise of the agreement begins far in advance of the second phase of the Heath administration incomes policy. As early as November 1972, for instance, Fawley management documents indicated that the implementation of the progressive approach was suffering from a loss of impetus and that a concerted effort by management and unions was required to find a way forward.

The progressive approach agreement itself got off to a bad start when the electricians' union (E.T.U.) refused at the outset to allow electrical permits to be processed by other trade groups (one of the flexibility provisions). This refusal by the E.T.U. was considered by management to have set an example of resistance to the rest of the workers in the yard. Other trade groups began to resist flexible working on the basis that no one union wanted to 'progress' at its own expense. Other craft groups, notably the boilermakers, made more direct challenges to the agreement. The boilermakers' union, on the basis of a protest about dwindling numbers within their trade group, withdrew cooperation over the agreement on 10 July 1972 (while continuing to be paid for participation in the deal). The deal was plagued, furthermore, by a rift which had developed between the craft and non-craft maintenance groups over claims by the non-craft groups for craft status (in line with the national trend at the time).

Post hoc rationales and reasons abound for the failure of the agreement. One manager noted that due to the long time it took to design and negotiate the agreement, many managers began to see the mere signing of the agreement as an accomplishment in itself.

Two different managers suggested that the timing of the agreement was altogether wrong. One suggested that

> ... basically we got the decade wrong with that one. The progressive agreement was like trying to develop an intimate relationship with a ghost. The employees received a large sum of money for agreeing to some future ongoing change that they had no intention of giving. (Interview with Fawley manager)

Yet another noted that

> ... The progressive approach simply took too great a leap. It built up barriers ... The ideas were right but the set of

134

> attitudes and culture of the time would not permit the agreement to work in any meaningful way. It was a pie-in-the-sky agreement, which didn't have a hope in hell of survival. We swung from a totally detailed and specific agreement, which had little success, to a totally open-ended agreement which had equally little success. (Interview with Fawley manager)

It is interesting to note that, despite management's stated intention to pay greater attention to the implementation phase of the agreement, the agreement nevertheless floundered. One of the main reasons for the small amount of progression within the progressive approach was identified by Fawley management as the stop–go attitude of management and the failure to keep the steering committee moving forward.

There appears to have been little adaptive learning on the part of Fawley management. One manager noted that

> ... our communication plan failed in the yard. To generate dialogue in the yard we needed a forum and subject-matter and we had none of these ... we were able to use one trade group against another to get the agreement in the first place, but the fact that the different unions had different aims and goals inhibited the implementation of the agreement. (Interview with Fawley manager)

It is, of course, one thing to put a 'statement of intent' deal between hard covers – and yet another to convert these stated intentions into reality. The packaging and assembling of the agreement could be described as high-profile, rewarding and as having a definable objective; however, the implementation and day-to-day maintenance of the agreement was often considered to be tedious and laborious, without any definable end point.

It would also appear to have been the case that there were internal management organizational problems associated with the implementation of the progressive approach. In particular, Fawley management identified problems associated with continuing changes in the representation of management over the different phases of a productivity agreement. This was a problem identified by many a Fawley manager and was seen to be one of the main lessons learned by the progressive approach experience. A desire was expressed for continuity of representation in order that a real commitment to change could be developed.

The problems associated with realizing progressive approach objectives did not, however, revolve strictly around management organization. Trade union groups became increasingly suspicious about the motivations behind the agreement. First, the agreement came to be seen as a means of easing trade union organization off the site. There was also a fear amongst

135

craft unions that all that was wanted (by management) was a refinery worker; an individual who was a 'jack-of-all-trades' who would have neither one trade nor a personal identity. Both the notion of 'personal assessment in a staff culture' and 'refinery worker' came increasingly to be interpreted by Fawley workers as a means of breaking trade union organization. The non-craft maintenance workers became especially suspicious of the agreement and claimed, for instance:

> The whole concept of the company's progressive approach is motivation by manipulation of participation (*sic*) ... To treat people like people not because they are people but because it pays. (Fawley, T.G.W.U. newsletter, 'Watchword', undated)

Union feelings on the site hardly appear to have been conducive to a type of productivity bargaining that was based on high trust. The Fawley Waterside Labour and Trade Union Liaison Committee came down with a particularly scathing indictment of the progressive approach as follows:

> Productivity, the word used by 'Big Business', is seen by workers as a dirty word. Hence Esso's switch to 'Efficiency' and the 'Progressive Approach'. All these names have the same meaning MORE PROFIT, HIGHER PRODUCTION and LESS JOBS for ourselves and our children. All this should be resisted by trade unionists. Shop floor workers have turned against productivity deals, unfortunately only to find local officials having said NO MORE PRODUCTIVITY DEALS would be contemplated, come the next round of talks it is back on the agenda again. PRODUCTIVITY has led, in Esso, to dramatic reductions in the labour force. Back in 1962 two years after the infamous BLUE BOOK agreement the hourly paid workforce was 2,301 TODAY there are 1,532 a reduction of a third, of which 433 were in the maintenance force. Plus a reduction of 50 apprentices, 70 employed now, as opposed to 120 in 1962. (Waterside Labour and Trade Union Liaison Committee, undated document, identified by steward as 'early 1970s')

Fawley management was not, however, to be disheartened by the failure of the progressive approach. Indeed management saw it as a valuable stepping stone to a further deal. The maintenance deal was struck in 1975 and is evaluated in the next section.

The 1975 maintenance deal: 'individuals working within related groups'

In the mid-1970s, the oil refining business was hit by the O.P.E.C. price rise and problems of rapidly falling demand. The result was the creation of surplus crude supplies and spare operating refining capacity. Needing to respond to reduced market demand, U.K. refineries pursued a variety of strategies, including the extension of 'shut downs' (for maintenance work) and the actual closure of refining installations. The Esso Milford Haven Refinery was itself running only at half capacity because of reduced demand. As an older refinery, Fawley faced the added pressure of competing with more modern and technologically sophisticated refineries. It was under such pressures that Fawley management turned once again to the productivity bargaining process in 1975.

In management's attempt to publicize and win some celebrity status for their new 1975 agreement, interviews were given to John Ellis of *The Financial Times* and to Eric Jacobs, the labour editor of *The Sunday Times*, wherein management described the problems of past agreements as well as the hope for the new 1975 maintenance deal. Unfortunately for Fawley, however, it seems that both Ellis and Jacobs chose to concentrate more on the problems of previous productivity deals than upon the hope for the future. Focussing on Fawley's self-critique, Ellis reported:

> On the debit side, however, the refinery found that the deals progressively became counter-productive as workers developed a special sensitivity over demarcation issues and managers had to spend an increasingly unproductive amount of time on the deals as each newly bought piece of flexibility brought its own crop of restrictions. (*The Financial Times*, 'Pressure for a new type of productivity deal', 14 May 1976)

In an article entitled 'The great productivity myth' (*The Sunday Times*, 20 July 1975), Jacobs summarized the recent state of productivity bargaining on a somewhat depressing note:

> The lesson of Fawley is that inefficiency is so deeply embedded in our industrial life style that it cannot be removed at a stroke by a single productivity deal. It takes years of negotiation of step-by-step change, coupled with persistent management exploitation of each advance that is made, to bring any useful results. (*The Sunday Times*, 'The great productivity myth', 20 July 1975)

Jacobs' article does report, however, on Fawley management's hope for the future. The article quotes the then refinery manager as follows: '(the refinery is) . . . on course for the 15–20 per cent improvement in its use of labour which should at last bring Fawley near to the top of the Exxon league.' Fawley's hope lay in two productivity deals, one for maintenance and one for process workers. The maintenance deal struck in March 1975 was subtitled 'Individuals working within related groups'. This agreement was, in spite of progressive approach problems, fundamentally based on the same philosophy as this 1972 agreement. 'The emphasis now was to be on general rather than precise aims' (E. Jacobs, *The Sunday Times*, 20 July 1975).

The agreement involved what is now an increasingly common approach to maintenance teams, the concept of 'individuals working within related groups'. The deal was set out in two phases. In the first phase, craftsmen were brought together in one of eight designated groups within which each individual could utilize both 'common' shared and 'individual' skills. Individuals would retain and continue to perform their core tasks but would in addition be expected to perform subsidiary or related tasks. Phase II of the agreement sought to extend this principle and was based on amalgamating the newly established groups into even larger bodies where the same flexibility principles relating to the use of common and particular skills would continue to apply. The agreement sought, therefore, to increase mobility and flexibility by bringing together and attempting to pool individual and shared skills using the group approach.

Importantly, the 1975 maintenance agreement was also significant in that it included provisions for both the extension of the utilization of contractor labour and for the movement of the warehouse personnel into a 'staff status' employment contract (a contract which meant the relinquishing of collective bargaining rights). In line with this philosophy, the warehousemen were transferred to 'staff status' contracts under this agreement. The 1975 agreement put it in these terms: 'In order to support the needs of a modern progressive warehouse organization, and to allow personal progression of the individual, this total group will be transferred to full monthly staff' (1975 maintenance agreement). The relevance of this staff status initiative is explored further in chapter 10.

Furthermore, the use of contractor labour was to be extended so that

> ... the use of contractors will no longer be restricted in order
> to generate overtime working for the owned (Fawley) forces ...
> It will be necessary to employ contractors for particular types
> of maintenance work. These fall into the following categories:
> low-skill work, non-refinery type maintenance work, declared
> events, peak lopping, specialist work. (1975 maintenance
> agreement)

Finally, the 1975 deal also sought to attack the old Blue Book 'bogeyman' of high overtime levels. The deal sought to bring overtime levels down, to obtain greater equalization in overtime payments between individuals, groups and trade unions and to wrest control and regulation of overtime working from the union.

The provisions of the 1975 Maintenance Deal included the following,

PHASE I:
— formation of related groups (total of eight groups)
— reduction/elimination of demarcation for all groups
— movement of warehousemen to 'staff status'
— reduction of permanent shift force
— introduction of 'assessment scheme' for T.G.W.U. maintenance workers (to facilitate reduction of the craft/non-craft differential)
— overtime reduction

PHASE II:
— formation of larger related groups (total of five groups)
— extension of contract labour usage
— make driving a common skill for all groups

How successful was Fawley management in actually realizing these objectives on the shop floor? It must be said that, overall, the agreement appears to have had limited success. First, phase II of the agreement was never implemented. Fawley's maintenance unions refused outright to partake in the second phase of the deal until such time as the agreed second pay increment could be paid out (this increment was not allowed to be paid out under the incomes policy in effect at the time). The message delivered by Fawley maintenance workers was clear, there was a price to be placed on cooperation and with no money there would be no cooperation.

It may not have been simply incomes policy, however, that prevented the implementation of phase II. The decision to put phase II 'on ice' appears to have been a long-standing desire (on the part of the mainten-ance unions). Once the maintenance unions were able to achieve the initial nine per cent increase in wages within the first phase they apparently lost interest in picking up the remaining six per cent in the second phase (the phase in which the unions believed they would be 'giving up the most').

Apart from the total abandonment of phase II, phase I of the agreement itself does not appear to have achieved much success. In summing up the overall effect of the 1975 agreement, one manager claimed that it had resulted in a very traditional and regressive view being progressed on all fronts. Another manager noted that 'there was a feeling that management was sinking into a progressive approach state; with prolonged discussion sessions where there was no real desire to make real progress'. Yet another manager noted that there was increasing resistance at all levels to any change (including overtime, welding, driving, phase I implementation, phase II introduction). Referring to the 1975 agreement, the Industrial

Relations Review and Report noted that '. . . as they (Fawley) progressed through their various stages (of the agreement) and the technology of the plant changed, the imperfections and limitations became clearer to both sides' (I.R.R.R., No. 282, 1982: 11).

Union documentation also reflects the idea of failure when referring to the 1975 agreement. The T.G.W.U. noted for instance:

> Conflict has arisen between groups as the interpretation of the deal develops a management bias or alternatively develops a union group bias. Outstanding claims for craft status, the feeling of jack of all trades master of none, loss of identity, and now in addition, the present pay legislation, are some complex and interrelated areas dominating the scene. (T.G.W.U. Branch 2/22, communication on 'Appraisal of problems, attitudes, principles', arising out of the 1975 efficiency deal)

On an item-to-item basis such negative assessments appear to have been valid. It could be said that Fawley management's success with the agreement was restricted to three specific areas: first, the warehousemen group were successfully transferred to 'staff status'; secondly, there was some manpower redeployment; and finally, there was a reduction in the permanent maintenance shift numbers (from 60 to 33). The flexibility, overtime and contractor provisions all appear to have gone by the board.

Unions and workers were able to defuse the flexibility provisions by engaging in long and time-consuming debates about the definition or meaning of words. As one steward put it, 'with each of the agreements we struck there were always a few key words which we could argue about. "Augment" was one of these words. In the 1975 deal we argued over the words "particular" and "common" ' (interview with senior shop steward).

Unions and workers also frequently made reference to safety issues as they related to flexible working. Workers could always claim that they were not properly trained to perform a particular job and that without proper training the job could not be performed in a safe manner. The T.G.W.U. maintenance workers themselves evoked these arguments in many instances. One T.G.W.U. steward claimed to management, for example:

> . . . the Hymax equipment had particular operating difficulties, particularly with steering and hydraulics that meant that people had to be very carefully trained and experienced in the use of this equipment. There have been three recent accidents in the use of this equipment and we don't want to see any more.

140

As a result, the T.G.W.U. steward was able to restrict the operation of the Hymax equipment to riggers, by appealing to safety considerations.

By October 1975, Fawley management was willing to admit that they still had not been able to achieve flexibility between craft and T.G.W.U. maintenance workers. One of the non-craft maintenance stewards explained the dynamics of the erosion of the flexibility provisions within his own group in this way:

> We would give up some of our jobs to the crafts ... for example we give them the right to operate the 'A' frame. The crafts were supposed to give us some jobs back in return. We soon found, however, that most of the jobs the crafts were giving us were 'dead' jobs (i.e. they were no longer done on site). Once we found out this we started to claw back our own jobs. We started to use the words in the agreement. They gave us protection. Sometimes we failed to train the crafts on our equipment – because we were 'too busy'. Other times we would monopolize equipment. We just wouldn't give it up – it was as deliberate as that. Supervisors in the end left us alone to do our jobs ... regardless of the deal. There was always a big difference between the print and the practice. (Interview with senior shop steward)

Moreover, at around this time, front line supervision increasingly began to complain about a '... lack of understanding of industrial-relations policy' and about '... the weight of past and current agreements'. In a training programme set up for front line supervisors, designed to help them implement the 1975 agreement, they were given information sheets covering some 100 flexibility provisions struck in past agreements in addition to the flexibility provisions of the 1975 deal. With this 1975 agreement, supervisors began to complain about the complexity and unwieldy nature of cumulative deals. After a series of 'briefing sessions' with first and second line supervisors in October of 1976, Fawley management was forced to come to the depressing conclusion that front line supervision was unaware of industrial-relations objectives (and that there was) 'no feeling of involvement'. One senior steward offered the following observation about front line supervision's understanding of the provisions of the various productivity deals:

> With little exception the stewards were more knowledgeable of the agreements than supervisors. Supervisors would often call us up to get an interpretation of a deal. Some of them were simply embarrassed to go to their own superiors to get an interpretation. (Interview with senior shop steward)

Few inroads were made with respect to Fawley management's objective of liberalizing contractor usage. Certain activities such as 'declared events' and 'peak lopping' always involved 'lengthy discussion' about contractor usage.

The attempt to rationalize the method of overtime allocation and administration was considered by Fawley management to be 'unsuccessful', partly because of management's decision not to progress overtime discussion at the time, but rather to concentrate on the flexibility initiatives. While actual maintenance overtime levels were reduced in 1975 to 3.7 per cent (from 16 per cent in 1974) and once again in 1976 (to 2.3 per cent), creep back in overtime levels occurred in 1977 (to 15.1 per cent) and in 1978 (8.1 per cent).

Fawley management's faith in the open-ended agreements looked as though it was beginning to wane. By the mid-1970s some managers even expressed the desire to see some harder nosed productivity dealing. The 1975 maintenance deal was matched with a parallel deal with the process operator group, and it is this deal that is addressed in the next section.

The process efficiency deal: 1975

Fawley management was to have greater difficulty in persuading the process group to enter into a productivity deal than it did in persuading the maintenance group. The process operators were, at the time, according to Fawley management, very suspicious of management motives and saw no need for further efficiency dealing other than the clause in the 1968 deal which assured them of retrospective payments for equipment and procedural changes which they had implemented in the previous year.

It was not until 1975 that the process operators were actually to conclude their next productivity deal. The deteriorating economic climate and the relaxation of pay legislation can be seen to have provided the environmental stimulus for the striking of this deal. While the earlier 1968 process agreement had provided a mechanism whereby major and minor changes to equipment would be recorded at a local level and reviewed on an annual basis, the 1975 process efficiency agreement took this principle somewhat further with the provision that the process work-force would accept not only changes of equipment but also changes of procedures and working practices, on an ongoing basis. The provisions included in this agreement are summarized as follows:
— ongoing reward for agreement on changes to equipment and work procedures and practices
— reduction of overtime to less than five per cent wherever possible
— availability of operator to carry out additional duties and render

142

assistance to other areas to be determined by chief operator and local supervision
— introduction of 5-grade operating structure
— reduction of operating establishment by 15 men

It can be seen that the main objectives of the agreements were, for the most part, recycled from past agreements. The productivity initiatives in the process area were, however, becoming increasingly linked to the introduction of new technology and associated working practices, as well as to the reduction of manning levels (resulting from the introduction of the new technology in the first place). In a letter to management, the process workers made the following forceful point:

> The company is not interested in real efficiency . . . but only in reducing the number of heads. The real 328 Branch problems as seen by the operators have been completely ignored by the Companies . . . While this situation is deeply regretted the 328 Branch inform the companies that the unpaid flexibility and cooperation freely given in the past in the interests of an efficient refinery will be indefinitely suspended. (T.G.W.U. Branch 328, letter to Fawley management, July 1975)

While, in late 1975, Fawley management was to claim that it had made some progress with the deal, by 1977 Fawley management was willing to admit that no significant progress had been made in 1976. Once again, the overtime problem was not able to be tamed. Overtime levels in the process area, for example, never dipped below 10 per cent for the period from 1968 to 1980. The 1975 process deal never came close to attaining its target of having less than 5 per cent overtime. While the percentage of overtime did drop from 15.9 per cent in 1974 to 11.7 per cent in 1975 and, in 1976, to 10.5 per cent, overtime levels did, however, increase once again as we move into 1977. In the period from 1977 to 1979, process overtime averaged above 14.5 per cent. Therefore, the 1975 process deal saw much the same kind of creep back as did the original Blue Book deal. On the overtime front, the status quo has reigned supreme.

It is also interesting to take a look at process worker manning levels for the period from 1968 to 1980. Despite negotiated reductions in manning levels in 1968 and 1975 manpower levels managed to increase from 510 in 1968 to 524 in 1980. What is particularly interesting about this pattern is that manning levels dropped after the 1968 and 1975 productivity agreements but in each case subsequently rose again.

The 'target approach' agreement: March 1978 (subtitled 'maintenance effectiveness measurement')

Fawley management's *affaire de coeur* with productivity bargaining was sparked again in the period around 1977–8 with the striking of an incomes policy linked productivity deal known as the 'target approach'. This agreement was heralded at Fawley Refinery as a new approach to linking productivity achievement with reward. Like many agreements before, however, it was to gain little ground and, in the end, was considered to have been more powerful in theory than in practice.

In August 1977, on the inception of phase III of the Labour government's incomes policy, Fawley management declared its commitment to move towards a 'self-financing' productivity agreement for its maintenance workers and, after some eight months of discussion and negotiations, this was concluded and labelled the 'target approach'. The 'self-financing' productivity agreement, struck in March 1978, was to be in effect until 31 March 1979.

The target approach was introduced in recognition that traditional productivity bargaining had not achieved expectations and that the value of old agreements was limited. Like many of the productivity deals struck under the influence of the 1977 incomes policy, the target approach agreement bore a greater resemblance to a group based bonus system than to a traditional productivity bargain, albeit prepared under the guise of, and within the language of, productivity bargaining. What is interesting is the extent to which Fawley managers themselves interpreted the target approach within the overall language and logic of productivity bargaining. The productivity bargaining technique remained sacred; it was still the reference point for all major industrial-relations initiatives.

The target approach represented an attempt to link productivity improvements to a payment system of ongoing reward. According to the agreement, Fawley management would monitor productivity improvements and these in turn would be converted, through an agreed formula, into a productivity based pay supplement. The reward accruing to individual maintenance employees could go up to a maximum of 10 per cent of the basic rate and was to be paid out in arrears on a quarterly basis.

What was supposed to be 'basically a simple system' turned out, however, to be a confusing one, where both management and the unions had a poor understanding of how the scheme worked. The formulae used in the calculation of the pay awards and the associated set of performance indicators ended up being far too complex, often obscuring rather than clarifying the link between effort and pay. As one manager put it, '... even our own management team had difficulty in effectively communicating the nuts and bolts of the target approach to our workers' (interview with Fawley manager). The text of the agreement itself even stated:

> The necessary consultation to jointly understand targets will require a minimum of one month from acceptance of this procedure . . . considerable development and understanding of the new system will be necessary for the full effects to be achieved. (Target approach: 1977)

The complexity of both the formulae and the associated performance indices may have led the workers to suspect that the productivity results could be fudged or fiddled, according to the whim of management.

Apart from the difficulty of measurement, there were various other problems that Fawley management confronted with the target approach agreement. It soon became clear that it was difficult to isolate the productivity of maintenance workers from the contribution that other refinery workers made to the efficiency of the maintenance group. Process workers, for example, could impede maintenance work by slowing down or holding up work permits that were required to carry out process related maintenance work. According to one shop steward, the holding up of these work permits, which were issued by senior process operators, was a fairly frequent occurrence. Within the maintenance area itself, it also became clear that certain work groups were in a better position to affect the performance indicators than others, so that motivations for productivity improvement were not evenly distributed across different maintenance groups at the refinery. Finally, it would appear that there were certain difficulties associated with the recording of work done and time-keeping due to the highly fluid and often non-quantifiable nature of maintenance work.

It is interesting to note that many of the identified constraints on efficient working of overtime and rigid work demarcations persisted during the life of the agreement. For instance, overtime levels for craft maintenance workers continued to be high and were running at an average of 8.1 to 12 per cent for the period from 1978 to 1979. In 1980 working practices at Fawley were found to be rigid between maintenance and process and it was said that rigid inter-trade demarcation still existed.

In addition to the above problems, Fawley management had also begun to feel that the philosophy underlying the target approach might be in conflict with the company's longer-term strategy of introducing 'individual' merit based pay, within the context of a 'staff status' employment contract. One personnel manager expressed his concern in this way:

> The target approach ran counter to all of our other agreements and objectives. We forgot our past emphasis on attitude

change and the need to reward individuals and not groups. We also forgot we are a cost centre and not a profit centre. (Interview with Fawley manager)

It was under the weight of these technical and philosophical problems that the target approach expired in March 1979.

Conclusions

This chapter has evaluated the third generation of productivity deals struck at Fawley. For the most part these can be described as 'open-ended' agreements. Much like the Blue Book with its detailed productivity clauses, and the similar type of productivity bargaining carried out in the second generation, the less structured agreements of the third generation also failed quite dramatically to attain their stated objectives. Management appears to have turned to this 'open' type of agreement to avoid the many problems associated with the earlier detailed comprehensive agreements. As McKersie and Hunter have noted, with detailed comprehensive agreements, there is

> ... the danger that strong resistance will develop to any proposals for change not embodied in the agreement and that newly arising needs for adaptation on the part of the workforce will be delayed until they can be incorporated into the agreement. In other words, where the specific *quid pro quo* approach is adopted, each possible innovation in practice or working arrangements may acquire a price which has to be paid before progress in its installation can be made. (1973: 136)

The Fawley open-ended agreements did not, however, solve Fawley's productivity problems. In the end, these agreements existed more as rhetoric than as real substance and they never really improved operating performance at the nuts-and-bolts level at all. Worker attitudes do not appear to have changed for the better; in fact they may even have become worse. Quite typically, what happened with each of the agreements described above was an initial surge of enthusiasm and excitement (restricted often to the design and negotiating group), followed, as time passed, by a loss of interest on the part of management, unions and workers alike.

By the end of this third period, Fawley Refinery was still to be found at the bottom of the so-called productivity 'league' tables. Moreover, according to management, in 1975 the maintenance work-force was working at a level of efficiency performance of less than sixty per cent of the best continental and U.S. experience.

The open-ended productivity agreements

Although the above open-ended agreements were each heralded as representing a fundamental change in philosophy (in that detailed changes to working practices were not written down in the formal manner of the previous two generations of productivity bargaining), they still did little to improve labour productivity.

9

Productivity bargaining in the 1980s: coping with the recession

Introduction

The early and mid-1980s proved to be a particularly difficult period for the oil refining business. The industry was characterized by both significant surplus crude supplies and spare operating capacity. After some considerable soul searching, Esso U.K. Ltd. felt forced to shut down its Milford Haven Refinery in March 1983, leaving Fawley as its only remaining refinery in Great Britain. In contrast to Fawley Refinery, Esso's Milford Haven Refinery was caught with much more limited 'up-grading' facilities and was not as capable as Fawley in responding adequately to the swing in the product market towards the so-called 'light end of the barrel' (even though Fawley was the older of the two refineries). It is within this difficult business environment that the most recent phase of productivity bargaining must be considered.

The Industrial Relations Review and Report notes the following about the use of productivity bargaining by various oil companies in attempting to overcome the difficult business environment confronting the British oil refining industry in the 1980s:

> In the manpower field the result has been a spate of productivity deals to improve working practices and cut manning levels in refineries. Mobil for example has reached a deal with maintenance workers at its Coryton, Essex, refinery, allowing for greater craft flexibility and interchangeability together with an agreement on manning changes with its process workforce (P.A.B.B. 69). Elsewhere, BP has been trying to win the agreement of process workers to demanning and efficiency measures at its Grangemouth site. (I.R.R.R. No. 282, 1982: 11)

During this period, productivity bargaining became principally a means (especially within the process area) by which to reduce manning levels. It provided Fawley management with a pseudo-scientific language that

148

could be used to justify or rationalize large-scale reductions in manning levels. Couched within neutral 'productivity' terms, it was management's hope that such manpower reductions could be made more palatable to the work-force.

On the process side, Fawley management introduced a 'hard-hitting' agreement in 1981 aimed at the shedding of labour, while on the maintenance side, Fawley management was to usher in a further open-ended agreement in 1982. Heralded as another revolution in productivity bargaining at Fawley, this agreement was, however, to be almost identical to the 1972 progressive approach deal.

The process productivity agreement: October 1981

As Fawley Refinery moved into the 1980s it was confronted with a dramatic down-turn in the demand for refined oil products, especially in what is known as the 'bread-and-butter' heavy fuel oil area. It was at this time that Fawley management was to conclude its first major productivity deal with the process workers since 1975, a deal referred to simply as 'the 1981 process productivity agreement'.

The 1981 process productivity agreement itself was preceded by an extensive management communications programme, involving both talks by the refinery manager to all groups of employees at Fawley as well as an elaborate written communication entitled 'Why change at Fawley?' (running to some 16 pages). This communication programme served to develop Fawley management's rationale for needing further productivity improvements and in particular for large-scale manning reductions. The message of the communication was clear. If Fawley could not demonstrate that real and substantial progress was being made towards a more highly efficient, better manned refinery, then there was risk that there would be a diversion of funds and projects to already more efficient refineries in Europe.

According to Fawley management, the 1981 process productivity agreement was a 'tough' agreement but was required because Fawley was among the worst performers in the European Exxon circuit. The reality was that in comparison with other European refineries with similar plants Fawley's manning levels were considered unacceptably high. The 1981 process agreement comprised four main objectives as follows:
(1) To reduce significantly the number of process operators working at Fawley over a two- to three-year period. The general plan was to cut about twenty per cent of the process work-force over the period to 1983. The agreement specified, however, that it was '... not the ... intention to have any compulsory redundancies at Fawley Refinery'

(although Fawley's commitment to this was qualified by a *force majeure* clause covering unforeseen circumstances).

(2) To shorten the training period (for movement to the full operator grade) to eighteen months.

(3) To introduce a new, single, fully rotating shift system, known as the five-man shift system. This new shift system would be based on a 39-hour week and compensatory rest time in the shift pattern. The new shift pattern was introduced partly to help reduce overtime levels to a maximum of five per cent.

(4) To achieve a flexibility agreement which specified that the process work-force would be willing to accept ongoing change in working practices and equipment, increased job mobility and additional work flexibilities (for example, acceptance and performance of maintenance work).

What, then, was the outcome of this so-called 'tough' deal? In an article entitled 'Oil industry – Fawley leads again?', the Industrial Relations Review and Report makes the following favourable assessment:

> apart from the normal teething problems associated with such major change projects the outturn looks good. Overtime work-ing has been reduced ... For the process workforce the esti-mate is a cut from fifteen per cent to seven per cent with further reduction envisaged as the plant consolidates the changeover of personnel into the new shift system ... In ad-dition, the necessary manpower cuts designed to reduce costs and improve competitiveness have been and, barring major disasters, will continue to be achieved in a controlled manner (Report No. 282, 1982: 15)

Such a favourable assessment does not, however, square with my own data. Of the process productivity agreement's four key objectives only the five-man shift system was implemented, and even this shift system did not have, as will be seen below, the expected ameliorating effect in bringing down overtime levels.

Before turning to this point, however, it is worth noting the rather obvious fact that this process agreement carries with it considerable repetition of items from previous productivity deals. The 'new' provision for the 'acceptance of ongoing change in equipment, procedures and work practices as the need arises ...' figured centrally in previous deals as did the 'new' provision relating to process workers '... doing maintenance work as part of the role of the process workforce subject to any necessary training being provided'. The resurfacing of these provisions, in almost identical language, can really only be interpreted as evidence of the failure of past agreements. What is even more interesting to note is that the rider 'subject to any necessary training' is also passed on from agreement to agreement – one of the riders that workers had already used in the past to circumvent flexibility provisions.

The 1981 process productivity agreement, which basically came to be known as a 'demanning activity', was Fawley management's most aggressive attack on manning levels within the process department. As one branch officer put it: 'The 1981 process deal wasn't so much a productivity deal in the true sense of the word, but it was really just an excuse to reduce our numbers.' It had gradually dawned on Fawley management that those productivity initiatives that relied on continuous planning and coordination had little chance of longer-term success. With the 1981 process productivity agreement, Fawley managment went for the direct shedding of labour. Even with these manpower reductions, however, Fawley management was less than completely successful. The process Transport and General Workers' Union branch, unable to block all 'demannings', turned instead to a strategy of slow resistance. All but a handful of the planned shift position reductions were bogged down in discussions, many of which required lengthy debate and negotiation in the 'Process Negotiating Committee'. Union sanctions were also frequently imposed on Fawley management to delay the demannings.

This bogging down of demannings is interesting in itself as it reveals some of the difficulties in achieving manpower reductions, even when such reductions have been agreed to by union officials. It is important to note, as well, that the pitched battles which surfaced over the demannings served to set up worker hostility to other productivity provisions and served therefore to devalue them. Moreover, workers became adept at using the demanning debates to gain improvements in other areas (for example, upgraded facilities).

Worker resistance to the demannings also casted doubt on Fawley management's ability to work out the implementation of a productivity deal in a 'joint' manner, that is, in partnership with the union. In the face of increasing opposition to the implementation of the agreement, Fawley management saw it necessary to impose change merely at the local level and to cast aside any pretence about 'jointly managed change'.

The difficulties encountered by management in attempting to achieve the agreed demannings only increased as time went on. In March 1982, management witnessed the strongest reaction yet to the agreement. The union branch officers suspended the agreement for eight days, bringing discussions about demannings and training programmes to a halt.

In May of 1982 the Transport and General Workers' Union suspended the agreement once again, this time as a sanction against management in pursuance of the union's claims in the annual wage negotiations. This tactic illustrates yet another means by which workers are able to 'renegotiate' the terms of a productivity deal should it come to be interpreted by workers as unfair. Productivity deals can, therefore, be used as a bargaining lever by workers themselves. Workers can and do threaten to withdraw cooperation and consent to past productivity deals unless their demands are met for the current round of negotiations. By formalizing the 'work' side of the wage–work bargain, management effectively provides a bargaining lever to workers. This highlights one of the dangers associated with formalization itself.

While Fawley workers were able to delay the manning reductions and renegotiate the original terms of the agreement, management was, in the end, able to push through (or in some cases impose) the majority of the shift position reductions. By January 1984 manning levels had been brought down by 79, a reduction of fourteen per cent from the 1981 level against a targeted reduction of twenty per cent.

Union and worker disenchantment with the proposed reductions of the 1981 process deal had, however, adverse effects on other aspects of the agreement. In response to the demannings, workers withdrew cooperation from other parts of the agreement. This was true for the flexibility items. Job flexibility was either withdrawn formally as a result of a lodged sanction, or informally, as a protest against the demannings. As one steward put it:

> Very few of the flexibility items were ever really implemented. If they were, they had a short life. We never did any spading, we never assisted in scaffolding and we didn't do much painting or flexing up. We made a big deal out of our few successes and these were a way of pumping up the agreement. (Interview with shop steward)

A supervisor put it this way: 'Because of the status reports we were under pressure to report good news in the flexibility area. Sure some flexibility got done, but it wasn't significant and it didn't last long' (interview with Fawley supervisor).

With respect to the aim of reducing overtime to a 'maximum of 5 per cent', a pattern similar to that for previous agreements is found, with an initial dip in overtime followed by a creep back to pre-agreement levels. While process department overtime levels were brought down from a 1981 average of 14 per cent to 6.75 per cent, they never reached the targeted figure of a maximum of 5 per cent. Furthermore, overtime levels had crept back to double figures as early as May of 1982 when overtime reached a level of 10.7 per cent.

Fawley management was able to implement successfully the 'training progression' provision, but only after lengthy negotiations and haggling. There existed a difference of interpretation as to the manner in which newly qualified trainees could be utilized before the completion of their 18-month training period. This had to be reconciled before the new training progression could be implemented.

Finally, it is important to note that the 1981 agreement appears to have had a significant and long-standing effect on the process department employees. By the end of 1983 Fawley management was willing to admit that process department morale had hit an all time low because of the demannings resulting from the 1981 agreement.

Following these observations and many others of the same view, Fawley management felt compelled to organize a major 'organization development' activity to help win back employee commitment and consent. A major change project entitled the 'Process planned change' was put in place in December 1983, with a view to improving process operator morale. The stated objective of this 'planned change' programme was to create opportunities for process workers to 'rejoin the company', to 'repair and develop some of the injured working relationships at the worker/supervisor interface'.

The 'planned change' activity consisted of a series of workshops in which process workers and supervisors were invited to discuss openly problems and to search for solutions for these problems. A number of problems were raised – many of which could be directly linked to the series of past productivity deals. Workers complained of 'tighter manning levels' and 'constant fears of redundancy'. They stated that there was a 'lack of contact from supervision and management' and a general feeling of 'isolation' on the units. They also suggested that process jobs were now 'dead end' jobs – 'with little or no real possibility for career progression'. Some workers harked back to the 'good old days' when a 'man had career prospects in the process department'. Young graduates were seen to have taken away the possibility for real promotion. In short, the planned change programme unveiled a growing problem of consent or commitment amongst Fawley workers.

The maintenance enabling agreement: March 1982

The value of an historical analysis of productivity bargaining at Fawley is that current practice can be interpreted in the light of past experience. In an historical analysis one has, in other words, the advantage of making sense of a productivity agreement in terms of past deals. The March 1982 maintenance enabling deal is one which has been heralded by both Fawley

153

management and by the popular trade journals as having '. . . ushered in an important new era of flexible working and the possibility of temporary shifts' (Industrial Relations Review and Report, No. 282, October 1982: 2). The agreement was reviewed by the I.R.R.R. under the flattering title 'Oil industry – Fawley leads again'. A quick reference back to the 1972 progressive approach agreement reveals, however, that the philosophy and key principles of the 1982 maintenance enabling deal are little more than a direct replica or copy of the 1972 deal. Couched under a new title, the 1982 deal was effectively being sold by a new generation of Fawley managers as a revolution in productivity bargaining.

Fawley management did, however, have considerable difficulty in gaining union agreement to the 1982 maintenance enabling agreement. Discussions between Fawley management and the unions about this 'new concept' dated back to early 1981. Both the design and the negotiation of the agreement were protracted, taking over nine months actually to negotiate the agreement. The price of increased worker cooperation remained hotly contested and open to question. The 1982 maintenance enabling agreement was finally concluded in March, however, and applied to both craft and non-craft maintenance workers at Fawley.

Like the 1972 progressive approach agreement before it, the 1982 maintenance enabling agreement was an ongoing or open-ended productivity deal. It sought to abandon the 'shopping list' approach to productivity bargaining (as employed in the Blue Book deal) as well as the problems associated with such an approach. For Fawley management the 1982 agreement was considered to be an 'enabling' agreement with an essential dynamic characteristic: 'The intent of the agreement is to enable both management and the work-force to make and accept changes now and into the future.' What apparently was being proposed was a 'significant culture change for Fawley'.

The 1982 maintenance agreement was deliberately entitled 'enabling' and sought to eliminate all workplace demarcations. No detailed changes were to be specified and the main emphasis was placed on the need to change attitudes. The basic aim of the agreement was to 'enable' the company to carry out maintenance work in the most efficient way, with no restrictions based on precedents or previous practices. The only qualifications to this were that the individual had to have the time and skill to do the work, and that the work had to be done safely. The underlying philosophy and main principles of the 1982 agreement were, for the most part then, identical to the 1972 progressive approach agreement. The specific objectives of the 1982 deal are summarized below:

— Full utilization of worker capabilities within 'time', 'ability' and 'safety' parameters. In deciding the allocation and method of work (that is who does what, how and when) the overriding need is to find the most efficient route, without restriction based on precedent or previous practices which may no longer be relevant. When, for instance, workload and efficiency considerations, advances in technology or changes in organization require new skills, new working practices or the assignment of individuals to different work areas in the refinery, the only limitations would be: the skill that people have or can acquire (with new training if necessary); the time available to perform tasks; and the requirements of safety.

— Planned reductions in the maintenance work-force (the actual amount to be cut was not specified in the deal but was laid out in the company manpower plan. Fawley management aimed to reduce the size of the total maintenance work-force from around 500 to between 450 and 470).

— Elimination of the need to consult with unions on a 'job-to-job' basis, about the use of contractors. Fawley management was now only to 'consult' with unions on a quarterly basis to provide an update and review of contractor usage. This provision was injected in order to allow management freer and more extensive use of contractor labour in 'peak lopping', 'specialist' work, non-refinery maintenance work and low-skill work.

— Overtime allocation and distribution responsibilities were to be taken away from the union and were to be unilaterally controlled by Fawley management.

— Abnormal conditions money, height money and call-in payments were no longer to be paid under any circumstances.

— Regular 'performance appraisal' discussions were to be held with workers.

The agreement also contained the following safeguards:

— No compulsory redundancy as a direct result of the agreement (the agreement reaffirms Fawley's commitment to this position on the personal security of employment for each individual, namely that no redundancies would occur as a direct consequence of the agreement).

— Management commitment to explain to unions, on a quarterly basis, manpower plans and policies and contractor usage.

— Management commitment that individuals or groups of individuals would not work unnecessarily high levels of overtime.

What is particularly interesting about the 1982 agreement is the extent to which the authors so blatantly sold this agreement as something new, innovative and novel. No reference was made by the authors of the agreement to the content and substance of the earlier 1972 agreement. It was as though the 1972 agreement had never existed.

When, however, shop stewards were asked about the similarities between the 1972 and the 1982 agreements, one shop steward claimed that the fact that the agreements were similar in the first place reflected not only the failure of the agreement that had been struck ten years earlier, but also the failure of other past agreements:

> The 1982 maintenance enabling is proof of the failure of all of our past deals. If the changes that management wanted to achieve in past agreements were really achieved, then why are they paying us now again to achieve the same things that were asked for in the past. (Interview with steward)

How successful was Fawley management in implementing the specific provisions of the 1982 maintenance deal? Perhaps predictably, management was to report the following favourable evaluation to the Incomes Data Services:

> There has been a marked change in attitudes. Working within problem-solving teams with considerable autonomy, individual craftsmen have been relieved of concerns about demarcation. The younger and most able craftsmen have responded particularly well. Most of the craftsmen consider that their work has become more interesting and demanding since more of their capabilities are now used. There is a 'good spirit'.
>
> In terms of increased efficiency, the companies consider that improvements of around 20 per cent have been achieved.
>
> Overtime working has been cut from around eight or nine per cent to about two or three per cent. (Incomes Data Services Study 322, September 1984: 18–19)

This favourable management assessment does not, however, correspond with my own case study data.

In terms of the flexibility initiatives my case study research reveals less success than that reported in the Incomes Data Services study. As early as August of 1982 Fawley craft unions claimed that management was abusing the flexibility provisions and, as a result, Fawley management was forced to add a rider to the flexibility provisions which sought to ensure '... as far as possible that no unnecessary flexibility takes place'. Interviews with managers, senior stewards and stewards all confirmed that little real flexibility had been achieved. The craft stewards estimated that craft workers spent little time actually working outside of their own craft. None of the senior stewards were prepared to say that Fawley workers spent more than five per cent of their time working outside of their craft. This estimate did not exceed the five per cent supposed amount of inter-craft flexibility that Flanders found to exist at Fawley soon after the striking of the Blue Book (1964: 177). Interviews with front line supervisors corroborated this view, each of which suggested that cross-trade working was minimal and happened only in major 'turn-around' maintenance work. Moreover, senior stewards noted that there were a lot of problems with the agreement at the outset, when the flexibility initiatives were being pushed by Fawley management. As one steward put it:

> It's inefficient to work outside of your trade. Sometimes I'll punch a hole through a wall, when I could have called a carpenter in to do the job. If I punch too big a hole I'll waste my time closing it down or taking the wall down. (Interview with steward)

In this way, constraints relating to the ability to do a job may sometimes be more serious than imagined, especially when one includes tacit skill as part of the ability to do a job.

On the overtime objective management seems to have fallen into the same 'creep back' pattern as did past agreements. Overtime did in fact drop to two to three per cent through to 1984, but by 1986 the 'pressure for overtime has risen again despite the agreement requiring individuals to be available for temporary shift-working' (Incomes Data Services Study 360, April 1986: 7). The decline in overtime levels after the 1982 maintenance agreement appears, therefore, to have been part of the 'decrease and increase' pattern that has been witnessed in past deals.

The drop in overtime levels from 1982 through to the end of 1985 needs, however, to be questioned. The decline in overtime levels in this period cannot simply be interpreted as a result of the more effective working practices of company workers. Rather, what we have witnessed in this period is the simple substitution of overtime with 'cut-price' forms of overtime, in the form of 'temporary shift working' and a higher priced form of overtime in the form of increased contractor labour usage (this point is developed further in the next chapter).

With regard to Fawley management's assertion (above) that efficiency had been 'increased by twenty per cent', it is unfortunate that the basis of such a calculation is not to be found. It would appear to have been, more than anything else, a simple management 'guess'. It is possible that, because manpower levels were reduced to about half of the targeted level that the efficiency estimate of twenty per cent may have been based upon these reductions.

Finally, unlike the temporary shift working provisions attempted in the Blue Book and in subsequent agreements, this time Fawley management was able to continue to use shift working arrangements under the 1982 agreement. Since the implementation of the agreement, however, Fawley management has been pressured into making a series of concessions in this area to its workers. These concessions included: (1) an agreement to provide meal chits for shifts longer than 10 hours (after saying that this would never be permitted); (2) agreement to ensure that, other than in the most exceptional circumstances, non-volunteers for temporary shift would not be asked to work non-standard shift patterns; (3) agreement to avoid, as far as possible, asking non-volunteers to work any temporary shifts; (4) agreement to be flexible towards volunteers if they have personal reasons for not being able to work any particular shift. Each of these concessions represent, once again, examples of how stewards can renegotiate the terms of an agreement even after it has been signed.

The single area in which I found that progress was being made was in the increased use of contractor labour, both for 'shut-down' work and for 'ongoing' maintenance. The more liberalized use of contractors has not, however, been problem-free. In spite of the fact that Fawley management no longer had to consult with the unions on a 'job-to-job' basis, many overtures were made to Fawley management, by stewards and workers alike, to keep contractor usage down. In spite of this pressure, however, contractor usage continued to grow. The implications of the growth in the contractor employment relationship is considered in the next chapter.

Addendum

In April 1984, Fawley management introduced a new 'personal incremental payments system' which provided a payment of 1.5 per cent a year for both process and maintenance workers in anticipation of 'continuing efficiency gains'. Under this system, the company pays Fawley workers 1.5 per cent a year until 1989, subject to continued satisfactory implementation of the 1981 process and 1982 maintenance deals. Up to 1985, these payments have been made as a result of mounting pressure from Fawley workers to 'revalue' the terms of the 1981 and 1982 productivity deals.

Conclusions

My review of productivity bargaining at Fawley, not only in this chapter but also in the previous three chapters, has demonstrated that, by and large, the process was not successful in enabling management to reach the objectives that were stated in the agreements. At the end of some 25 years of productivity bargaining the Fawley operations manager admitted that '... Fawley is still posted at the bottom of Exxon's league table for efficiency and productivity'. In 1960, there had only been one of the Exxon league table indices in which Fawley had stood favourably and that was in the area of wage levels, which at that time were low compared to the wage levels of other Exxon circuit refineries. By the mid-1980s, Fawley Refinery had even lost that one small competitive advantage, that is in the area of low pay.

It is perhaps appropriate to end my overview of twenty-five years of productivity bargaining by sharing some Fawley observations, made at different levels of the organization, about the impact of productivity bargaining at Fawley over the last 25 years.

SENIOR SHOP STEWARD:
What was agreed to was quickly clawed back. Very few practices were ever stuck to. We have been successful in clawing back about eighty per cent of all the deals.

FRONT LINE SUPERVISOR:
I can't really identify a single positive effect of any of the productivity deals. If I was forced to think about one, I'd say they gave me formal approval to do some things I was already doing in the yard anyway.

MANAGER:
Our productivity bargaining was an extended educational experience but it was largely a sterile experience. It has been a frustrating experience in which we didn't accomplish a lot. We may have held the line or kept our employees happy in a period of wage restraint but we haven't moved that far ahead. We've taken a few steps forward and maybe that's all you can ever expect.

10

Offshoots of productivity bargaining: the staff status initiative and the increased use of contractor labour

Collective bargaining in industry is the equivalent and counterpart of democracy in politics. Its extinction would be a denial of freedom of association and representative organization and would put an end to trade unions and employers' associations. No one is seriously suggesting that. (Flanders, 1975: 175)

Introduction

It has been seen above that, from the Blue Book onwards, productivity bargaining failed to reach most of the objectives stated in the agreement and that many of the productivity provisions kept appearing and reappearing in subsequent agreements. This chapter argues, however, that productivity bargaining at Fawley played an important role in helping management to facilitate two subsidiary industrial-relations 'strategies' – (1) the long-term withdrawal of collective bargaining and, ultimately, trade union organization from the site and (2) the increased use of contractor labour. Both of these subsidiary 'strategies' were intimately related to Fawley's dominant productivity bargaining based strategy and can, in fact, be seen as offshoots of this strategy.

The growth of the staff status initiative

Flanders had always been critical of the 'traditional' or 'authoritarian' style of management. He described such an approach as rejecting '. . . any division of or sharing of authority within the firm' (1975: 172). Flanders did not consider the 'authoritarian' approach to be viable and noted that 'cooperation in the workplace cannot be fostered by propaganda and exhortation, by preaching its benefits. Nor does it depend primarily, although this is an important factor, on improved communications . . .'

(1975: 172). According to Flanders, British management needed to move to a new style or strategy – one of 'joint regulation'.

For Fawley management, however, it would appear that productivity bargaining had very little to do with integrating the union into the management decision-making process. It is argued, in fact, that Flanders' well-known evaluation of productivity bargaining at Fawley was coloured or distorted by his own vision of what 'ought' to have been, by his own personal philosophy which was rooted in the notion of 'workplace democracy'. It could be said, as well, that Marxian scholars themselves were blinded by the rhetoric of 'reformism' and simply assumed that the rhetoric of the reformist movement had been taken seriously and was actually implemented by British management. Due principally to his own ideological blinkers, Flanders was unable to appreciate the extent to which Fawley management remained hostile to the idea of direct union participation.

Flanders suggested that 'Esso had no subtle intention to weaken the unions, nor was this the outcome of the changes introduced' (1964: 218–19). Contrary to Flanders' convictions about the role of productivity bargaining in democratizing workplace relations and extending the scope of the collective bargaining agenda, the opposite actually occurred. It is maintained here that productivity bargaining came to be used to minimize rather than to enhance the collective role of the union. If Flanders' vision for Fawley was the creation of a new spirit of 'joint control' then he could not have been further from the mark. It is argued, in fact, that an important hidden or covert dimension of productivity bargaining at Fawley related to Fawley management's longer-term 'de-unionization' strategy, a strategy to be embodied in its staff–status programme.

The staff status programme developed at Fawley was management-conceived and management-led. It represented a strategic choice about how management wished to manage industrial relations at the refinery. Staff status did not originate with the unions (as, for instance, in the toolworkers agreement at Chrysler in 1972), nor did it merely represent a process of 'harmonization' whereby, through the process of normal collective bargaining, staff-wage differentials would be gradually reduced. Rather, the plan to shift trade union employees to staff status represented a strategic choice on the part of management in terms of whether it would conduct its industrial relations with or without the institution of collective bargaining and ultimately with or without trade union organization.

At Fawley, the staff status initiative was directed principally, but not exclusively, at the craft maintenance trade union groups. The process workers, in general, organized through the Transport and General Workers' Union, were seen to be too large and unlikely to move to staff

161

status. However, any attempts at moving workers to staff status within the process department were directed at the most highly skilled group in this department, the 'chief operators'.

Fawley management did not imagine that the transfer of craft workers to staff terms would be easily realized, and for this reason management articulated the goal within a long-term horizon, planning to target group after group rather than attempting the wholesale movement of all maintenance union groups to staff terms in 'one fell swoop'. This step-by-step or group-by-group conversion was to take place in accordance with management's perception of the ease of the transfer and the group's strategic importance to the production process. This was a strategy of 'gradualism' whereby it was hoped that the conversion of one group would lead eventually to the wider application of staff conditions down the line. This gradual conversion process was to begin in the early 1970s.

Management first aimed at the warehousemen in the stores and equipment division. The warehousemen were seen to be an excellent first target group as they were both small and relatively self-contained, reducing the immediate problem of how to reconcile the side-by-side working of unionized with non-unionized men. Furthermore, the warehousemen only represented a small part of their union's membership (30 of 160) so that the loss of this group would not mean the complete withdrawal of the union from the site.

Management saw the warehouse group as a small, highly organized trade union group in a strategic position in the event of a dispute. Staff status, was seen, further, to reduce this strategic hold and to provide individual incentives which could increase commitment and cooperation. The warehouse group had also recently been through a considerable change in work organization as a result of the computerization of the stores department. This computerization had gone even further in concentrating strategically important jobs in the hands of a few. Finally, Fawley management felt confident that the warehouse group would be one of the more likely groups in the refinery to accept staff status terms. Successful application of staff status to this group could be viewed as a major stepping stone in refinery-wide application.

The Fawley management proposal to move this group to staff terms and to remove their collective bargaining rights came, however, to be contested by the Transport and General Workers' Union, the bargaining agent for the group, which saw the proposal as the '. . . thin edge of the wedge . . . designed to wrest away control from the unions'. The hostility against the plan by the Transport and General Workers' Union was expressed in an internal Transport and General Workers' Union memo directed to Fawley management. It stated that '. . . we are concerned about the continuing pressure being used on the warehouse personnel on the question of staff status . . . we have no intentions of discussing staff status, now or in the future' (September 1974). By the end of September 1974, Fawley management was able to reach a compromise solution with the Transport and General Workers' Union, whereby the warehousemen would give up collective bargaining rights but would still retain individual membership in the union. Individual membership was, however, relatively meaningless and was rendered even more meaningless in the future as new recruits into the warehouse were not compelled or pressed to join the union.

Thus, following the gradual approach, management was successful in transferring the warehouse group to staff status in 1974. With the move to staff status the warehousemen were given all staff related benefits as well as an annual guaranteed salary. Increased pay appeared to be the primary motivating factor for the warehousemen to accept staff status and give up their collective bargaining rights. Importantly, pay was to be linked to performance through the annual staff appraisal salary scheme. This change in the method of payment represented the sublimation of the 'collective' interest in favour of the interest of the 'individual'. Fawley management was seeking to gain greater control of the distribution of workers' pay, by making compensation a function of performance and loyalty.

With the successful transfer of the warehousemen to staff status, management sought to identify other strategic groups within the refinery. The craft group considered by Fawley management to be most strategically located within the production process was the instrument fitters group. It was the responsibility of this group to maintain the automated computer control equipment on the refinery site. The failure of this group to perform its job could quickly result in the refinery grinding to a halt. With ever increasing computer control, the servicing and maintenance of such equipment was becoming ever more critical.

Discussions regarding their transfer first arose out of the 1977 productivity discussions and, by 15 November 1978, management had put forward a proposal to the instrument fitters which outlined the terms and conditions of the transfer. These terms were also to apply to all subsequent groups transferred. Once management had detailed the terms and conditions of staff status and presented these to each member of the group, management withdrew from any further active solicitation and left it to the individual members to put pressure on the union hierarchy. It was therefore the workers themselves who, in the end, approached their full-time officials to request a move to staff terms (while those wishing to remain 'hourly paid' could do so). By placing the onus on the union members themselves to push for staff status, management was seeking to free itself from the possible allegation that it was leading a 'deunionization' campaign. British Petroleum Chemicals, also pursuing a staff status programme, had based their staff status programme on a similar set of tactics: '... the company (B.P.) claims that pressure for the deal (staff status) has come from the employees at the plant' (Bassett, *The Financial Times*, 6 December 1984).

Thus, management was able to gain the full-time officials' and the union membership's agreement to permit a transfer of the instrument fitters to staff status on 23 November 1979 (a total of 70 unionized workers were transferred to staff terms). The E.E.T.P.U. full-time official, faced with unanimity amongst his members to move to staff terms, did not actively oppose the change (although the union 'expressed continued concern about the loss of collective bargaining rights'). As part of the deal, management made a commitment to each staff transferee that no one would fall below the 'top' craft rate after any annual salary review.

The provision of the contract stated that, under staff status there were to be 'no recognized unions although individuals can and do belong to unions'. This meant 'no collective bargaining rights'. Greater use was to be made of line communications and group meetings within departments. Remuneration was to be based, further, on 'annual salary, merit payments, salary bands, and opportunity for salary group progression'. Finally, the disputes procedure, rather than being '... geared to collective representation and action with union involvement', would be '... set out and based on individual issues – (with) facility for accompaniment by friend or staff representative'. Consultative systems were to play a key role in the staff status environment. Fawley management felt that, as a result of the significant savings of management time which had been devoted to negotiations, they would now be able to concentrate on achieving 'excellent' communication and consultative systems (interview with Fawley manager).

With the movement of the instrument fitters to staff status, Fawley management sought to bring out into the open its desire to move other groups to staff status. The third group to change to staff status terms, the boilermakers' group, came three years later, in 1982. The transfer of the boilermakers is interesting in itself, as this group had traditionally been regarded as the most militant and recalcitrant group on the site. Flanders himself described the boilermakers as a

> ... closely-knit body of men who look on their union almost as
> an impregnable fortress ... The union, proud of its past and
> conscious of its strength, tends, as the ship-building industry –

its main province – bears witness, to be militantly conservative in its outlook. (Flanders, 1964: 116)

Flanders even pointed out that, given this kind of tradition, it was not surprising that the boilermakers were suspicious of the Blue Book: 'That the B.M.S. (Boilermakers' Society) at Fawley – members and stewards alike – should have had their doubts about the Blue Book is not remarkable' (Flanders, 1964: 116).

What is surprising, therefore, is that some 22 years after the striking of the Blue Book agreement, the members of the Boilermakers' Society, as historically militant as they were, gave up their collective bargaining rights, like the two other refinery groups before them. What were the factors that precipitated such a turnabout?

The 1982 maintenance enabling agreement proved to be a critical agreement for the boilermakers and one which, certainly for this group, was to raise the question of the value of collective bargaining rights. Prior to the striking of the 1982 maintenance enabling agreement, boilermaker overtime was running consistently high relative to other groups on site, and such high overtime levels came to be interpreted as an expected and normal part of their compensation. Furthermore, the wage differentials resulting from such overtime earnings came to be seen by the membership as right and just; particularly since it was overtime that led the boilermakers to see themselves at the top end of the trade group hierarchy.

With the introduction of the 1982 maintenance enabling agreement and its provision to reduce overtime levels and to take the control of overtime allocation away from the union, the boilermakers came to believe that their earnings would be more adversely affected than other trade groups on site. Management's pledge to drive down overtime levels was seen by the boilermakers as a direct attack on their earnings levels and that it would, therefore, have a negative effect on their position in the trades group status hierarchy. In particular, the boilermakers were already feeling that their status position had eroded vis-à-vis the instrument fitters (the group which had already transferred to staff status and was receiving a salary above and beyond the normal hourly paid rate of the boilermakers).

Why did the boilermakers suddenly feel that Fawley management was going to be successful in reducing overtime levels when, in the past, management had not been successful? First of all, the boilermakers felt that because there was such a significant differential between the overtime level of their group and that of all other trade groups, they would be the hardest hit. Secondly, because in the 1982 maintenance agreement management had succeeded in gaining control of overtime administration from the union, the boilermakers believed that this represented a firm management resolve to reduce overtime.

The boilermakers felt that the maintenance enabling agreement would benefit other groups in the refinery more than its own, and therefore decided not to sign the maintenance enabling deal and to pursue other avenues which would keep their earnings up relative to other groups. The boilermakers began to see staff status as the only route which could guarantee to retain its earnings differentials compared to other groups. Accordingly, they made the request to Fawley management that they be transferred to staff status.

Given the militant history of the boilermakers, management maintained that it would agree to such a request only after the boilermakers had first demonstrated that they would, in fact, work with 'staff like attitudes'. The transfer to staff status came to be used as a carrot to induce 'high levels of commitment and productivity'. In the case of the boilermakers, Fawley management enforced a probationary period of one year in which there were to be '. . . no industrial-relations problems or threats of collective action . . . no disputes, low absenteeism and a commitment to achieve maximum efficiency by making full use of the working day'. In line with what could be called their 'instrumental orientation', the boilermakers met such criteria and were transferred to staff status by the end of 1983.

The fourth group of workers to be considered for staff status was the welders, organized by the Amalgamated Union of Engineering Workers (A.U.E.W.). Management's attempts to move this group to staff status, however, was to mark the watershed of union resistance to the programme and was to put a temporary hold on any future transfers to staff status. Working only low overtime levels compared to other craft groups, the welders were motivated to increase their base rate to the higher rate that was offered under the staff status arrangement. On 17 August 1983, the welders voted to consider whether or not to move to staff terms. The results were clear and with a majority of 12 to 1 the welders were brought on to staff terms.

Rather than following the same kind of pattern of union resistance as in past transfers (i.e. initial protests from the full-time officials and eventual acquiescence to pressure from work groups) the move of the welders to staff terms precipitated a strong wave of reaction from the balance of the trade groups. One day after the welders' vote, on 18 August 1983, the manual employees of the Fawley maintenance department, minus the welders, put down their tools and walked out of the plant. This marked Fawley's first work stoppage in many years and signified a break in what can only be classified as a relatively conflict-free working relationship between management and the maintenance unions.

166

Staff status and contractor labour

With the successful withdrawal of collective bargaining rights from three trade union groups and the proposal for a fourth transfer, the maintenance workers said that they '... had had enough' and sought '... to put an end to the plan to get rid of us' (interview with Fawley maintenance senior shop steward).

The walk-out took the form of a mass meeting, in the late afternoon of 18 August, at which the union members voted to impose a series of sanctions on management. These sanctions included (1) the withdrawal of the 1982 maintenance enabling flexibility provisions, (2) the withdrawal of the temporary supervision role and (3) the refusal to work side-by-side with any 'staff status' welders. As a result of these sanctions management was forced to accept a compromise solution whereby the welders who moved to staff status could remain under staff terms only provided that management would hire four new welders who were deemed to be *surplus* by management and who, as union members, would have collective bargaining rights. This compromise solution was accepted and the welders moved to staff terms.

While the turbulent transfer of the welders did put a temporary halt to the plan to move all trade union groups to staff status, there is no indication that the plan has been set aside permanently. Staff status is still seen as a realistic strategy to pursue, one that will need time and money to implement. As one Fawley manager put it:

> At this point, despite the resistance we've experienced with the welders' transfer, we still think that it is really a question of money. The men in the yard are waiting for the right sum.
> We'll offer that right sum sooner or later, and when we do the long string of productivity deals will come to an end. (Interview with Fawley manager)

One personnel manager claimed, in fact, that '... full staff status, will be the productivity deal to end all productivity deals ...'.

The compatibility of the staff status initiative with productivity bargaining

Productivity bargaining needs to be seen directly in terms of Fawley's staff status objective. It was perhaps with the so-called open-ended or indirect productivity agreements that Fawley management's 'unitarist' hand was most clearly exposed, for it was with these agreements that Fawley managers actively began to appeal to workers to identify their interests with company objectives. It was with the 1972 progressive approach agreement that Fawley management first began to talk in terms of a staff status culture and about the possibility of introducing individual perfor-

167

mance appraisals for wage personnel. Within the negotiation of this agreement, Fawley management first developed its 'devil' or 'staff status bargain' whereby workers were offered staff status employment conditions in return for relinquishing their collective bargaining rights. Such a bargain was clearly, however, not yet palatable to the bulk of Fawley workers. As a Fawley maintenance workers' union newsletter put it,

> ... some people say that management are concerned that they
> have not the control over the unions they would like ... that
> all the overtures made by management are designed in the
> short term to wrest control from the unions ... perhaps there is
> something in this as management have maintained a personal
> assessment in a staff culture. If you are well liked by your
> supervisor and you have the right colour eyes and you don't
> complain too much, perhaps then you may have a secure job.
> (Watchword; Maintenance Workers' Union Newsletter, 5th edi-
> tion, 1972)

It would appear that the objective of these open-ended productivity agreements was to reduce jointly determined formal workplace rules and thereby reduce union control at the point of production. Under open-ended agreements, union officials and stewards would no longer negotiate over the substance and content of any one particular rule nor were they responsible for the interpretation and application of workplace rules on the shop floor (simply because there were to be no rules!). Instead, management would have the discretion to manage work processes in accordance with managerially defined efficiency and productivity criteria. The objective on Fawley management's part was to push union organization out of the control process.

It is important to note, as well, that the productivity bargaining process was used increasingly as a communication tool or device to develop Fawley management's philosophy about the importance of the 'individual' over the 'collectivity'. The language of the agreements is particularly revealing. The text of the agreements, and especially the preamble to the agreements, was for the most part decidedly 'unitarist'. The agreements themselves stress the need to emphasize the 'common' goals of management and labour, and the need for the worker to work in such a way as to be unfettered from trade union restrictions or constraints. The word individual is accorded special attention and is equated directly with efficiency and productivity, while the notion of collectivity is equated with restrictions to output and inefficient working practices.

So far, it is the 1982 maintenance enabling agreement which has stressed the emphasis on the 'individual' the most. The agreement was based on a

philosophy of 'individual motivation and efficiency'. It called explicitly for
'... improved individual motivation, leading to more effective working'
and for '... maximum input for the individual'. The agreement also
included a provision for regular 'individual' performance reviews and,
while these reviews were not to be tied to pay, it was agreed that every '...
opportunity will be taken to talk to individuals on a regular basis, to
discuss their personal contribution and how this can be enhanced by
training, personal development, behaviour changes ...'. Whether or not
the language of the agreements had any real impact on changing worker
attitudes is open to question but the different language does, nevertheless,
exist as a testimony to the shift in management philosophy towards the
elevation of the 'individual' over the 'collectivity'.

It was, moreover, with the 1982 maintenance enabling agreement that
the maintenance stewards sold away two significant control dimensions:
control over (1) overtime administration and allocation and (2) contractor
usage. Both of these control dimensions had special meaning for union
members as both had either a direct or an indirect effect on membership
earnings' levels. While control over working practices had been eroded in
the past, the union's loss of control over overtime and contractor usage
was new. The loss of control on overtime allocation was particularly
significant as a large part of earnings was directly tied to overtime
earnings. Moreover, overtime administration was a highly visible activity
and one which workers readily identified as a key role of senior shop
stewards.

Management's new right to control and influence contractor usage
marked another significant loss of union power. Prior to the introduction
of the 1982 maintenance enabling agreement, union approval had been
required for both major and minor non-capital construction and maintenance work. Union membership saw the union's role as critical in this area,
particularly as contractor usage was seen to have a direct effect on
overtime payments (as contract labour could be used as a substitute form
of overtime working). The union's role in controlling contractor usage
was also seen to be critical in terms of maintaining reasonable levels of job
security (as increased contractor usage was seen as potentially leading to
job loss).

With the gradual loss of key control levers, it appears to be the case that
some union members began to lose faith in the ability of union representatives to deliver anything of value or substance to their members. With the
redefinition of the union's role, workers increasingly came to rely on their
own devices to retain control on the shop floor.

The progressive loss of steward control made it increasingly difficult for
the stewards to command loyalty from their membership. This paved the

way for worker acceptance of the 'devil's bargain' – the relinquishing of collective bargaining rights in return for an 'individual' staff status employment contract. Any agreement on behalf of the union membership to give up their collective bargaining rights could really only take place once the membership had come to believe that real union control had been diminished. Doubtless, other complex motivating factors were at play in leading workers to give up their negotiating rights, but it would appear that the impact of productivity bargaining on union control was indeed one motivating factor. This research did not focus upon the issue of staff status, but, rather, upon the use of productivity bargaining in general, and therefore the conclusions drawn here would, ideally, require additional, more specialized, research.

It is important to note, however, that the loss of union control was by no means complete – far from it. This is evidenced by the fact that management's steady progress in the area of staff status initiatives was eventually blocked and also by the fact that other union groups on site continue to ward off the 'devil's bargain'. It is only suggested here that a certain degree of union power and influence was eroded over the years – and that this power diminution has led some union members into giving up, or thinking about giving up, their collective bargaining rights.

The rationale and logic for Fawley's movement to staff status

The idea of moving to a 'union-free' environment provided a certain appeal to Fawley management in that it presented management with the opportunity to align itself with the parent company's (Exxon Corporation) industrial-relations strategy of operating without unions wherever possible. The managers of Fawley Refinery had continually been plagued by unfavourable productivity comparisons with other Exxon circuit refineries, many of which were operating in a union-free environment. It is not unreasonable to assume that some Fawley managers came, as a result, to believe that productivity improvements could really only be made in a union-free environment. While, for certain obvious reasons, there was no apparent direct mandate from the parent company to pursue such a strategy, it is suggested that such a philosophy may have been transmitted somehow via less direct processes (e.g. through the exchange of company personnel between U.K. operations and the parent company). Flanders (1964: 27) himself was aware of the parent company's '. . . reluctance to deal with "outside unions" ' but may have underestimated the extent to which the parent company's influence actually affected its subsidiaries.

For Fawley management, staff status had its own internal logic. First, the growth in the complexity and expense of new capital equipment in the continuous process industry was resulting in the need for increased worker responsibility in operating and maintaining the equipment. The potential to disrupt production, at considerable cost, had fallen into the hands of smaller and smaller groups of workers. This group was to be represented by the 'front end' of the maintenance department, notably high skilled craft workers such as the instrument technicians.

It was Fawley management's belief that those trade groups placed in certain strategic locations in the production process would be better managed within the context of a 'staff' as opposed to a 'collective' employment contract. The possibility of collective action by strategically located groups was seen by Fawley management to be lessened once a group had been pushed into a staff status contract. This unitary view of the enterprise was based upon the belief that by extending staff conditions of employment to manual workers, a 'non-manual' attitude to work and an identification with company objectives would be the result. As Wedderburn and Craig note, differences in objective terms of employment and subjective terms of status have an economic origin:

> ... the need to buy the loyalty of workers who were to be 'l'homme de confiance' or the 'employers substitute' ... this employer–employee relationship was predicated on the assumption that the employee shared his employer's interests and his definition of responsibilities. (1974: 158)

In attempting to remove collective bargaining rights from the site, Fawley management tried to command a sense of responsibility and consent from workers. Managers often told me, for instance, that they believed that the introduction of staff status contracts would serve to eliminate the so-called 'them–us' attitude and would unleash a high internal commitment to the firm's objectives. It was believed that this 'unitarist' approach, which advocates one source of power and authority and one focus of loyalty, would lead to worker behaviour that would be self-motivated and self-disciplined. It would be the basis for 'self-' or 'internalized' control. It was hoped that workers would come to respond to work situations like every other staff member, so that the need for explicit surveillance and evaluation would be reduced and ultimately eliminated.

Sir Ronald Edwards, the former chairman of Electricity Supply, provides his own logic on the value of staff status. Regarding his 1964 staff status deal he suggests:

> There are many tasks in the field of electricity supply ... where one is dependent, in the last resort, not on the stick or carrot

but on a man's sense of loyalty, pride and belief in the services which he is there to give ... One cannot, on the one hand seek, when it comes to wage and salary settlements, to make the hardest of bargains. We thought that by raising or seeking to raise the social status of industrial workers we should increase their sense of responsibility in an industry where this is of crucial importance. (Quote referred to by H. Phelps-Brown, in Edwards and Roberts, 1971: xv–xvi)

The Incomes Data Services has reported that the majority of staff status programmes are to be found in large capital intensive industries, operating in the high technology sectors (IDS Study, October 1980: 3). This may relate to the need felt by management to buy the loyalty and commitment of a strategically powerful work-force in these particular industries.

While there may be various benefits associated with Fawley management's pursuit of staff status, it is important to note that such a strategy also carries with it its own set of problems and contradictions. Who is to say, for instance, that the transfer of trade groups to staff terms would somehow magically transform worker behaviour on the shop floor? Furthermore, is it possible that the transfer of workers to staff status might serve to foster élitism and consequently heighten the bargaining awareness of the staff group? Is it also possible that non-staff workers would taint the purity of staff status groups, so that the performance differences between the two groups would be more cosmetic than real? Newly transferred staff workers could possibly take advantage of the benefits of their new status while simply carrying on their old ways. Furthermore, the threat of reunionization could always be used as a sanction on the part of workers. Finally, might not the unionized or non-staff status groups begin to use the staff status groups as a reference point for their own bargaining, and would this not lead to 'leapfrogging'? For instance, Fawley's non-staff status groups reportedly quite frequently asked the disturbing question 'Why should we be paid less than the staff groups when the only difference is that the staff status groups have relinquished their bargaining rights?' Each of these questions need to be weighed against any supposed benefits of Fawley's staff status programme.

The growth of the contractor employment relationship

At the same time as Fawley management was busy trying to eradicate collective bargaining rights from the site it was also increasing its contractor labour force. This increase in contractor usage should, however, not be seen as part of a grand management strategy, but rather as a simple response to the failure of productivity bargaining itself.

The absolute number of contractor employees has grown steadily since the mid-1960s, with an additional surge of activity since 1976. This growth has occurred exclusively in the following maintenance areas: capital construction, 'turn-around' (involving the temporary shut-down of an operating unit for major maintenance work) and ongoing maintenance of the low-skilled variety.

Interestingly, the growth of contracted maintenance labour is directly paralleled by a steady decline in the numbers of company maintenance workers. The ratio of Esso maintenance workers to contractor workers on 'turn-around' maintenance work, for instance, has changed significantly since the mid-1960s, with the contractor group taking on an increasingly greater proportion of this work. This growth in the use of contractors for turn-around maintenance work is significant, because in the refining industry, it is 'turn-around' and not day-to-day maintenance that is considered the most substantial and important work conducted.

The use of contractor labour in day-to-day maintenance has, perhaps, been the most sensitive issue in the eyes of Fawley trade unions (contractor labour issues in this area, for instance, have generated more grievances than any other single issue). Traditionally, Fawley unions carefully guarded day-to-day maintenance work on the site, and this has been particularly true for the non-craft maintenance workers who were threatened the most by contractor involvement. The precise increase in contractor labour in this area was not revealed to me (partly due to the sensitivity of the issue), however, interviews with both management and trade union personnel confirm that '. . . there has been a significant inroad made in the substitution of contractor labour for Esso employees . . . especially in the low-skill areas' (interview with management personnel). In 1969 the proportion of contractors in total maintenance and capital construction was twenty per cent while in 1979 this had risen to forty per cent (interview with management personnel).

The essence of the Fawley contractor strategy was to have higher-skilled work performed by Esso forces, with semi-skilled and unskilled work being contracted out. All peak labour demands, such as 'turn-around' maintenance work, was also to be handled by outside maintenance contractors.

Why increase the use of contractor labour?

Interestingly, the advantages normally associated with the use of contractor labour do not always hold in the Fawley case. Contractor labour, for instance, is traditionally considered to have the advantage of being sensitive to fluctuations in work demand, an advantage that would clearly have relevance for the refining industry, due to the need for the intermittent shut-down of the refining units for major maintenance work. Because a unit must be 'turned around' as quickly as possible, it is advantageous to tap a large pool of labour.

Furthermore, as a result of changes in plant technology, the use of contractor labour on 'shut-down' maintenance work has become more and more important. The increased reliability of operating equipment has meant that the amount of time between one plant turn-around and the next has been extended and that the plant 'downtime' has itself been shortened. This has placed pressure on Fawley management to increase its 'numerical' flexibility, i.e. to increase its ability to draw in and out of the organization large pools of labour to cover for the intermittent shut-downs.

While there is some logic in the need for contractor labour in such turn-around maintenance work, what is odd in the Fawley case is the extent to which the contractor labour pool actually remains relatively stable in numbers. While some extra contractor labour is pulled in for these turn-arounds, the bulk of the contractors tend already to be on site. There does not, in fact, tend to be a wide fluctuation in the use of contractor labour over time. For many contract workers at Fawley, contract employment sometimes implies 'life-long' employment on site. As one shop steward put it,

> ... the story that contractors only remain on the refinery for a short period of time is at an end. No one believes it any more. Many of the contractors at Fawley have enough service to warrant long service awards. (Interview with Fawley shop steward)

Some of the contractor workers even expressed confusion as to who was their real employer. Many of the contractor employees I spoke to identified themselves as 'Esso' as opposed to contractor employees (this is not surprising as some had been employed on the site more or less continuously for twenty years or more). The confederation (the bargaining agent for the contractors) had even pressed for the introduction of pensions for long-serving contractor personnel on site. This reality of 'life-long employment' for contractors appears to contradict a basic tenet of the so-called 'dual labour market' theory. The Fawley case might even be seen as turning the 'dual labour market' theory on its head by operating a system of relative employment security for contractor workers, while

174

internal company employees are subjected to one redundancy programme after another.

Further, according to 'dual labour market' theory, contractor labour is generally associated with the 'cheapness' of wages. Once again, the theory does not hold in the case of Fawley Refinery. Looking at the basic pay rate, it is well known on site that contractor pay is only marginally less than that of Fawley employees. If the contractor wage rate supplements are added (overtime opportunities, travelling money, and special conditions money) compensation between the groups tends to equal out.

Fawley management has estimated that there are direct cost savings to be made by contracting out low- and semi-skilled maintenance work (ten to fifteen per cent) and a 'break-even' cost for basic maintenance work. These savings would appear to result, given the approximate equivalence in wages between contractor and Esso workers, in 'overhead' costs (and most likely 'management' overhead costs).

The increased use of contractor labour at Fawley did, however, appear to have one benefit for Fawley management, but this was declared to be unintended and was considered a wind-fall by management. The extension of contractor labour served to fracture or divide the labour components at Fawley so that conflict engendered by the capital–labour employment relationship tended to be reconverted or redirected to conflict between competing labour groups. For example, Fawley workers interpreted contractor employees as a 'threat' and, as a result, met them with hostility. A kind of Esso status élitism developed between contractors and internal employees, which served to break up or split labour unity. Such élitism was expressed, for instance, (trivially) in the refusal by Esso employees to permit contractor employees to share the internal workers' general facilities on site. One worker put it this way: '. . . we have to be better than the contractors . . . we have to know more because we tell them what to do'. Another stated that, '. . . there are contractors and there's us'. 'Us' was symbolic of company or Esso membership and this type of membership could be considered as a kind of cost-free normative control for management.

There appears to be at least one other motivation for Fawley management to be interested in extending its contractor component, and this relates to the failure of productivity bargaining itself to reach or attain its stated objectives. As I have already pointed out, both Fawley's manning and overtime levels were out of step with the parent company league tables. It would appear to be the case that contractor labour increasingly came to be used by Fawley management to 'fiddle' or 'fudge' the extent to which any real progress was being made in bringing manning and overtime levels down. In other words, management also turned to the use

175

of contractor labour to disguise the extent to which any real progress was being made in improving efficiency.

It has been shown above, for instance, that, as far back as the Blue Book era, contractor labour was used as a substitute for overtime working. This usage effectively disguised the extent to which real overtime levels were being realized. The 1975 maintenance deal overtime reduction target was itself premised on the fact that contractor usage would be increased to 'assist' in the drop in overtime levels. Furthermore, the reduction in manning levels that Fawley attained over the past two-and-a-half decades needs to be seen in the light of an increase in the use of contractor labour. Contrary to what many would believe, it has, therefore, not simply been the case that Fawley workers have become more efficient, in the sense of maintaining the same or more capital equipment with fewer men. Rather, what has happened is that there has been a simple substitution of one form of labour for another. Therefore, the apparent success of productivity bargaining technique in reducing Esso Fawley's manning levels has been somewhat 'cosmetic' and does not take into account the extent to which contractor labour substitution has taken place.

Problems associated with the use of contractor labour

The use of contractors who work on the premises (as opposed to those who carry out assigned work elsewhere, off the site) brings with it a number of constraints and problems. These constraints and problems tend to be a function of the physical proximity of the two labour groups, that is company and contractor workers.

At Fawley, the proximity of the 'on-site' contracting group with the internal work-force ensured that the contractor group's employment conditions were kept up to some minimal level. For example, Fawley unions exerted their influence to ensure that all contractors would themselves be unionized and that standard employment conditions would be met for all workers. Fawley unions also pressed management to ensure that no 'cowboy' or 'cheap' contractors would be allowed on the site. This pressure by Fawley unions has effectively inhibited Fawley management from taking advantage of the type of non-standard employment conditions (relaxed safety standards, 'sweat shop' working conditions etc.) often afforded in the 'off-site' contractor employment relationship. In fact, in the 1983 contractor wage negotiations, Fawley management was pressured into issuing a special statement of intent indicating that it would pursue a higher standard of industrial relations for its contractor workers. This statement pledged Fawley management's commitment to ensuring that contractors do not '... introduce dubious working practices which would be detrimental to both the employees involved and the high standards and consistency of industrial relations at Fawley . . .' (Incomes Data Services Report 413, November 1983: 5).

One of the purported advantages of 'contracting' out work is that the labour control problem is itself contracted out. With the type of 'on-site' contracting relationship that Fawley had, however, labour control continued to be a problem. At Fawley, control over the contractor group is seen to be essential in order to ensure that any labour problems on the contractor side do not 'spill over' to the company side. Contractor labour problems associated with 'turn-around' maintenance work could mean, for instance, that an operating unit would not be 'turned-around' as quickly as it should, thereby losing valuable production time.

In keeping with Fawley management's notion of labour control over the contractor group, there are two full-time personnel professionals employed by Fawley to monitor and control contractor industrial relations. These Fawley personnel people work so closely with the contractor outfits that it is sometimes difficult to understand whether this personnel staff is working for the contractor or for Fawley. The traditional control of contractor industrial relations by Fawley management includes (1) the bid review process used in the selection of contractors to ensure industrial-relations 'suitability', (2) the indoctrination of contractors into Fawley's industrial-relations philosophy and (3) the day-to-day monitoring of contractor industrial relations.

Fawley management's control of contractor industrial relations actually includes the joint devising of wage negotiation strategies. The extent to which control is exerted by Fawley management is evidenced by the fact that it will actively intervene in the hiring or firing of the industrial-relations personnel of the contracting companies. In more than one instance Esso was instrumental in terminating the employment of a contractor industrial-relations manager (interview with Fawley manager). Such a direct involvement in contractor industrial relations can hardly be interpreted as a 'contracting out' of the labour control problem.

The proximity of the internal work-force and the contract labour group also means that there is a tendency for each group to use the other as a point of reference for wage claims. Both types of labour group have, for instance, utilized 'leapfrogging' tactics to increase wage awards. In the 1981 contractor wage negotiations, for instance, 1,100 contractor workers went out on strike in order to achieve pay comparability with Esso's permanent employees (although parity was not achieved, the contractor group was able to pressure Fawley management to issue an additional and separate statement of intent which answered some of the contractor workers' grievances).

177

The quest for productivity

Fawley workers also continually made reference to contractor wage levels and to contractor benefits such as 'travelling' money to try to increase their own wage settlement. As one craft union wage strategy document put it:

> The erosion of the value of the base rate has forced a need to look at comparability with people working on the site, namely the main contractors who for some years have gradually made inroads in our maintenance type work. We notice with grave concern that the contractor has quite a lot of freedom in updating travel allowances and fringe benefits – benefits that have already been eliminated for us through productivity bargaining. (Internal union document)

Another craft union wage document notes:

> ... we believe that in comparison to the contractor group, the Esso maintenance man is not as privileged and well paid as he is made out to be and total rewards he receives need to reflect the loyalty and commitment he has to the company. (Internal union document: wage strategy for the 1977 wage claim)

There were, in fact, to be many referencing problems related to the productivity provisions struck for Esso workers and the more traditional working practices arrangements for the contractor group. For example, the reintroduction of the temporary shift working arrangement through the 1982 maintenance enabling agreement had direct interface problems with the contractor group. While Esso workers were working 'shift' arrangements on weekends, contractors were, at the same time, receiving overtime premium rates for this work. There are obvious problems associated with employees making references to the pay and the conditions of a nearby work group.

This referencing problem appeared also to affect worker attitudes, serving to engender a spirit of worker militancy among company employees. The proximity of the two labour segments also meant that any industrial action or worker militancy on the part of the contractor group was highly visible to Esso workers. The normative control engendered through the construction of Fawley's internal labour market may, then, have been disturbed by Esso workers' imitation of contractor industrial relations. There was a feeling amongst a number of managers that the many strikes involving contractors, some involving heavy picketing, had produced a general mood of militancy on site. While it is difficult to measure such a diffusion process, it is not unreasonable to assume that highly visible industrial action on the part of the contractor group, and the

178

extent of their success in obtaining their objectives, would have some adverse effect upon trade union behaviour at Fawley.

The many references made by company employees to the contractor group may serve, at least partially, to explain the failure of some of the key provisions of the productivity agreements. It was difficult, for instance, for innovative working practices to be introduced in the shadow of the traditional working practices of the contractors. Esso workers could always tell themselves that if the contractors were not changing their working practices then why should they, especially since the contractor wage rates tended to be equivalent to Esso's own wage rates. Similarly, Fawley's overtime reduction objectives might have been difficult to achieve because Esso workers could always point to the high levels of contractor overtime working.

In addition to the problems mentioned above associated with the 'proximity' of the two labour groups, there is, of course, a range of further problems which can generally be attributed to a contractor employment relationship. First, there are costs associated with training contractor workers to pick up the necessary skills and knowledge to do the particular job. Secondly, there are certain risks associated with the quality of work. Inferior workmanship can be costly to fix and can mean prolonged down time of operating units. More seriously, poor quality work can have a dramatic impact on health and safety standards.

Conclusions

This chapter has discussed two subsidiary industrial-relations 'strategies' at Fawley – the staff status arrangements and the extended use of contractor labour. Both of these strategies are seen to be intimately linked and dependent upon the dominant productivity bargaining based strategy.

Are these two subsidiary strategies part of a grand management strategy of labour market 'segmentation'? That is, were the groups of employees who were in a position to intervene critically in the production process 'pushed up' closer to the firm (into 'staff status' contracts), while those employees who were marginal to the production process were 'pushed down' (and sometimes out) or replaced by contractor labour? It is tempting to interpret the movement to staff status and the increased use of contractor labour in these terms, but this interpretation would, I believe, be giving management too much credit for strategic thinking. Certainly, in the case of the increased use of contractor labour, it would appear that management was more interested in supplementing, and camouflaging the failure of, the productivity agreements.

11

The control implications of productivity bargaining reconsidered

Introduction

This chapter reconsiders the control implications of productivity bargaining that were described in chapter 4. Productivity bargaining was associated with (1) a movement from a 'half-pay/half-effort' strategy to one of 'full-pay/full-effort' (representing a strategy of labour market 'internalization'), (2) a movement to a pluralist based strategy of 'joint control' and (3) a movement to restore order at the workplace through the increased formalization of rules.

After studying the many generations of productivity bargaining agreements at Fawley over twenty-five years, it was seen that management ended up with little to show for its pains. This leads one to wonder why management failed so repeatedly in achieving the objectives of the agreements. If only a few agreements had gone awry, one could provide a number of reasons to explain this failure – such as 'lack of careful preparation' or 'lack of follow-up', but considering that *each* agreement had, in the end, run aground it would appear that certain more fundamental problems existed. This chapter argues that there were *fundamental* control problems and contradictions inherent in the productivity bargaining process.

This chapter now takes a renewed look at the three control claims of productivity bargaining.

The dream of full-pay/full-effort; the strategy of labour market internalization

It was the hope of Bill Allen, the architect of the Blue Book, that the productivity bargaining process would serve to 'internalize' Fawley's labour market. Fundamentally, 'internalization' was a micro-corporatist strategy which involved an attempt to bind the labour force to the company through high wages and employment security in exchange for greater flexibility of movement between jobs. This strategy was to mark a departure from high manning and high overtime toward a greater reliance on the internal labour market. Ideally, productivity bargaining was to result in the creation of a highly skilled and highly paid 'internal' work-force, working at high levels of productivity. Productivity bargaining was, in other words, to create an internal labour market where none had existed in the past.

The concept of the 'internal labour market' is itself deceptively simple. Employees within internal labour markets are seen to be showered with favourable employment conditions: high wages, extensive fringe benefits, high levels of job security, favourable working conditions and so on. Promotion is afforded through a complex job progression system. Firms offer such favourable institutional inducements to secure high levels of commitment from their employees, to ensure stability of skill supply due to high, firm-specific training expenditures and to minimize turnover. The logic behind the internal labour market relates to the firm's desire to induce long-term commitment from workers or employees.

Those firms characterized by high levels of capital intensity, market stability and relatively large size are considered to be particularly prone to creating internal labour markets as the jobs in such firms are generally associated with high levels of skill and responsibility and with high training requirements.

More recently, the concept of the internal labour market has been developed within what is known as 'dual labour market theory', which stresses the growing polarization of the work-force into one 'core' and various 'peripheral' groups (for the British case, see Atkinson, 1984). Core workers are portrayed as that group which enjoys increased levels of job security and favourable career and promotion prospects, involving the acquisition and deployment of new skills. For this group, employment security is usually seen to be won at the cost of accepting 'functional' flexibility both in the short term (involving cross-trade working, reduced demarcation and multi-discipline teams) as well as in the longer term through career changing and retraining (Atkinson, 1984: 29). The peripheral group, on the other hand, is seen to be composed of employees experiencing reduced job security, minimal job-specific training pro-grammes, low pay and generally deteriorating employment conditions. Firms are seen to employ peripheral workers in order to take advantage of what has been referred to as 'numerical' flexibility, i.e. they can hire and fire such workers in accordance with shifts in product demand.

My own case study data reveal that Fawley's attempt to move toward an internalization strategy largely failed. It is possible to argue, in fact, that Fawley management never did fully appreciate either the philosophical basis or the complexities of such a strategy. In the end, high pay, job progression schemes and 'life-long employment' – each considered to be essential aspects of an internalization strategy to induce worker commitment and consent – were not pursued. It is perhaps not surprising, given management's failure to create an atmosphere of life-long allegiance to the company, that many of Fawley management's efficiency objectives, such as their drive for increased flexibility, did not succeed.

Some time after the striking of the Blue Book agreement, the objective of pursuing a 'high wages' strategy appears to have weakened. It had only been pursued in an uneven and halting manner, with Fawley management striking a productivity deal which increased wages (isolating them from the external labour market), but then letting wages gradually slip in relation to the local labour market. It has been seen that Fawley's movement forward and then the subsequent loss of relative wages occurred as early as during the historic Blue Book deal itself. The non-internalization of the labour market on the wages side is further reflected in the relative absence of differentials between the wages of Esso company employees and those of outside contractors.

It does not appear that Fawley management ever had the confidence necessary to pursue this strategy to a point of cutting itself off from the local labour market. Faced with the frustration of falling short in its labour productivity objectives, in other words, facing the spectre of high wages combined with low effort, Fawley management chose to let the 'high wage' strategy slide.

Arguably, the importance of the 'high-pay/high-effort' strategy, originally touted by Bill Allen in 1960, does not appear to have caught the imagination of British management in general and to an even lesser extent that of the current British Conservative government. The Thatcherite anti-inflation policy, and the administration's belief that higher wages would result in a loss of international competitiveness has set the tone for a 'wage suppression' based strategy (although this strategy has not been realized – as we have witnessed higher wage increases in the 1980s than in any other period since the 1950s). It could be said that the 'high wages' based strategy has not taken off for two reasons: first, because of British management doubts about its *own* ability to extract the extra effort required from workers to run a 'high-wage/high-effort' strategy and secondly, because of wider government policy which does not fully appreciate the notion of the internal labour market. The former suggests deficiencies in management organization, structure and effectiveness.

Apart from management's lack of success in moving to the 'high-wage' aspect of the internalization strategy, Fawley management also diverged from a pure internalization strategy in other ways. For instance, the reduction and collapse of job hierarchies and job progression schemes figured centrally in a number of productivity deals at Fawley. Such proposals basically meant moving in the opposite direction from what internal labour market theorists like Edwards (1979) would suggest. Within the process department, for instance, there were 22 different pay grades in 1959 which ended up being reduced to two pay grades in 1984. For Fawley management complex job progression schemes were interpreted as a *problem*. Job progression schemes were seen to place 'boundary conditions' on the expenditure of effort. It was believed that workers limited their work to the defined job specifications of particular jobs. As a result, it was believed that increased worker flexibility would be enhanced by the break-up of these job ladders and progression schemes. Rather than interpreting job ladders and clusters as functional to the organization (by serving to induce ideological commitment as a basis for organizational control), Fawley management viewed job ladders as 'restrictive' in themselves.

The desire to break up existing complex job ladders in order to win increased worker flexibility was to result, however, in Fawley workers' discontent regarding diminished promotional opportunities. In 1984, process workers were themselves to claim that there was 'no financial incentive to move, and this is caused by a lack of differentials between ranks'. One process worker claimed that the lack of job progression opportunities

> ... is a sore point. For most of us, we start and end in the
> same job. If you're lucky you can get to a chief operator's job.
> There's no chance anymore to get a supervisors' job. The
> supervisors' jobs are taken up by graduates who don't know
> anything about the units. (Interview with process worker)

Ironically, one Fawley manager, reflecting back to the pre-Blue Book era, suggested that the complex job hierarchies of that period were precisely what was needed at the refinery today. For him, the break-up of the job progression system had resulted in a 'commitment crisis'. It would appear, therefore, that there is an inherent *conflict* or *contradiction* between the need to reduce the complexity of job hierarchies in order to obtain more flexible working and the need to retain these same hierarchies as a device by which to induce ideological or normative commitment from workers. Thus, there may be inherent contradictions between management control strategies – in that the optimization of one may result in the sub-optimization of another.

Finally, in terms of the employment stability aspect of the internal labour market strategy, it has been seen that this did not exist at Fawley.

In fact, the majority of the agreements were directed at the shedding of labour. As one personnel manager put it: '... we must be careful not to give an impression that Esso negotiates productivity deals which give a guarantee of job protection. I think we must accept that productivity deals will mean fewer people if they are any good.'

Management's desire to reduce the size of the work-force was, however, to run in direct *conflict* or *contradiction* with some of the other productivity aims and objectives that required commitment and consent from the work-force. In fact, the principle of 'life-long employment' – perhaps the cornerstone of the Japanese internalization strategy – was ignored in each productivity agreement as management attempted, time after time, to reduce the size of the work-force. The message that was left in the minds of the workers was that they were dispensable and surplus. If management was expecting high levels of commitment from its work-force, this might not have been the best message to convey. The need to shed labour, while at the same time trying to win high levels of employee commitment, could be considered a fundamental *paradox* of many a productivity deal. Indeed, it is somewhat surprising that so many a productivity deal has attempted to achieve simultaneously the mutually exclusive goals of 'labour shedding' and 'commitment generation'.

Fawley management does not appear to have had any great interest in gaining the commitment of workers through the fundamental principles of 'life-long employment' and job progression opportunities. The opportunity to generate commitment through the possible venue of close and compassionate supervision was also ignored. Management created considerable damage to the supervisory role, in the eyes of the workers, by reducing the numbers and levels of supervisors, by introducing multicraft supervision and by removing the supervisors from the union. The thrust of Fawley management's approach to supervision was to increase the authority of supervision (by taking it out of craft control). Supervisors were to become the direct agents of management on the shop floor. Pressure was placed on supervision to police the agreements. This was to result in a qualitative shift in the nature of the supervisory role, the overall effect (at least in intention) being the heightening of the 'coercive' role of the supervisor. As a result, worker commitment and consent which, in the past, had been gained largely through 'compassionate' supervision was eroded. An example of this loss of commitment was seen many times, when Fawley workers withheld 'informally' granted flexibility – flexibility which flowed spontaneously from close and compassionate working relationships between supervisor and worker. The reduction in actual numbers and layers of supervisors over the years only served to exacerbate this situation.

184

Control implications of productivity bargaining

Just as worker commitment and consent was being eroded by a changed supervisory role – so, too, was it being diminished by a change in the role of the personnel/employee relations department. It would appear that, over the years of productivity bargaining, workers increasingly came to see the personnel department as a direct agent for productivity improvement as opposed to a kind of independent mediator between management and labour. A number of workers and union stewards suggested that the personnel department had grown 'tougher over the years' and 'was no longer so much on our side'. The redefinition of the role of personnel as an agent of productivity appears to be endorsed by some recent writers (e.g. Schumacher, 1981) – without their appearing to understand its possible costs, i.e. loss of worker consent (see Legge, 1978 for a discussion of some of the ambiguities inherent within personnel management).

Part of the advantage implied in a firm's use of productivity bargaining is that the nature of work and the decisions as to who does which type of job would be bought away from 'external' control (i.e. union or craft control) and that management could now tailor these items to the specific 'internal' needs of the company. The case study has demonstrated that such internalization was not, in fact, attained. What is perhaps surprising about this is the *extent* of management's failure (i.e. almost total and complete) to win inroads in job redesign and increased flexibility. This is most interesting considering the extent to which recent flexibility initiatives have been held up as a key strategy for change in the 1980s (Brewster and Connock, 1985 have, for instance, seen flexibility initiatives in this way). In fact, many scholars tend to assume that flexibility is being won in accordance with the written objectives of the agreements rather than assessing their effectiveness in day-to-day operation (for example, see Willman and Winch, 1985; Brewster and Connock, 1985).

It is only recently that a few researchers have started to question the actual effectiveness of flexibility programmes and initiatives. Atkinson's and Meager's survey of flexibility programmes in 72 large British companies reveals, for instance, that,

> ... although the observed changes were widespread, they did not cut very deeply in most of the firms, and therefore the outcome was more likely to be marginal, *ad hoc* and tentative, rather than a purposeful and strategic thrust to achieve flexibility. (1986: 26)

After years of celebrating the virtues of flexibility initiatives, the Incomes Data Services have themselves begun to backtrack on their earlier claims and started to question the *actual* success of various companies' attempts at realizing flexibility improvements:

The quest for productivity

> Myths about the advance in flexible working practices in manu-
> facturing have misled many people into thinking that funda-
> mental changes have taken place on a very wide scale. On the
> contrary, the fundamental changes are extremely narrowly con-
> centrated in particular corners or, very occasionally, particular
> sectors of industry. And even where these changes have been
> taking place, they can be incomplete, halting or superficial. The
> stated aims of the companies have often been only partially
> achieved. (Incomes Data Services, Study 360, April 1986: 4)

It would appear, therefore, that the craft system or external labour
market approach to regulating the standards and conditions of particular
tasks has proved more immutable than was generally believed. It could be
argued that, at Fawley, management's failure to achieve improvements in
flexible working was the direct result of its inability to understand that
there is a price to be paid in pursuing what would now be called a
'Japanized' internalization strategy. Such an internalization strategy requires that worker consent and commitment be won through high pay, job
security, job progression systems and so on. Without these inducements
such concessions as flexible working can only be a distant management
dream.

It could be suggested that a fundamental *conflict* existed within Fawley's 'internalization' strategy. Operating with a legacy of high manning
levels, Fawley management chose to pare down the size of the labour
force – in doing so, however, it served to reduce the consent and commitment of the work-force. Likewise, in eliminating job progression systems,
Fawley management eliminated one of its prime inducements to worker
commitment and consent. It is possible to argue that Fawley management
was caught in what could be called a *'productivity/commitment' paradox*.
Such tactics as manpower reductions, cost-cutting, and the elimination
of job progression opportunities were each essential for productivity
improvement – yet it would appear that each served to reduce the level
of worker commitment that would have been required for other critical
management objectives such as job flexibility.

The *'productivity/commitment' paradox* was perhaps most vividly
revealed in Fawley management's 'hard-hitting' 1981 process productivity
agreement which sought to drive down process manning levels
significantly. It was seen that progress in the area of demannings resulted
in a 'crisis of commitment', manifested in increased grievances and
lack of cooperation, which in turn forced Fawley management to delay
some demannings and to start up an 'organizational development' activity
in order to win back worker commitment (in the words of one

manager 'to look to ways in which process workers can "rejoin" the company').

While the use of productivity bargaining at Fawley had little, if any, effect on labour market internalization, the technique facilitated the reconstruction of Fawley's labour market in another way, that is by paving the way for the extended use of a 'secondary' labour pool in the form of contractor labour. The extension of a secondary labour market was partly due to the failure of productivity bargaining itself rather than to a conscious and deliberate management strategy. Productivity bargaining at Fawley had, therefore, more to do with the 'externalization' of labour markets (the increased use of secondary forms of labour) than with processes of 'internalization'.

In relation to dual labour market theory, what could be considered unusual about Fawley's 'peripheral' contractor work-force is that it tends to have labour market characteristics that are more closely aligned with so-called 'core' or internal company workers. In some ways contractors are more 'internalized' than Fawley's own 'company' workers. Contractor employees can expect, for instance, relatively high levels of employment security. Ironically, the spectre of redundancy loomed larger within Esso (as a result of a series of productivity deals) than within the contractor forces (indeed contractor employment has grown steadily). Moreover, contractor pay rates have remained high relative to Esso Fawley workers and have at times been in excess of Esso workers' rates (when wage supplements such as overtime and travelling money are included). In terms of increased management control through internalization, it must be said that the elegant dual labour market model does not apply to Fawley.

Increased management control through the pluralist based strategy for joint control

The overview of Fawley's productivity bargaining over the 25 years which followed the signing of the Blue Book suggests that Fawley's industrial-relations strategy could best be described as 'individualist' as opposed to 'collectivist'. In relation to Fox's (1971) typology of management frames of reference, the Fawley approach would clearly fall into the 'unitarist' or even a union avoidance category rather than the 'pluralist' democratic category. By moving employees to 'staff status', management was making ongoing attempts to 'individualize' the worker and to break up the integrity of collective interests on the site. Interestingly, in spite of Flanders' hopes that productivity bargaining would lead to a new higher-order pluralism, he was himself forced to acknowledge that he found a 'unitarist' orientation amongst Fawley managers at the time of the Blue Book:

> Such a belief (unitarist) appears to have been part of Fawley management's philosophy and to have been responsible for unrealistic expectations about the results of the Blue Book in producing a better spirit of cooperation. (1964: 200–1)

It would appear that the relationship between productivity bargaining and a higher-order pluralism existed more in the minds of theoreticians than it did in the minds of practitioners. Nightingale's study of productivity bargaining at I.C.I. and British Oxygen Company has shown that, while management in each firm did, to some extent, shift towards a strategy of pluralist based control, '... this break was not total' (1976: 350). With respect to I.C.I., Nightingale found that the work of behavioural scientists such as Herzberg and MacGregor underlay much of the company's productivity bargaining:

> Their ideas fitted more readily into the 'Human Relations' tradition and denied a number of propositions crucial to pluralist writers. To the extent that their influence was reflected in managerial ideology and practice, the emergence of a new pluralistic situation – one which gave anything like equal power to management and organised labour – was limited. (1976: 350)

Likewise Nightingale found that managers at British Oxygen Company '... contrived to place heavy stress on the "Scientific Management" traditions of work study and the like, in their effort to establish managerial controls' (1976: 350). For Nightingale, therefore, '... the managerial style associated with productivity bargaining revealed a positive, though by no means total, commitment to the "new philosophy" of pluralism' (1976: 351). The situation at Fawley revealed an even less positive commitment to a new pluralist management style. From the Blue Book onwards, Fawley management was to see productivity bargaining in an essentially conservative manner, as a means by which to buy out union control by developing unitarist notions of 'mutual' and 'common' interests.

It was perhaps too much to expect that productivity bargaining would serve to alter or change deeply rooted managerial ideologies. By their very nature, ideologies are deeply rooted and cannot be easily shaken. It is possible to argue, in general, that industrial-relations academics, with their slavish fascination with notions of pluralism, have been blinded to the extent to which techniques such as productivity bargaining have actually been interpreted and used by managers in unitarist ways. The argument could be made that unitarist based strategies have been, and continue to be, favoured by British managers (even though they may be constrained in operating in such a way) and that British managers may not have so readily endorsed collective bargaining or 'institutionalization of conflict' based strategies. While the unitarist position and associated labour strategies have been buried under the weight of the pluralist debate there is some recent evidence to suggest that the unitarist position is much more in existence than might have been earlier assumed. A recent survey by Poole et al. of a sample of British managers reveals, for instance, that

> ... the bulk of British managers maintain a preference for a 'unitary' system of decision-making control within the enterprise. No obvious preference was demonstrated for the joint determination of rules and rule making procedures whatsoever. (1982: 304)

Flanders' declared link between productivity bargaining and a new pluralism may have been a function of his own ideology or frame of reference. His own deep feelings about the importance of democracy at the workplace may have coloured his own interpretation of the productivity bargaining process. In other words, Flanders may have been seeing what he so desperately wanted to see.

The extent and depth of Fawley management's 'unitarist' perspective was, as was seen, reflected, tangibly, within the staff status programme. Many other multinational and British companies have also jumped on the staff status bandwagon. Their interest in, and experiences with, staff status programmes have, for the most part, been described in relatively innocuous terms, typically presented as resulting from a 'joint' agreement amongst workers and management to harmonize employment conditions. It needs to be noted, however, that they are, for the most part, management led. Lawler (1981: 63) has noted that unions have expressed little widespread support for the idea and that some see 'all salary' plans as a strategy to prevent unionization. Rarely have these staff status initiatives been seen as part of a management strategy directed at either 'deunionization' or the prevention of unionization in the first place.

It is important to note that both 'single' (all employees on staff status) and staff status programmes have been used as an 'anti-union' technique. Most of the single status companies in Britain are entirely non-unionized and while many would not openly admit it, the covert purpose of such programmes has been to fend off union organization. Such organizations as I.B.M., Texas Instruments, Smith Cline Corporation, for instance, operate without collective bargaining rights and with wage increases being based largely on individual performance merit criteria. As we have seen at

Fawley, staff status initiatives can be used as part of a strategy to get rid of the unions and as a step-by-step process towards the eventual introduction of single status arrangements. Such programmes can be used to isolate workers who are strategically placed in the production process by shunting them up into more quiescent 'staff' bargaining units or, as in Fawley's case, they can be used as an inducement for workers to cede their collective bargaining rights altogether.

Esso does not appear to be alone among oil companies in pursuing a 'deunionization' strategy. Others in the industry have also shown signs of moving to a staff status employment relationship with workers. British Petroleum Chemicals attempted, for instance, in December of 1984 to secure a deal with its plastics plant in Barry, South Wales, which would give workers staff status and strip the plant's Transport and General Workers' Union of their negotiating rights. It has been reported that

> ... Union leaders fear the deal could set a precedent in the
> company and might lead to attempts to reach similar agree-
> ments at other BP Chemical sites. Some BP managers would
> like to see the deal repeated at other sites, though they accept
> that few plants are likely to display immediately the factors
> leading to its implementation at Barry. (Bassett, *The Financial
> Times*, 6 December 1984)

Other refineries have had more far-reaching success. Both Gulf and Conoco have managed to eliminate collective bargaining rights at some of their refineries.

Industrial-relations strategies devoted to anti-unionism have, for the most part, escaped the attention of industrial-relations scholars, and it is suggested that their significance has been underplayed. At least part of the reason that industrial-relations academics have refused to accord suffi-cient attention to this area can perhaps be attributed to their own tenacity to their particular frame of reference. Just as a pluralist frame of reference may have held Flanders hostage in terms of appreciating the strong 'unitarist' basis of productivity bargaining at Fawley, it may also be the case that industrial-relations academics have not fully acknowledged anti-union industrial-relations strategies for similar reasons. It is only very recently that we are seeing some attention paid to 'unitarist' and union-free industrial-relations strategies (e.g. Bassett, 1986).

Interestingly, my own findings appear to be at odds with Gallie's (1978) important work on management strategies in British Petroleum oil refineries in Britain and France. Gallie suggests that the British refineries were based on a 'semi-constitutional' strategy, while the French were based on a 'paternalist' strategy. The French management strategy took

190

care that a considerable portion of the workers' income would remain entirely within management's discretion. It sought to 'individualize' members of the work-force by making their financial status in the organization not merely a product of skill or market position, but also a result of workers' seniority in the firm and management's view of their degree of commitment and loyalty. Gallie suggests that the French paternalist system

> ... expressed a unitary conception of the firm in which problems were held to be harmoniously resolvable through discussion, and which emphasized representation of the community as a whole and denied the legitimacy of separate organized interest groups. (1978: 183)

In contrast, British management adopted a semi-constitutional strategy, the aim of which was to win the loyalty of the work-force by making sure that the terms of employment and the rules of work organization had secured the explicit consent of the workers' representatives. In the British system, the workers' salary was negotiable in its entirety, and there was no system of bonuses that tied the workers' income directly to management's good-will. According to Gallie, the British system

> ... represented a definition of relations as pluralistic, and hence an acceptance that manager/worker relations could only be stabilized on the basis of the procedures that allowed the expression of divergent points of view, and the negotiation of compromises that could obtain 'consent' and hence morally bind members to the system of organizational rules. (1978: 184)

Gallie's depiction of the British Petroleum industrial-relations strategy could not have been closer to the reformist dream. Evidence from Fawley suggests that Fawley management has itself been moving towards Gallie's French management strategy in that it has been moving gradually towards an 'individualist', as opposed to a 'collectivist', strategy. It is interesting to note that even British Petroleum, as we have seen above, has been moving towards an 'individualist' strategy, within the context of its staff status initiative.

Control over workers through the formalization of rules

It was seen in chapter 4 that productivity bargaining has been commonly associated with increased management control not only via the supposed internalization of the work-force or the extension of 'joint control', but also via the formalization of rules.

The quest for productivity

The detailed comprehensive style of the Blue Book and of many subsequent agreements did indeed lead to the formal recording of workplace rules; the Fawley case study, however, stands as a testimony to the problems associated with increased formalization and rule based control. The process of formalizing workplace rules at Fawley was seen to (1) heighten the significance of past custom and practice rules, (2) create a situation of rule proliferation, (3) be manipulated by workers and the union, (4) conflict with management attempts at worker flexibility and (5) contradict Fawley management's pleas for 'cultural' change. These are discussed below.

A number of problems associated with the formalization of rules became apparent. First the process of formalizing workplace rules was ironically seen to *heighten* the significance of past custom and practice rules. In the exercise of creating new formal rules, Fawley management found itself constantly bringing up past custom and practice rules as a reference point for working practices. Also, in the day-to-day operation of these new formal rules, management often needed to refer back to old custom and practice rules in order to define the meaning and substance of the new formal rules. The need to refer back to the many informal working practices that had been taken for granted not only at the time of creating the rules but also when maintaining them, served, in the end, to give them new significance and meaning.

Moreover, the process of rule creation served to foster rule proliferation. As specific formal rules of the productivity agreements were applied on the shop floor, it became apparent that such rules could not cope with the complex contingencies of shop-floor life. The result of this was the creation of an even more complex set of rules. After the Blue Book, for instance, it was seen that Fawley management estimated that, for every one negotiated rule three additional rules were created on the shop floor. Fawley management considered these to be restrictive, and possibly even more restrictive than past custom and practice rules (e.g. demarcation lines). It was for this reason that Fawley management began, in the post-Blue Book period, to complain that little had been accomplished in reducing demarcations and that, in the end, the Blue Book had merely served to 'shift the location of the demarcations' – from former custom and practice demarcations to newly determined formal demarcations. Fawley management had simply found itself with its hands tied to a new complex web of rules.

Another aspect of organizational life that thwarted any anticipated increase in management control through the use of formalization lay in the talent of Fawley workers to turn formal rules back on their makers. For instance, workers at Fawley were able to bog down the implementation of a particular rule by extending discussions about how a rule should be applied in various situations. As a reversal tactic, union negotiators developed productivity riders or clauses, such as training or safety clauses which could be used to defuse the substance of the agreement on the shop floor. Moreover, many of the shop stewards were proud of their ability to twist and turn key words within particular productivity provisions, such as 'augment' or 'supplement', so as to make them virtually useless. Referring to the formalization brought on in the 1960s reform period, Batstone himself notes that

> ... the general nature of rules provided considerable scope for negotiation over whether, which and how rules should be applied to particular situations; this was particularly important since new rules were sometimes contradictory and workers often attached greater legitimacy to the old rather than the new rules. (1984: 8)

Thus, the creation of a new set of formal rules, engrained in the detailed productivity bargaining process, enabled workers to *choose* those rules selectively, whether formal or informal, that were advantageous to them at the time.

The fourth problem stemming from the formalization of rules relates to the *fundamental mismatch* between Fawley management's need for increased worker flexibility on the one hand and bureaucratic, or rule based, control on the other. The kind of flexible working arrangements pursued by Fawley management implied a high degree of job discretion and, theoretically under such arrangements, workers' jobs become increasingly despecified and non-routinized. The attempt to encourage flexibility, however, made it increasingly difficult to predict the precise nature of work problems, procedures and methods required to carry out a task. By definition, flexible working (less fragmented work, with greater degrees of automony) defies the notion of control through rule. No matter how detailed, bureaucratic control simply cannot take into account the multiplicity of tasks normally associated with flexible working arrangements. The high degree of uncertainty and unpredictability of flexible working arrangements makes it difficult, if not impossible, to impose precise patterns of work behaviour through detailed and highly specific rules.

It stands to reason, therefore, that flexible work arrangements might be best controlled through non-bureaucratic normative or ideological control strategies. By their nature, bureaucratic control strategies are likely to be best suited to jobs which are precise, specific and low in discretionary content or, in the language of scientific management, those jobs which

193

have a maximum task breakdown. Management's rule based approach simply conflicted with the desire for flexible working arrangements. Fawley management was caught, therefore, in a *control conundrum* whereby the control device no longer fitted the task structure.

Finally, it was seen in the case study that the formalization aspect of productivity bargaining came into direct conflict with management's hope for a revolution in worker attitudes. It was seen that, throughout much of the productivity bargaining process, management expressed the desire to make cultural change at the workplace – to increase levels of worker commitment and consent. The attempt to win high levels of ideological commitment did not, however, prove to be compatible with management's strategy to gain more control by rule based formalization of industrial relations. The increase in rules could easily be interpreted by workers as coercive and implying a certain management distrust of labour.

The need for the codification of workplace rules stands in direct conflict, therefore, with the need to make fundamental cultural change. Fox himself argues that, in striking the Blue Book deal, Fawley management was unaware of the dynamics governing trust relations. Fox suggests that Fawley workers '... perceived management's proposals to reduce their discretion as a low trust initiative to which they countered with low trust responses ...' (1974: 129). Management's hope for 'high trust' worker responses – to be generated through appeals to the common interests of management and unions – was effectively dashed as workers came to interpret new rules as a low trust response on the part of management. As Fox suggests:

> In this study of the Fawley productivity agreements, therefore, we see another example of how changes initiated by one side which were perceived by the other as being in a low-trust direction led to greater specificity, formality, and inflexibility of rules and relations. Management's move to strengthen its control over the workgroups was countered by workgroup moves to contain and limit that enlargement of control by precise definition and rigorous policing of new frontiers. In applying that countering strategy, the workgroups showed that the degree of trust they felt towards the company was significantly less than management has supposed. (1974: 130–1)

Thus, there can be and often is a *fundamental conflict* between the objective of formalization or rule based control and the objective of ideological or normative commitment.

It could even be suggested that the formula for industrial-relations reform carried with it a *fundamental tension* between the need for high levels of commitment and the need for direct control (or to see that what needs to be done, does in fact get done). This reflects the tension between a strategy based on imposing 'control' and a strategy based on eliciting commitment. It is within this tension that the very heart of the problem of 'management' is exposed. Managers require some assurance that the work that needs to be done will actually get done and, to obtain such assurance, managers attempt to intervene in the employment relationship with various control devices (e.g. rule based control, direct supervision). By introducing such controls, however, managers run the risk of losing the spontaneous commitment and consent of the work-force. If, on the other hand, no controls are put in place, management can never be assured that what needs to be done will actually get done.

It was precisely this tension that existed between Fawley's 'detailed' and its 'open-ended' approach to productivity bargaining. The detailed agreements were based on a strategy of 'control', principally rule based control, while the open-ended agreements were based on a strategy of 'commitment'. The deep tension between these two strategies was revealed in the actual operation of the open-ended agreements. At least at Fawley, these open-ended agreements tended to be accompanied by some form of 'joint advisory' committee which was responsible for the implementation and day-to-day operation of the agreements. More often than not these committees were quick to take on a role of recording or detailing those changes which were taking place over the course of the agreement. Fawley management, anxious to record any advances made under these agreements, shifted slowly and unwittingly back to the old direct approach to productivity bargaining (and to all of the problems associated with such an approach). Fawley management's back and forth 'yo-yo' like movement from the detailed approach to the open-ended and back again, is indicative of the tension between control and commitment strategies.

The above discussion of some of the formalization problems associated with the detailed or listing approach to productivity bargaining is not presented as a kind of defence for the open-ended or indirect agreements. Indeed, as was seen at Fawley, these agreements were to have their own problems and were so loose and abstract as to be of little real value. The open-ended agreements existed more as rhetoric than in substance.

Conclusions

The three main claims that have been made in the literature about the way in which the use of productivity bargaining increases management's control over workers (internalization, joint control and formalization) were not seen to correspond to the Fawley experience. First, it was seen that Fawley management made few inroads in labour market internalization, 'chickening out' of its original pursuit of a 'high wages' strategy in the face of its inability to win higher levels of effort. It was suggested that there was a fundamental conflict between the reduction of job progression ladders and manning levels and the need for the high levels of worker commitment to achieve other productivity objectives such as flexible working. Fawley's productivity bargaining did serve, however, to reconstruct its labour market in another direction – that is through the extension of contractor labour usage. Ironically, Fawley's 'peripheral' contractor workers were seen to have labour market characteristics more closely aligned with the so-called 'core' workers or internal company workers. The contractor group appeared, in fact, to be more 'internalized' than Fawley's own workers.

Secondly, claims that the advent of productivity bargaining represented a new strategy of pluralist joint control did not apply to productivity bargaining at Fawley. It was suggested that, rather than embracing the higher ground of pluralism, management came to pursue a decidedly 'anti-union' strategy.

Although there was an absence of pluralist philosophy amongst Fawley managers, this did not mean, however, that there was no 'joint control'. Indeed, Fawley managers found themselves quite unwittingly tied to a new set of jointly determined formal rules (in addition to the old custom and practice rules).

Thirdly and finally with respect to any supposed management control advantages to the increased formalization of rules, it was seen that Fawley management actually confronted more disadvantages than advantages. A number of deep and fundamental control contradictions and conflicts were exposed. It was shown that there was a mismatch between a bureaucratic rule making device and the objective of obtaining flexible working arrangements. Finally, the deeper tension between control and commitment based strategies was explored. This deep tension was reflected in the distinction between the detailed (control based) and open-ended (commitment based) types of productivity bargaining.

12

Problems with operating a rational strategy: the relevance of the political approach

Introduction

There is much that can go wrong in designing, negotiating, implementing and maintaining a productivity agreement. The case study reveals the typical problems that can arise when translating management intentions into reality. Much of the literature from both the reformist and the radical schools assumes that the process is relatively unproblematic. Such analyses take for granted that the stated objectives of productivity agreements can be, and are, translated into operational reality with relative ease. There is an assumption that management is both fully capable of organizing and operating an effective control strategy.

This chapter develops an alternate view of productivity bargaining which highlights some of the political influences that were involved in disturbing Fawley management's productivity bargaining based strategy. The case study reveals that productivity bargaining operated within a world of 'instability and change', as a result of pressures from subordinate groups, from intra-managerial conflict, and from change in the internal and external environment. For the purposes of analysis, the productivity bargaining process has been divided into four key stages: design, negotiation, implementation and day-to-day operation. This chapter considers the various political forces that were at play at Fawley over each of these discrete phases.

Problems of design

Fawley's productivity bargaining design problems could be traced, for the most part, to the isolation of those designing the agreement from those who were to carry it out. The design phase of the many productivity agreements was, typically, restricted to either a group of senior managers or a group of senior managers and senior stewards. This isolation appears to have had two effects. First, it meant that critical bits of information

197

were excluded from consideration in the design stage. Secondly, it seemed to restrict commitment to the agreement to only those individuals who were actually involved in the design (to the extent that one accepts that participation in a change will tend to foster commitment to that change). Speaking about I.C.I.'s experience with the 'M.U.P.S.' productivity deal, Roeber noted similarly that: 'Once it was signed, the ideas that had been worked out and agreed within a small group meeting in isolation had to make their way in a world which had no part in their formulation – no *ownership*' (1975: 63).

Fawley management did increase the input of various actors, including front line supervision and local stewards, as the process evolved, but these groups were never, in the end, central to the design process. At best, they were brought in to provide input to a central design team and there was never a guarantee that input from these subsidiary groups would figure in the final design. Many supervisors were to interpret senior management's declared interest in their input as mere 'lip service'. As one supervisor put it:

> ... sometimes we were asked to come up with ideas, other times we were given training programmes on specific productivity agreements ... but somehow you always felt that no one was really interested in what we had to say. (Interview with front line supervisor)

It is perhaps not surprising that Fawley supervisors rarely had a burning commitment to the productivity bargaining process. They were described, in the post-Blue Book period, as 'lacking involvement' and as 'having a poor understanding of both the agreements and broader industrial-relations objectives'.

Perhaps most unusual was the lack of any input from the *workers* on the shop floor. It could be said that the productivity bargaining process itself effectively denies direct worker participation. It could also be said that productivity bargaining, in contrast to the current quality circle vogue, has effectively abstracted the worker out of the analysis. Productivity bargaining is, in a way, strangely élitist. Much of the focus of productivity bargaining is on *management* itself – on the need for management reorganization and education and on higher level negotiations. Great emphasis is placed on the role of experts in carefully analysing the work situation and prescribing the exact means by which productivity is to be improved (Bastone, 1984: 151). The commitment of top management is seen to be an essential starting point for the success of the process. Little is ever said about the role of the worker himself or on his direct contribution to workplace efficiency and productivity. Workers are considered to be central to the process only to the extent that they are defined as 'the problem'.

198

The relevance of the political approach

There does not appear to have been much interest in having the workers themselves actually participate in designing a solution to the 'problem'. While there was a call, as well, for union partnership in the resolution of the productivity problem, it was management, at the end of the day, that was seen to have the tools (the 'sophisticated' techniques) to resolve the problem. It is little wonder, therefore, that there was such a low level of commitment to the process where it mattered most, on the shop floor.

Seen in this light, productivity bargaining could be said to have served to legitimize management's right to manage. To the extent that those endorsing productivity bargaining repeatedly reinforced the idea that it was management and only management, through 'complex' and 'sophisticated' techniques, that could resolve the problems of the workplace, the managerial role was legitimized. As Flanders put it, 'they (management) alone are in a position to take the initiative to place it on a satisfactory foundation and to encourage the growth of more stable and co-operative relationships within the plant' (1975: 171). Productivity bargaining was, after all, first introduced at a time when management's legitimacy was being put to question.

It needs to be noted, however, that the general idea of worker participation was not always welcomed by either union representatives or by workers. In more than one deal, union stewards simply refused to participate in the design of the agreement, indicating that they preferred to let management design the agreement and to enter the process only at the negotiation stage.

The competing objectives of the design group can sometimes affect the design of any one agreement, recognizing that organizations are entities '... through which a number of often competing and ambiguous practices of calculation and assessment pass' (Thompson, 1982: 237). While optimizing the performance of one sub-group, a particular productivity provision may result in the sub-optimization of another. As Batstone suggests,

> ... managers have vested interests in particular patterns of action; the policies contained within schemes for improved productivity may conflict with other priorities or endanger various modes of intra-managerial and management–worker accommodation. (1984: 151)

The problem of designing a productivity agreement against a competing set of needs is that management can never be sure which set should be given priority. Indeed, it may often be the case that the needs that are agreed upon are not necessarily the most important but merely reflect the state of the managerial power structure (with the most powerful groups

199

defining the need, whether optimal or not). This leads us to ask questions about the nature of management structures and organization itself.

Further limits on the effectiveness of designing a rational strategy lie in the fact that the objectives of the management group will not only be competing over time but also shifting over time. The constantly competing and shifting objectives of various members of the design group makes the design process a complicated and almost impossible task.

Problems of negotiation

Even the best designed agreement is useless until such time as it is successfully negotiated. Fawley unions had a number of tactics at their disposal to defuse productivity agreements at the negotiation stage. First of all, they could and did block a deal entirely by refusing to be a party to the agreement. Fawley unions refused outright, for instance, to agree to the proposed 1974 'Pink Book' productivity agreement proposal and the 'Plan '80' productivity proposal. Both proposed agreements consumed considerable amounts of management time in the planning and design stage – only to be shelved by union refusal to be party to the agreements. As Flanders himself has noted, union representatives became increasingly disenchanted with productivity bargaining after the Blue Book deal was struck and began to impose stricter conditions on agreements (see Flanders, 1964). On a number of occasions, the Transport and General Workers' Union at Fawley placed embargos on any and all productivity bargaining (they refused, for instance, to conclude a productivity deal in the early 1970s which was meant to run parallel to the 1972 maintenance deal).

The unions could also simply refuse to accept the *specific* provisions of any one particular deal. Virtually all of Fawley management's first drafts of productivity agreements differed substantially from what was even-tually concluded. In other words, there was always a watering down or erosion of the terms of agreement from when they were first drawn up. The length of time taken by Fawley management to negotiate the productivity deals varied, with some of the agreements 'on the table' for a year; this suggests a 'watering down' of the original proposals. It is partly for this reason that Fawley managers were to come to the conclusion that '... progress could only be made at a reasonably acceptable rate'. In fact, as a result of the 'watering down' of management objectives over the negotiation period some Fawley managers started to question the value of the agreements in the first place. As one manager put it,

    ... by the end of the negotiation period many of us began to

wonder whether the agreement was actually worth it. By that
time we had spent so much time and effort on the deal that
many of us were willing to sign the agreement even if it was far
less than we intended. (Interview with Fawley manager)

It would appear to be the case that there were certain advantages to
managers concluding a deal even if it were one that had been substantially
'watered down'. At the design stage many of the productivity agreements
had already received Esso U.K. Ltd. board approval and this meant that
local Fawley managers were under certain pressure to conclude an
agreement, if only to meet the expectations of the board. One manager
suggested that

once we had obtained a go-ahead from London, we were
forced to deliver a deal no matter what it looked like. A
proposal to the board for a productivity deal was like any
other proposal. Once it had gone that high, you knew you had
to come up with something. (Interview with Fawley manager)

An extreme example of workers blocking management proposals at
Fawley can be found in the refusal of the craft workers, in the 1975
maintenance deal, to agree to allow process operators to engage in craft
related work. This was done even though management had, just a few
months earlier, successfully negotiated an agreement with process workers
to engage in craft related work.

If, on the other hand, a specific provision itself cannot be blocked from
an agreement, unions can at least seek to soften or dilute the power of the
provision. This can be done by injecting various qualifying clauses; for
instance, that certain types of flexible working can only be carried out
'once a man had been fully trained on the equipment and that such
training had been properly logged'. The qualifying phrases of 'Training
Ability and Safety' injected into both the 1972 and 1982 maintenance
agreements were continually evoked by workers to hold back flexible
working objectives.

Unions themselves can, of course, inject into the agreement their own
provisions or safeguard clauses. In Fawley's case, such clauses related to
'mutuality', no-redundancy and termination clauses. Mutuality clauses
were meant to keep the agreement open and subject to continual negotiation. Sometimes Fawley's mutuality clauses came in the form of an explicit
statement, such as in the 1975 maintenance agreement which contained
the following wording: 'This agreement ... may be amended by the
mutual agreement between the companies and the maintenance unions
...' In other instances, mutuality clauses came in a less formal manner, in
the form of a commitment to form advisory or joint consultative bodies to

monitor the progress of an agreement. The 1982 maintenance enabling agreement, for instance, contained the provision that

> an appropriate body (or bodies) will be set up comprising of trade unions and management representatives, whose purpose will be to review at regular intervals the application of that part of the agreement headed 'full utilization of capabilities'. The terms of reference of this committee are:
> (a) . . . to monitor the operation of the safe-guards contained in this section . . .

These 'mutuality' clauses meant that the unions could continually put to question the substance of particular provisions.

As well as the mutuality clause, the unions also made great use of termination clauses which placed considerable constraint on management action. Unions could either threaten to terminate an agreement as a bargaining tactic to soften the 'hard edges' of an agreement or they could actually drop the deal if they should feel that the terms were no longer acceptable. Fawley productivity agreements usually had a safeguard that either party could terminate an agreement with three months' notice and any one signatory would be sufficient to terminate the agreement.

It should be noted also that once a productivity deal has been struck there is nothing to prevent unions from 'revaluing' the agreement at subsequent wage negotiations. For instance, in those years when there was no productivity bargaining, it was commonplace for Fawley unions to attempt to justify higher than normal wage increases on the basis that the terms of the original agreement were no longer 'fair'. The 1984 annual wage negotiations in the process department resulted in a special productivity bonus that related back to the 1981 process productivity deal. If Fawley management did not acquiesce to such claims, then the unions typically would evoke a temporary sanction on the productivity deal.

Much like other types of bargaining, it is characteristic of productivity bargaining that the process does not end at the bargaining table; it is inevitably extended to the shop floor where agreements are subject to a continual and never ending set of informal negotiations. It is here that the 'work' side of the wage–work bargain is subject to continual renegotiation (in terms of what is deemed to be 'fair' by workers and 'efficient' by supervisors). This leads us into the next stage of the productivity bargaining process, that of implementation.

Problems of implementation

The problems associated with implementing an organizational change project have been well documented in the organizational theory literature (see, for instance, Pressman and Wildavsky, 1973). Basically, each of these problems is applicable to the productivity bargaining process. There is the problem, for instance, of 'managerial fatigue' resulting from the long and protracted process of designing and negotiating the agreement itself. In the Fawley case, as we have noted above, many of the agreements took in excess of a year to design and negotiate, leaving the management team in a declared 'state of exhaustion'. As one manager put it:

> By the time you've put one of these agreements together you really don't want anything to do with it any longer. You just want to wipe your hands of the whole shooting match. (Interview with Fawley manager)

This fatigue phenomenon has been noted by Gottschalk and Towers, who suggest that productivity bargaining is often a long drawn out process whereby the parties to the agreement '. . . may be too exhausted as a result of the process to actually take advantage of the agreement' (1969: ii). Pettigrew also suggests that I.C.I.'s management experienced such a problem:

> Having taken so long to gain acceptance of a need for change, having delegated the design of the vehicle for change to a small group, and now having assembled the political will to act in the productivity area, ICI now found themselves with a beached whale, a strategy they could not implement. (1985: 102)

This waning of energy in the implementation phase can have disastrous results, especially when management resources get shifted from productivity bargaining priorities into other areas. Fawley's training department, for instance, complained bitterly to senior management after the introduction of the Blue Book, claiming that not enough resources and energy were being directed to the training effort. A concerted training follow up was required to realize certain flexibility provisions since flexible working only becomes a practical proposition where the workers affected have been given the proper training and possess the necessary skills to carry out the tasks required of them. The training tasks related to Fawley's productivity agreements always fell under the category of implementation – precisely that phase in which senior management interest in the process was starting to wane.

It is important to note as well that, at least for Fawley, there were marked status and power differences between the designers and implementors of the productivity agreements. The designers were generally made up of certain senior managers who were considered 'the power brokers' in the organization, while the implementors – principally front line supervision and the training department – were of much lower status, lacking in both power and resources. Because the implementation of change is inevitably a politically charged activity, involving, for instance, the break-up of coalitions and groups and the alteration of time-honoured traditions, implementation appears to be a task more suited to the 'power-brokers' than to those situated lower down the organizational hierarchy. The training department's own staff was willing to admit that 'it is a forgotten department within the refinery'. This seems hardly the department upon which to rely to launch a major training programme to break up such practices as long-lasting and cherished job demarcations.

The waning of energy at the implementation stage appears to have resulted from more than mere managerial fatigue; it seems to have been a natural part of the cycle of change, with the 'honeymoon' days of design and negotiation being replaced by 'humdrum' and boredom of the implementation phase. Looking at Fawley, it would almost appear part of human nature to get excited about a project, to start it up at a cosmetic level and then to let it slide. Like a child with a new Christmas toy, interest in productivity bargaining waned after the first few spins of the top. It is the rare manager who thrives on the humdrum of an extended implementation process (and perhaps even rarer – an organization which rewards such humdrum activity!). Roeber has described this cycle in terms of I.C.I.'s own weekly staff agreement:

> The energy level of the programme ran down. Interest flagged once the first discussions were completed. Managers having satisfied the requirements of their supervisors in introducing the programme turned their interest back to the day-to-day problems of management; unions turned their energies to issues where further concrete benefits could be obtained. (1975: 210)

There is, of course, also the problem of communicating excitement and enthusiasm 'down the line'. While the designers and negotiators of a productivity deal may become excited and imbued with a newly found spirit of change, it is quite another thing to communicate this excitement into the yard. At Fawley this problem appeared to have been particularly acute for open-ended or indirect agreements focussing on worker 'spirit' and 'attitudes'. This certainly was the case for the 1972 progressive approach agreement in which senior management and stewards had locked themselves into lofty discussions about the philosophy and mechanics of cultural change only to find, during the implementation and operation of the agreement, that '... no one really had a clue what we were trying to do' (interview with Fawley manager). The consciousness raising activity had been restricted to a small group of managers and senior stewards, and rarely went beyond the smoke-filled negotiating rooms.

The distance of the implementors from the designers and negotiators creates problems with respect to the actual understanding of the agreements, especially in terms of implementing both the 'letter' and the 'intent' of the agreement. Many of the front line supervisors at Fawley suggested that the senior stewards and branch officers often had a better understanding of the agreement (since they had been party to the negotiation process) and, as a result, would defer to them for advice over the interpretation of the agreement. The notion of 'intent' came to be used by Fawley stewards to control the interpretation of agreements. Stewards would sometimes suggest to front line supervisors that they had not been at the negotiating table and therefore did not appreciate the spirit of the agreement. This problem may be more common than imagined. Parker et al.'s study of productivity bargaining in eleven firms found that

> ... insufficient attention was given in most of the eleven firms to preparing managers, workpeople and their representatives for the changes introduced. Even where some attempt was made to explain the main points of the new arrangements it became clear, as the changes were implemented, that considerable misunderstandings remained. (1971: 69)

Smith notes a similar problem with the steel industry 'Green Book' productivity deal:

> Many foremen, and some of their immediate supervisors, claimed that their shop stewards had been better informed of the progress of negotiations and therefore understood the Green Book agreement far better than themselves. This point was made in another way when one trade union official said that it had taken six months for junior management to get to know the mates' agreement. (1971: 411)

The successful implementation of any agreement requires that there exist a good fit between the provisions of the agreement and the operating contingencies of the shop floor. In most cases such a fit is less than perfect as the rules and provisions which are generated by productivity deals are time and situation specific and as circumstances alter, certain provisions become progressively less significant. Management controls tend to have an internal focus, but pressure on controls can also be properly seen as existing outside the organization. The refining industry has been especially prone to change over the last twenty years, and this has meant that many of the past agreements at Fawley (especially the listing type agreements) have in effect been made redundant by some change or other (in spite of the fact that Fawley management had already paid for these agreements).

Fawley management was itself to note in 1974 that '... our agreements are somewhat confusing in that a number of areas within them are outdated and not relevant to today's situation'. This means that management may pay for some provision today which will be redundant tomorrow. Management cannot, of course, simply 'roll back' wages to adjust for redundant provisions, but must continue to pay for these changes (for ever more) through inflated base wage rates.

The Industrial Relations Review and Report has itself pointed to this problem:

> ... some companies have found that the pace of technical change is now so rapid, and impacts so profoundly on working practices from year to year, that simply to list a set of working practices one year can serve to trap them in a time band. By the next year the technology may have changed so significantly that the 'new' practices become outdated and are seen as restricting efficiency. (I.R.R.R., Report 316, 20 March 1984: 6)

Finally, another difficulty associated with implementation is the problem of pacing. For example, it may be tempting to implement the agreement too quickly and harshly, thereby risking a backlash from workers; or too slowly, thereby risking that the programme peters out or fades away. The Fawley case study suggests that both extremes had occurred at different times, each resulting in the demise of various agreements. In the case of certain flexibility initiatives, for instance, some over-zealous supervisors pushed vigorously for the implementation of one particular flexibility item and subsequently lost worker cooperation in other areas.

In another case, a Fawley supervisor noted that some supervisors '... tried to rush the implementation of the agreement and would force-fit provisions which just wouldn't make any sense' (interview with front line supervisor). Another supervisor claimed that this 'force-fitting' of provisions sometimes reached the absurd, thus jeopardizing the credibility of the deal: 'We would have pipefitters doing welding jobs and welders doing electrical work. Everyone would be working outside of their trade; but no one was working efficiently. This just didn't reflect well on the shop floor' (interview with Fawley supervisor). Flanders himself noted an incident at Fawley whereby supervisors '... had possibly acted over-zealously to enforce the clause in the new agreement which abolished washing time' (1964: 144).

206

The relevance of the political approach

Problems of day-to-day operation

While the problems of implementing organizational change have been reasonably well developed in the organizational theory literature, considerably less attention has been placed on the problems associated with the day-to-day operation of an organizational change programme. At Fawley this is the phase of the productivity bargaining process which was perhaps the most difficult phase for the management group, not least because – once the original excitement and enthusiasm associated with the design, negotiation and implementation of the agreement had waned – management began to pay less attention to the actual operation of the agreement.

Productivity provisions can be slowly and progressively altered during the every-day operation of the agreement. This alteration recognizes that the content of any one productivity provision will not be stable but will be open to day-to-day negotiations. There are rich enough academic traditions which have accounted for this process. Proponents of 'negotiated order theory' (Strauss et al., 1963; Bucher and Stelling, 1969; Benson, 1977; Day and Day, 1977) have all argued that organizational arrangements are continuously being negotiated through the day-to-day encounters of participants. In Benson's language:

> The arrangements reached through negotiation are seldom stable and often represent merely surface agreements which mean different things to different people. The working relationships between occupational groups, for example, are developed in this way and are gradually modified through ongoing interactions and periodic crises. (1977: 12)

Similarly, in industrial-relations terms, Batstone et al. have noted:

> The signing of a formal agreement is only a starting point: case law has to be developed and this occurs through debates and disputes, which serve ultimately both to develop a consensus upon the interpretation of specific clauses, and a network of informal agreements and custom and practice which make the agreement meaningful in particular contexts. (1978: 52–3)

What this kind of an analysis implies is that the relationship between formal written rules and actual behaviour cannot simply be assumed but must be investigated empirically.

In addition to the tampering of productivity provisions by workers, various sections of the management group may also come to subvert the content of the provisions. In this instance, various management groups enter the subversion process either because the provisions are too restrictive and conflict with production demands or because management needs to relax a provision in order to command cooperation and consent from workers. Productivity provisions may, therefore, be interpreted by management personnel as dysfunctional and requiring 'joint tampering'. A classic example of this can be found in one of Purcell's case studies. In one company he studied, the detailed labour flexibility clauses which had been agreed earlier actually had to be relaxed by management during a moment of crisis in order to achieve the most efficient level of performance (1981: 178). The agreement needed, in other words, to be tampered with (or, as in this case, actually ignored) by management to attain an efficient level of performance. This was a common occurrence at Fawley during major 'shut-down' maintenance work. As one steward put it to me,

> ... during shut-down work we all muck in. We're working at the highest pace possible for three to four weeks. All of the rules are broken. We just go out and do what's right. (Interview with shop steward)

Management objectives may vary between management functions. A classic case of conflict in managerial objectives at Fawley related to the different priorities of improving the 'health and safety' statistics (Fawley has lagged behind other Esso refineries in this area), while at the same time striving for increased flexible working. It was safety regulations that often acted as the factor limiting Fawley management from moving towards more flexible working. Fawley workers were always, for instance, able to make reference to management safety programmes when discussing whether or not a new flexible working practice was viable.

The objectives and needs of front line supervisors were also often at odds with the requirements of the various productivity agreements. Front line supervisors at Fawley admitted, for instance, that they particularly disliked the administrative controls put in place (e.g. various log books) to ensure that the productivity provisions were indeed being implemented. Such controls were considered to be too time-consuming and cumbersome, as well as impeding work. These controls, in the form of log books, '... were not always filled in properly or not completed at all' (interview with Fawley supervisor).

There was also the problem of the sheer weight or volume of the agreements themselves. In spite of the training programmes put on for Fawley supervisors to update their understanding of various agreements, supervisors were still not able to cope with the complexity of the various agreements. It was partly for this reason that many supervisors were to put the deals 'in the drawer' and to continue to rely on past custom and practice rules – rules with which they were most familiar and comfortable. It was far easier for supervisors to make a case based on custom and practice rules (rules which both parties understood) than on a set of rules which were foreign and new. It is little wonder that one supervisor commented: 'Sometimes I think that all the different productivity agreements just served to confuse us. Many of us simply forgot the agreements and got on with our jobs' (interview with front line supervisor). Custom and practice rules, as a result, never disappeared but coexisted – sometimes in an uneasy way – with formal productivity bargaining based rules. This situation of two conflicting sets of rules opened up the possibility for workers to choose selectively between these, depending on their particular interests at the time.

One senior manager at Fawley claimed, further, that the productivity agreements themselves were sometimes seen by Fawley management as exposing weaknesses in supervisory planning ability. As this manager put it:

> Our open-ended agreements have meant that supervisors have now to be more sophisticated in their planning. When we operate out of a rigid set of trade demarcations our supervisors can always hide around these. With the restrictions removed supervisors are left with no more excuses. (Interview with Fawley manager)

Supervisors, in other words, could no longer blame job demarcations as a reason for a slow-down on a job. Demarcations in this sense were functional for supervisors themselves, as they gave supervisors an excuse for poor production results.

It is also important to note that the actual ratio of supervisors to workers was in decline over the years. This drop in the supervisory ratio made it increasingly difficult for supervisors to implement the various agreements properly. Faced with time constraints, supervisors invariably looked to the 'tried and true' old ways and methods of doing a job.

Supervisors at Fawley also had an interest in subverting agreements in order simply to keep peace on the shop floor. As one supervisor put it: 'In the end we were not pushing them (productivity deals). Management would always back down when faced with a confrontation. If they didn't, then they risked having the whole agreement being tossed away' (interview with front line supervisor). The extent to which supervisors were willing to back off from conflict situations was reflected in the following remarks by a non-craft maintenance steward:

> Craft workers were trained on lorries and rigging equipment and could run this gear just like our own men. To stop them from using this gear we just used to say to supervisors that we wanted a rigger to do the job and the supervisor would come

up with one. This still happens today. (Interview with branch officer)

Front line supervisors were often really only interested in the cosmetic implementation of the successive productivity deals. Thereby they could satisfy senior management that the agreements were indeed being implemented, while at the same time maintaining peace on the shop floor. The front-line supervisory group became particularly adept, therefore, at operating simultaneously on two fronts – appeasing management with cosmetic implementation (for instance, with the fudging of reports on the success of the agreements) and the striking of 'informal bargains' on the shop floor with workers, in order to take the harder edges off the agreements.

Conclusions

This chapter has sought to develop the relevance of the political approach in understanding Fawley's productivity bargaining based strategy. Complex political processes were highlighted at the design, negotiation, implementation and day-to-day phases of the productivity bargaining process. Productivity bargaining was defined in terms of instability and change. Such instability and change was seen to result from pressures from subordinate groups, intra-managerial conflict, and from changes in the internal and external environment.

13

The perpetuation of productivity bargaining: the relevance of the symbolic approach

Introduction

Why did Fawley persist in the use of productivity bargaining when, at least at the rational level, the agreements failed to attain their objectives? Why, in other words, did productivity bargaining come to form the very essence of Fawley's industrial-relations strategy over twenty-five years, when it was so clear that the stated objectives of the productivity agreements were far from being realized? What was behind Fawley management's reason for clinging to productivity bargaining?

The opportunity that productivity bargaining presented in terms of circumventing various incomes policies over the years cannot itself be seen as the driving force, since Fawley engaged in productivity bargaining both within and outside of incomes policy periods. In fact, Fawley management maintained that the most significant productivity deals were struck outside those periods when a productivity rider could secure wage increases that were higher than the ceiling imposed by the government. It is clear from the case study that productivity bargaining was being perpetuated for reasons other than incomes policy.

This chapter discusses some of the hidden reasons behind the continued use of productivity bargaining at Fawley. It is argued that productivity bargaining at Fawley had a deeper set of meanings than those laid out at the rational level, that is at the level of stated objectives, and that it is only within this deeper set of meanings that the perpetuation of productivity bargaining at Fawley begins to make sense. These deeper meanings relate mostly to the important array of symbolic functions that productivity bargaining played at Fawley. The symbolic significance of organizational behaviour has frequently been bypassed. Researchers have, for the most part, simply ignored '. . . the metaphoric and symbolic bases of organized life that create and sustain . . . organizational ideas' (Smircich and Stubbart, 1985: 727).

So far, this research has mainly been directed at the 'rational', objec-

211

tively identifiable processes associated with productivity bargaining. This focus upon the 'rational' has, for the most part, precluded a deeper investigation into productivity bargaining in terms of any underlying symbolic basis, that is, in terms of its function as 'myth', 'ritual' and 'rhetoric'. It is argued in this chapter that productivity bargaining at Fawley had more than just 'rational' objectives; it had also become imbued with powerful symbolic functions.

Others who have found limited value to the productivity bargaining experience have restricted their research to the rational level of analysis. For example, in summing up I.C.I.'s experience with productivity bargaining, Roeber stated: 'The management got their agreement, or a form for it; the craft unions got their pay increases. Neither side got much else' (1975: 233). This may be true at the purely rational level, but it is possible to argue that both sides did, in fact, get something else. At least at Fawley this appears to have been the case. This 'something else', it is argued, relates to the cultural or symbolic consequences of the productivity bargaining process. In fact, the case study research at Fawley reveals that productivity bargaining was a richly symbolic activity. In order to understand the meaning of productivity bargaining it is, therefore, necessary to uncover its symbolic significance.

A symbolic frame of analysis suggests that organizational structures and activities may have meaning and significance above and beyond the purely rational functions normally attributed to them. The symbolic frame of analysis redirects our attention away from overtly stated goals and rational objectives, seeking instead to uncover the hidden messages and meanings of apparently rational action and processes. The symbolic approach suggests that organizational phenomena may have a complex set of double meanings – some readily observable while others are hidden or tucked away.

While certain management activities at Fawley were failing at the rational level, they were still providing important hidden functions at the deeper symbolic level. This would suggest that, even if management programmes and initiatives do not produce concrete results or attain their stated goals or objectives, they may still be important in other ways – for example, as arenas for negotiating new understandings and meanings, as devices to convey important messages or impressions, or as a means by which to create or maintain legitimacy. It is possible, therefore, that various management activities and initiatives which appear to have failed, when interpreted in terms of their ostensible rational purposes, may in fact be logical with regard to their deeper symbolic functions.

At Fawley, while productivity bargaining was failing at the rational level, it was a logical and predictable process in view of its symbolic

212

functions. In this chapter it is argued that productivity bargaining at Fawley was used (1) as an important symbol in the management of uncertainty and crisis, (2) to give various groups (Exxon company board, U.K. board, the government, Fawley employees and the general public) the *impression* that 'something useful was being done', (3) as a vehicle for the enhancement of careers (both within line management and within the personnel function).

Productivity bargaining as a symbol for the management of uncertainty and crisis

It is possible to argue that productivity bargaining was used in a *ritualistic* way by Fawley management to deal with organizational uncertainty and crisis. During the years from 1960 to 1985, Fawley management was buffeted by a series of business crises and, moreover, plagued with a continual and apparently unresolvable labour productivity problem (compared with other Exxon refineries). These problems presented themselves, in other words, as 'complex', 'mysterious' and 'random'.

It is suggested here that productivity bargaining at Fawley came to be institutionalized as a ritualistic 'way out' of a crisis. As Schein suggests, an organization's culture is, in part, a defence mechanism to avoid uncertainty and anxiety, pointing out that it helps to '... manage the unmanageable and explain the unexplainable' (1985a: 31 and 1985b: 80). Schein argues that myths and stories tend to occur around critical events in an organization's history, especially events that are difficult to explain or justify because they are not under organizational control. He notes, for instance, that certain management techniques and processes often tend to be viewed as 'the way' to get out of trouble. He cites the 'task force' under the leadership of a 'heroic' manager and the use of 'high-powered' consultants as ritualistic 'ways out' of crises.

Schein also argues that '... when a situation arises that is similar to a prior crisis, it will arouse anxiety and cause the group to do what it did before in order to reduce the anxiety' (1985a: 24). Ritualistic ways of thinking and feeling are evoked in order to avoid, as much as possible, the reliving of the discomfort and pain of past crises. According to Schein, solutions to external and internal problems that have 'worked' in the past come to be '... taught to new members as the correct way to perceive, think about and feel in relation to those problems' (1985a: 19–20). Similarly, in a study of organizational crises, Nystrom and Starbuck (1984) found that crises often result precisely because managers cannot unlearn old ways of seeing the world; they just keep 'solving' problems in the same way, clinging even harder to habits when confronted with poor results.

It is possible to suggest that the productivity bargaining process came to be Fawley management's ritualistic way out of its 'irresolvable' productivity problem. The source of Fawley's productivity bargaining ritual was, of course, the Blue Book deal. At the time, the Blue Book was heralded as a major revolution in the management of industrial relations and, as a result, it had a powerful effect on British management. It is clear from my field work that the impact of the Blue Book had an even more powerful effect on Fawley managers themselves. In each of my interviews with Fawley managers, the Blue Book deal was invariably raised by them as a point of discussion. As the interviews progressed, I developed great interest in noting the point in time at which the Blue Book deal was brought up by the interviewee. In many instances, I did not have long to wait as, more often than not, it was raised at the outset of the interview. It became clear, early in the interview process, that the Blue Book deal had been enshrined as a deep and powerful myth within the organization.

The Blue Book fits the definitional requirements of myth as '... myth always refers to events alleged to have taken place long ago' which 'explains the present and the past as well as the future' (Lévi-Strauss, 1963: 208–9). For Lévi-Strauss, the substance of a myth lies in 'the *story* which it tells' (1963: 208–9). It exists as a type of extended metaphor, with the implicit assertion that 'the story told in the myth stands in a metaphoric relationship to real events' (Pondy, 1983: 159). Moreover, myths also serve '... to legitimate the present in terms of a perhaps glorious past, and to explain away the pressures for change which may exist from the discrepancies between what is happening and what ought to be happening' (Pettigrew, 1985: 44–5).

The Blue Book clearly represented for Fawley management something of a 'glorious past'. The celebrity status which was accorded the Blue Book meant that productivity bargaining had become engrained within the management culture as 'the way of doing things'. When confronted with a crisis or problem, Fawley managers came naturally to refer back to the Blue Book era, to the days when all eyes were on Fawley and when it was thought that Fawley 'could do no wrong'. Whether or not the objectives of the Blue Book were actually carried out (and the case study has demonstrated that they were not) was not important; what was important was the extent to which the Blue Book was thought or believed to be successful, for, as Pondy notes, a myth '... evokes rich and emotional detail that bypasses logic' (1983: 163). 'Furthermore since, in myth, the ordinary rules of logic are suspended, anomaly and contradiction ... can be resolved within the mythical explanation' (Pondy, 1983: 163).

Thus, the Blue Book paved the way for productivity bargaining to become a key ritual or ceremony for subsequent Fawley managers when dealing with crises and problems. One manager even suggested that '... Ever since the Blue Book, Fawley has been known as highly innovative. This ethos of innovation has simply perpetuated itself over the years' (interview with Fawley manager). In this regard, Maanen and Barley have noted that there may be a natural set of forces leading to a patterned behaviour amongst managers:

> ... as people move toward the higher ranks of an organiza-
> tion's hierarchy, it becomes more difficult to know what others
> consider to be desirable performance. In doubt about what is
> expected and therefore fearful about standing out in the crowd,
> newly appointed upper-level managers sometimes play it safe
> by emulating perspective behaviours already prevalent amongst
> their newfound colleagues. (1985: 46)

While productivity bargaining itself was to take different shapes and forms over time, the design, negotiation and implementation rituals were fundamentally similar – a 'crack' or 'top flight' senior management team would be assembled, 'brain-storming' and 'creative-problem' solving sessions would ensue, 'answers' and 'solutions' to the productivity prob-lem would be identified, followed by negotiations with union representa-tives. Out of this process a neat and well-packaged productivity deal or 'book' would be produced. Finally, certain commitments were made about the importance of good follow-up and implementation.

The ritualistic nature of the whole process was revealed most vividly in the 'packaging' of the deal itself. It was critically important to the whole process that a concrete and tangible 'book' be produced. Whether the deal that was being struck was a complex detailed fifty-page agreement or a three-page open-ended agreement was not important – each of the deals was to be neatly presented in the old Blue Book style. Stapled and covered, the deals stood as concrete affirmations that action had been taken. The colour coding of the various agreements was critical to this whole process. There were to be 'Blue Books', 'Orange Books' and 'Pink Books'. Even if a particular productivity deal was not, at the outset, formally assigned a colour code by management – such deals soon came, informally, to be referred to in 'colour' terms (the 1981 process productivity agreement came to be known, for instance, as the 'Yellow Book'). The packaging and colour coding of the agreements were essential parts of the ritual. The content and successful implementation of the deal had become less important than the ritual of 'packaging' which connected Fawley's past with the present.

Over the twenty-five years covered by the case study, the fundamental principle of productivity bargaining was always to remain sacrosanct at Fawley. While Fawley managers would, themselves, criticize particular *aspects* of past or former deals – the fundamental principle of productivity bargaining itself was never put to question. Productivity bargaining existed as a 'sacred totem', a totem that could be touched up with paint, adjusted slightly – but never taken down, never totally dismissed or rejected.

Fawley managers, when faced with a series of business difficulties such as long-term decline in demand for refined oil and continually poor standings in the international league tables, repeatedly turned to productivity bargaining to relieve their own personal anxiety as well as the anxiety of superiors and subordinates. It is perhaps no coincidence that productivity bargaining was seen to have the '... character of a new religion' (McKersie, 1966: i). According to Schein, there also appear to be various functions associated with an organization's reliance on past formulae and ways of doing things:

> As the founder's prescriptions for how to do things are
> adopted, they help to stabilize cognitively how to deal with the
> new world and they help to structure the initially unstructured
> relationships among the new members. (1985b: 222)

In another way, Bolman and Deal have noted that 'a good story provides a way of responding to an unpleasant fact' (1984: 158). It appears that, at Fawley, productivity bargaining was used as a 'good story', as a means of creating various desirable *impressions*. It is to this aspect of the symbolic significance of productivity bargaining that we now turn.

Productivity bargaining: the management of impressions

It has been noted that much of organizational symbolism is concerned with the 'management of impressions'. Morgan et al. note, for instance, that

> ... organizations are pre-eminently involved with the business
> of impression management, in relation to the general public,
> other corporations, consumers, employees, government, and
> other significant actors capable of influencing their well being.
> Individuals too are required to produce and sustain appropriate
> symbolic images of their relation to 'the organization', their
> managers, colleagues and the like. Modifying the words of the

well-known song, the theatrical approach to organizational symbolism suggests very clearly that 'There's no business *without* showbusiness.' (1983: 20)

At Fawley, it would appear that management used productivity bargaining to create various impressions simultaneously, on three fronts: with regard (1) to its U.K. and parent company boards, (2) to its employees and (3) to the general public. In this way, productivity bargaining came to be used by Fawley management as a *rhetorical* device to disguise its inability to manage the productivity problem. It became a way and means of reaffirming or validating management's legitimacy to manage in the eyes of both the board and of employees.

Due to both periodic business crises and an apparently intractable labour productivity problem, Fawley found itself under (almost continual) pressure from both its own U.K. board and parent company boards to improve productivity and efficiency. Fawley management was able to, and did, use the productivity bargaining process as a 'smoke screen' to take the heat off the board's various mandates to 'buck up'. Productivity bargaining appears to have been used in this way, both unconsciously and consciously. Its conscious manifestation was revealed in what was referred to by many supervisors as a 'cycle of good news reporting'. Many supervisors who were interviewed suggested that, at the time, there was a kind of subtle pressure placed on them to report back good news on a productivity deal even though little progress was taking place. Whenever early formal evaluations of the agreements took place, they were often filled with platitudes about the success of the agreement. The harsher realities of the failure of the agreements were only made known in later documentation. One manager explained this 'cycle of good news reporting' in this way:

> It's the nature of our organization that we adopted an orientation of success reporting. Nobody wants to hear bad news in this organization. Especially those people who were directly involved in the deals. This success reporting ended up creating some tall tales. (Interview with Fawley manager)

As could be expected, it was precisely these platitudes and positive assessments which were included in most of the reports that were fed back to the U.K. board, as a testimony that the 'problem' had now in fact been resolved.

One supervisor explained the audit process in this way:

> We knew that the agreements would be important for senior management and therefore made some attempts at implement-

217

ing them. Some of our supervisors even began to report success even if we weren't having any. (Interview with Fawley supervisor)

Another supervisor explained this process in more calculative terms as follows: 'The boys upstairs needed to hear good news. My career and job was on the line if I couldn't provide them with what they wanted . . . so, as a result, I gave them what they wanted to hear' (interview with Fawley supervisor).

A senior manager himself admitted that 'good news reporting' was, in fact, a key feature of the overall process. Referring to a recent deal, this manager put it this way:

> When we go to the board looking for approval to do a produc-
> tivity deal, the board gives us the money with the expectation
> that they'll get something in return. In order to protect our
> own integrity we hardly could report back that the deal back-
> fired on us. (Interview with Fawley manager)

It is interesting to note, as well, that the unions often themselves collaborated in the 'good news reporting' process. As one branch officer put it:

> I used to tell the stewards that we shouldn't slag the deals too
> much in front of management because if management sus-
> pected that we were not working hard or according to the spirit
> of the productivity agreement, then – when the next pay nego-
> tiations came around – management would be reluctant to give
> us a big wage award. If we told management that the deal was
> working well and we were working hard, then we could always
> ask for more money when the current rates expire. (Interview
> with branch officer)

As many of the productivity agreements were based on phased or instalment payments (i.e. to be made only after certain objectives had been achieved), there was even greater incentive for unions and workers alike to report good news about the agreements.

The effect of productivity bargaining on working practices came increasingly to take on a mythical quality. What was being reported back to the board was not the 'hard truth' (of little, if any, change) but rather that great progress was being made. This 'cycle of good news reporting', therefore, served to relieve some of the pressures placed on Fawley management from the top by assuring the board that there were indeed clear answers to important questions and clear solutions to difficult problems. It would also appear plausible, although there is no firm evidence of this, that the U.K. board itself used upcoming productivity deals to 'take the heat off' any pressures from the American Exxon board. By telling the board of the parent company that its faltering Fawley Refinery was about to negotiate, or in the midst of negotiating a new productivity deal, the U.K. board was able to assert that it was on top of the problem and that the problem of poor productivity was indeed being dealt with.

It is argued here that, for many levels of the organization, productivity bargaining had become a ceremony which 'beamed' the message to interested audiences that 'all was alright'. The activity served as a ritual to provide reassurance. As Morgan et al. have suggested:

> Many organizations consciously attempt to create complex symbol systems which are intended to signify the desirability of engaging in rigorous patterns of rational, instrumental and pragmatic action. Symbols reinforcing the pursuit of excellence, achievement, aggressiveness, competitiveness and intense commitment to organizational ends provide good examples. While intended by management to symbolize the characteristics of success, and to encourage the pursuit of success, for some organizational members they may stand as a symbolic structure which expresses their perceived inferiority and inability to cope. (1983: 13)

Productivity bargaining, therefore, can be seen to have served as a self-justification mechanism for management. If real productivity gains could not be achieved, then Fawley management could at least use the rhetoric of productivity bargaining to justify its bad standing to the U.K. and parent company boards. In this sense, management's claims and exhortations about being involved in a productivity deal came to be more important than the results themselves.

Productivity bargaining also provided Fawley management with a convenient communication tool which could be used to develop a rationale for, or to defend, desired action. In this sense, it served as a valuable ruse for management action. Like the rhetoric of bureaucratic control, productivity bargaining presented itself as '... highly expressive language that constructs and legitimizes managerial prerogatives in terms of a rational goal-directed image of organizational effectiveness' (Gowler and Legge, 1983: 198).

The productivity bargaining process provided management with a 'pseudo-scientific' language with which to justify to workers what they would consider to be unpalatable aims and objectives. These aims could be disguised under a wider rationale of efficiency and productivity. In other words, Fawley management was able to point to the anonymous objectives of 'efficiency and productivity' rather than to its own particular logic, when attempting change. Through the productivity bargaining process, management could argue that it was caught in a battle 'with the march of progress' against the ever-increasing efficiency of other Exxon refineries.

Thus, productivity bargaining could be, and indeed was, used as a means of deflecting blame away on to the neutral and intangible forces of progress. This hidden function of the technique was perhaps most evident with reductions in manning levels where productivity bargaining could be seen to provide some form of pseudo-scientific rationale. The use of productivity bargaining as a rhetorical device tended to increase at Fawley as time went by (although productivity bargaining also provided the monetary inducement to effect reductions in manning levels). Many of the later productivity deals, for instance, were to be accompanied by substantial management manifestos outlining the philosophy and rationale behind the agreement.

Fawley management was also able to use productivity bargaining as a means of reaffirming managerial legitimacy with its own workers. Each productivity deal served as an attempt to signal to workers that management 'was in control' and that the refinery would be saved from financial ruin. In this way, productivity bargaining can be seen as a device for buttressing management's legitimacy within the context of organizational difficulties.

As the case study has shown, however, management had far from total success in gaining employee consent through the use of sophisticated rhetoric. Workers did not merely 'swallow the eyewash' (to use Cliff's term, 1970: 142) but often took this rhetoric with a 'pinch of salt'. Still, it must be recognized that the propaganda machine, which productivity bargaining was so much about, did at least provide management with a set of 'arguments' to help justify various programmes.

Yet another level at which productivity bargaining was used to create desirable impressions was with the general public. Fawley management was the author and owner of the historic Blue Book deal and, as such, there were internal motivations to keep the Blue Book myth alive and well. No one wants their most prized possession to be criticized or debunked. Indeed, there appears to have been a rather well-orchestrated attempt by Fawley management to suppress any negative statements about either Fawley's Blue Book productivity deal or subsequent productivity deals. The lack of success of these deals was hidden, in other words, from the wider public. It has already been noted, for instance, that the written and oral evidence submitted by Esso Fawley about the Blue Book to the Royal

Commission on Trade Unions and Employers' Associations (Tuesday, 7 June 1966) did not fully square with its own internal audit of the same agreement. Further, it was seen that, when Fawley was forced to admit to the National Board for Prices and Incomes (N.B.P.I. Report No. 36) that there had been a creep back in some areas of the Blue Book, notably, in the overtime objectives, it did so in a way which sought to protect the integrity of the agreement, that is by suggesting that the rise was not due to management control problems but rather due to an '. . . unpredictable rise in the number of fires and breakdowns . . .' (N.B.P.I. Report No. 36). The N.B.P.I. itself was happy enough to accept this explanation and was, as suggested earlier, most sympathetic to Fawley's position.

While it is beyond the scope of this study to investigate the N.B.P.I.'s reasons and motivations for encouraging the perpetuation of productivity bargaining, it is noted that the N.B.P.I. appeared to settle for Fawley's own, biased evaluation of its productivity bargaining. Fawley's own myth may have been useful, therefore, to the N.B.P.I. and other industrial-relations boards and committees in encouraging the 'reform' of industrial relations along the lines of productivity bargaining. This argument is not so implausible as, doubtless, the careers and jobs of employees within these boards and committees were linked to the success of such initiatives as productivity bargaining.

The extent to which Fawley management was sensitive about keeping the Blue Book myth alive is demonstrated neatly with regard to an article published in *The Sunday Times* in 1975 entitled 'The great productivity myth' (*The Sunday Times*, 20 July 1975). This article contains a series of critical comments on the Blue Book based on information leaked from one of Fawley's own managers at the time, who appeared to be interested in aggrandizing one of his own deals at the expense of running down the Blue Book myth. Senior management's reaction to this article was swift and clear, coming in the form of a chastisement for those involved in the leak. This senior management sensitivity about 'bad press' was reflected in a memo issued to a manager who was about to publish an article on his particular experience with post-Blue Book productivity bargaining. In fact, this memo forbade the manager to proceed with publication.

Fawley management's desire to control the impression that the general public held about productivity bargaining at the refinery was, therefore, apparent in many ways and for many reasons. It could be argued, for instance, that because the Blue Book agreement was one of the best known and most celebrated industrial-relations interventions of recent years in Britain, current Fawley management has a custodial pride in maintaining the impression of success; through the impression of success, managers themselves would gleam with residual triumph. Fawley managers had developed personal stakes, pride, reputation in productivity bargaining and did not, therefore, want to bring to 'public' disgrace such an important set of values and practices. One of the benefits of impressing the notion of success on the wider business community is that this notion gets reinforced and fed back to Esso at many levels of the organization, including the board of directors.

It would appear, furthermore, that some journals (notably the Incomes Data Services (I.D.S.) and the Industrial Relations Review and Report (I.R.R.R.)) have also contributed to sustaining the myth of success and achievement through productivity bargaining. Article after article appearing in both the I.D.S. and I.R.R.R. have extolled the virtues of Fawley's productivity bargaining. A 1975 issue of the I.R.R.R. on productivity bargaining at Fawley entitles its article 'Fawley leads again . . .' (I.R.R.R., Report 282, October 1982). It could even be suggested that such journals feed off the myth of success for their own ends, that is, to sell 'new' and 'relevant' changes in the world of industrial relations.

It was, therefore, in a variety of ways that Fawley management was involved in the art of 'impression management'. The result of such effective image building was to create a complex tissue of lies, a large and quite fantastic myth about the productivity bargaining process. It is only very recently, after twenty-five years of productivity bargaining in Britain, that this myth might be beginning to 'crack' as journals start to question the *actual* progress made with some productivity and flexibility deals (see, for instance, Incomes Data Services, Study 360, April 1986: 4).

Productivity bargaining and careerism

Productivity bargaining at Fawley played a powerful role as a vehicle for the development of individual management careers and in this sense came to take on what I will refer to as an important 'careerist' function. Within the language of the organizational symbolism literature, productivity bargaining came to be interpreted as an important 'rite of passage'.

'Rites' serve to reduce anxiety associated with personal confrontation of the unknown. In organizations, rites can take on several forms: for example rites of passage (induction), rites of degradation (firing), rites of renewal (annual retreats), rites of enhancement (seminars), rites of conflict reduction (collective bargaining) (Trice and Beyer, 1985). A 'rite of passage' usually consists of a set of activities or an 'ordeal' which accords to the initiate either a formal or an informal stamp of approval. In organizations it relates directly to the notion of 'organizational membership'. As Trice and Beyer note: 'A prominent feature of genuine rites of passage is some sort of ordeal by which the initiate is symbolically separated from past identities so that the new identity and its obligations can be better assumed' (1985: 373–6).

During my research at Fawley, it became apparent that productivity bargaining had become transformed into an important 'rite of passage' for Fawley managers. In this sense, productivity bargaining had become related directly to the career objectives of the management group, not so much for its contribution to overall organizational effectiveness and efficiency, but rather as a way or means of advancing careers within the managerial hierarchy. For both personnel managers and line managers, career advancement became, in fact, almost synonymous with the ability to put together a productivity deal. To enter the upper reaches of the Fawley management hierarchy almost required, in other words, that the productivity bargaining 'rite of passage' must first have been 'negotiated'.

With productivity bargaining so firmly entrenched within the management 'folklore' or 'culture' since the days of the Blue Book, subsequent generations of managers began to interpret productivity bargaining as a means by which to advance their own careers. The high organizational and public profile which was accorded the Blue Book ensured that further generations of Fawley managers came to interpret subsequent productivity bargaining as synonymous with their own career success.

The Blue Book productivity deal had already served to propel the careers of many a Fawley manager – through promotions not only within Esso but also through advancement outside the organization. As one commentator put it, 'the world of industrial relations is now strewn with ex-Esso managers anxious to grab a little piece of the reflected glory of such a pace-making event' (J. Elliott, *The Financial Times*, 'Pressures for a new type of productivity reward', 14 May 1976). Both knighthoods and company chairmanships have, in fact, been the rewards of association with productivity dealing at Fawley. In an interview one ex-Fawley manager put it to me (candidly) in this way:

> I and many of my ex-Fawley colleagues have effectively traded on Fawley's productivity mystique. There's no question that there have been a whole raft of Fawley managers who have capitalized on their association with Fawley's productivity bargaining ... and have got big jobs out of them ... It doesn't matter whether you were associated with the big deals like the Blue Book ... any Fawley productivity deal is good enough to make a move upwards either inside or out of Esso. (Interview with Fawley manager)

Once two or three generations of productivity deals had been struck at Fawley, and once it had become clear that those involved in these deals were being looked upon favourably by Fawley's senior management, productivity dealing came to be accepted as an important rite of passage. As one Fawley manager put it to me, '... it became clear to me that if I wanted to progress in this organization, I too would need to put together a deal, or at least be a part of one' (interview with Fawley manager).

Much of Fawley's productivity bargaining revolved around managers' attempts to win their own Blue Book notoriety through the discovery of a new or different form of productivity bargaining, one which could finally resolve the elusive productivity 'problem'. The rewards for this discovery were highly coveted – career success. This feverish attempt to attain a kind of a Blue Book notoriety reached the point of the absurd when one Fawley manager who was anxious to publicize the discovery of his new and 'revolutionary' type of productivity bargaining was told to 'back-off' from making any claims to the press as this type of deal had already long been discovered and used by other British companies.

The task of becoming a key member of a team which was involved in the creation of a productivity deal was often difficult in itself. Places were few as, once admitted to these teams, managers jealously guarded and coveted these positions. Much manoeuvring and posturing reportedly took place in getting on to one of these teams. As one supervisor put it:

> I never really got close to any of the management teams who did the deals. Sometimes you felt that there was a small club operating up top ... it was a club you heard little about until you received a copy of an agreement or read some minutes.
> (Interview with Fawley supervisor)

The juggling and in-fighting for direct participation in the creation of a productivity deal meant that various coalitions or political forces blocked the participation of rival management groups. The extent to which a 'club' mentality existed may, itself, explain part of the failure of the agreements. The fact that the negotiation of a productivity agreement carried with it a 'careerist' dimension, meant that widespread participation in the production of the deals was limited. This 'club' mentality meant that only a small cross-section of ideas and perspectives were being considered and processed in any one deal.

It appeared to be the case that both line management and personnel management at Fawley used productivity bargaining in a 'careerist' manner. The status of Fawley personnel managers appeared to be particularly high compared with that of personnel managers in British industry in general. Productivity bargaining has, no doubt, been at least partly responsible for this higher status. The process also served to integrate the personnel function with the line management functions.

Through the productivity bargaining process, personnel became involved in the every-day activities of line managers, in the planning and scheduling of work and in the restructuring of working practices.

The relatively high status of Fawley's personnel department is reflected symbolically in the positioning of management offices. According to Fawley management, it is apparently customary within the Exxon organization to have the operations manager's (the line position immediately below the refinery manager) office located next to the office of the refinery manager, with both managers sharing a common secretarial resource. At Fawley this situation was *altered* so that the personnel manager's office was positioned next to the refinery manager's office (i.e. where the operations manager would normally be located). The symbolism of this office arrangement can be seen to be a testimony to the power of the personnel function and was resented by a number of senior line managers. As one of these put it:

> There's a feeling around this place that personnel is too power-
> ful. Sometimes some of our engineers think that the refinery
> manager isn't running the place, but that it is really being run
> by 'X' (the personnel manager). Sometimes you think that he
> (the personnel manager) is telling him (the refinery manager)
> how to run the refinery. (Interview with Fawley manager)

In this way, it can be seen that productivity bargaining was to have important implications for the power and status of the personnel function.

With productivity bargaining established as an important career tool, it behoved line managers to 'get close' to the personnel function. It was the personnel function which, like the 'rain makers' or 'witch doctors', held the magic formulae to produce the potions (to make the deals) and if the line managers wanted the formulae, they needed, to some extent, to align themselves with the personnel function.

The 'careerist' interpretation of productivity bargaining fits in neatly, as well, with the performance appraisal and career cycle systems at Esso. Esso operates from a well-structured performance appraisal system which is deeply engrained in the organization's culture and well respected (and often feared) by its employees. This appraisal system places great onus on the initiation and development of activities and programmes that go above and beyond the every-day duties normally associated with the particular job. High performance, in other words, is largely defined by the demonstration of a willingness to go above and beyond the functions and responsibilities specified in the written job descriptions. This emphasis on 'initiating' places pressure on managers to come up with high profile and high glamour projects. Esso's career cycle system is itself based on a two-

225

to three-year review period, in which high performance is rewarded with a promotion either within the unit in which the employee is already working or, ideally (to escape the tedious task of implementation), a transfer to another unit.

In view of the type of performance appraisal system and the short career cycles, it could be said that a productivity deal was an ideal career tool. A productivity agreement could easily be laid out in a manager's annual performance objectives and could be designed and negotiated within the context of the short career cycle. The high level of acceptance of productivity bargaining within the Fawley culture made it even more attractive as a career device. Moreover, by departing from the scene immediately after the design and negotiation of the agreement (usually due to a promotion) the manager is, more often than not, spared the problems of implementation and day-to-day operation of the agreement. The manager, in other words, leaves in the 'honeymoon' period and escapes the scene before the real effects of the productivity deal become apparent.

It is suggested here that the performance appraisal system and the tendency towards short career cycles may also serve to explain why productivity bargaining failed at the surface level at Fawley. These business methods placed the highest premium on short-term 'glamour' projects, while underplaying the importance of the more difficult and laborious tasks associated with the implementation and day-to-day operation of the agreements. It is well recognized that the 'glamour' or 'high profile' phase of any change project is in the conception and design phases, while the implementation tends to be met with less fanfare and glory.

From a career perspective, therefore, it was often sufficient for managers simply to design and negotiate an agreement in order to secure promotion, leaving the tedious implementation and monitoring phases to a new management team or to lower levels of the management hierarchy. The performance appraisal points scored for the design and negotiation of a new productivity agreement usually meant that the members of the management coalition who were involved in these stages were soon promoted to new jobs. In turn, this meant that an incoming manager became responsible for the implementation and maintenance of the agreement (i.e. inheriting the legacy of some past manager's activity). In the case of some agreements, this type of turnover had definite negative implications. As one manager put it:

> There is nothing worse for a new manager to be saddled with than the programmes and plans of past managers. New management is always more interested in developing its own new

programmes and agreements than in carrying out the agreements of past managers. (Interview with Fawley manager)

At Fawley, new managers wishing to follow in the footsteps of past fame and glory, tended, therefore, to be more concerned with creating their own new projects than with reworking or monitoring an agreement that was associated with a past manager. Another Fawley manager described the situation in this way:

> One of the big reasons why agreements slipped a little bit was a lack of ownership. A manager would do a deal one day and be gone the next. It's hard enough to keep a project going that you have designed yourself . . . but if it's someone else's programme I'd say its almost impossible. (Interview with Fawley manager)

The fact, moreover, that a career premium was placed on the design and negotiation of the agreement meant that the crucial implementation and monitoring activities were neglected. This is what happened, according to Roeber, at I.C.I.:

> Many managers achieved the clear objective of introducing WSA (the Weekly Staff Agreement) in their works but subsequently lacked the energy and enthusiasm needed to keep up the pressure in the interests of less obvious gains. (1975: 216)

While Roeber does not specify what these 'less obvious gains' are, in the Fawley case these would relate directly to diminishing career advancement returns.

In the early 1970s Fawley management began to show some awareness that the lack of management continuity affected the outcome of productivity bargaining, but did little to change the situation. The continued practice of promoting management personnel shortly after the striking of a deal itself resulted in problems relating to the interpretation of the agreement. The managers who replaced the newly promoted managers, not having been party to the design and negotiation of the agreement, did not have the same understanding of the content of the agreement or of the 'spirit' of the agreement. The union representatives were well aware of management's problems relating to this lack of continuity and claimed to exploit this to their own end. According to one senior steward:

> If we were asked to do something and we didn't think it was fair we could always say that it wasn't in the spirit of the agreement. With some of management's old negotiating team

227

gone to other jobs it was hard for them to say that that wasn't what we intended. (Interview with senior steward)

Discontinuity on the management side was matched by continuity on the worker side, which made this tactic all the more powerful.

Other evidence of management concern over the career dimension of productivity bargaining can be found in what was referred to above as the 'cycle of good news reporting'. The tendency to build up the extent to which a productivity agreement was meeting its objectives is itself a testimony to the significance of the careerist interpretation of productivity bargaining. The anxiety of authors and designers of the agreement who are banking their own career on one of these deals, can easily be filtered down the organization. It became increasingly important to feed back success stories about the agreements themselves to senior management. 'Good news' was required if managers were to be promoted. This cycle of good news reporting had its own negative impact on the evaluation of the agreements by skimming over, or camouflaging, problem areas that needed to be rectified.

Another result of the careerist aspect of productivity bargaining was that management became more vulnerable to worker demands. With career development so blatantly linked to the ability to design and negotiate a productivity deal, Fawley managers became more and more prone to yield to union pressure in the sense that the focus was more on signing the deal than on securing initially desired provisions from the workers or the union. Therefore, in some cases, Fawley managers would do almost anything to get a deal successfully negotiated in order to reap the professional rewards. At least one of the senior stewards was aware of this situation and noted that:

> There usually came a point in our negotiations when we could feel that management was softening. We would have been working on a deal for over a year and you could sense that they really wanted the deal. They wanted it wrapped up in a nice parcel. We usually could take out a lot of the more hard hitting items at that time. (Interview with senior steward)

The extent to which productivity bargaining was interpreted in 'careerist' terms is reflected in the way that the authors of subsequent productivity deals were so keen not only to strike an agreement but also to 'publicize' what they saw as their own productivity deals. The trade journals are filled with accounts which sing the praises of some new Fawley productivity agreement or other. These articles and reports represent, in many instances, attempts by post-Blue Book managers to capture the same kind of notoriety and success as that associated with the original Blue Book deal.

The relevance of the symbolic approach

Conclusions

This chapter has argued that, at Fawley, productivity bargaining developed over the years a powerful symbolic significance and that such significance helps us make sense of the perpetuation of productivity bargaining despite its failure at the rational–technical level. At the deeper symbolic level, the productivity bargaining process was seen to (1) aid in the reduction of uncertainty, (2) manage impressions both within and outside the company and (3) provide a 'magic carpet ride' to a bigger and better job.

14

Conclusions

This research explored the evolution of Fawley's industrial-relations strategy from the striking of the historic Blue Book in 1960 to 1985. In doing so, it has sought to investigate the meaning of strategy for industrial relations. The Blue Book agreement was not a 'one-off' initiative but rather, there was a total of 21 significant productivity agreements struck over the 25-year period. In this way, productivity bargaining came to define the very essence of industrial-relations strategy at Fawley.

Just as productivity bargaining continued to thrive at Fawley, so did it maintain its importance in Britain in general. Although the technique may, at times, have faded in popularity, it keeps on coming back. Despite the literature's relative silence on productivity bargaining in the post-1970 period, it was seen in chapter 3 that there were indeed two strong surges of productivity bargaining activity after 1970.

The advent of productivity bargaining in Britain provided a fertile ground for debate about the management of industrial relations. In fact, productivity bargaining came to be heralded as the first legitimate attempt at the *strategic* management of industrial relations in Britain (Lupton, 1966). It was seen to have marked a departure from the *ad hoc* to the systematic management of industrial relations and to have forced management into accepting human resource management as a critically important function in its own right:

> The trouble with the greater part of the best of line management in British industry from top to bottom is that it does not want to accept the responsibility for the human aspects of its job, what is sometimes called, although I dislike the term, man-management. (Flanders, 1975: 62)

Productivity bargaining has stood, in fact, at the very heart of British industrial relations (with the small irony that the birth of productivity bargaining was to occur at the subsidiary of an American firm).

230

Conclusions

Different people were to pin different hopes and dreams on the technique, in accordance with their own ideologies and beliefs. Bill Allen, the American consultant who was the architect of the Blue Book, stressed labour market 'internalization'. He made an impassioned plea for Britain to move out of its 'half-pay/half-effort' syndrome towards a strategy of 'full-pay/full-effort', and he saw productivity bargaining as the means towards achieving this end.

For Flanders, the Oxford academic who was invited to Fawley to record the productivity bargaining experience, the technique held the promise of democratizing workplace relations by extending the collective bargaining apparatus and integrating union stewards into the heart of the management decision-making process. According to Flanders, productivity bargaining was to form the technical basis of a new pluralism in industrial relations. The use of productivity bargaining would, no less, lead management to a higher ground, to a new moral order in workplace relations. The very act of engaging in productivity bargaining was seen to infuse management with a regard and respect for democracy in the workplace. Productivity bargaining was seen as '... the stuff of democratic politics' (Flanders, 1975: 209).

The case study investigated Fawley's productivity bargaining at three different levels of meaning: (1) the rational, (2) the political and (3) the symbolic. At the rational level, it was seen that, for the most part, the many generations of productivity agreements failed to achieve their stated objectives. Working practices proved far more difficult to change than might have been imagined.

With respect to Allen's dream for a 'high-pay/high-effort' strategy, it could be said that, in 1985, Fawley was still locked into roughly the same kind of 'low-pay/low-effort' strategy that Allen had identified in 1958. To be sure, some progress was made in changing working practices over the 25-year period, but certainly not to the extent that Allen might have wished. His hope for labour market 'internalization' was not realized. Instead of pursuing an 'internalization' strategy, Fawley management opted for 'externalization' – in the form of the increased use of contractor labour. Furthermore, the case study results revealed that the secondary sector labour market characteristics normally associated with the use of contractor labour did not necessarily hold true for Fawley. Indeed, it was found that the elegant dual labour market theory had been turned on its head, with 'core' workers sharing some of the labour market characteristics of 'peripheral' workers and 'peripheral' workers enjoying many of the characteristics of 'core' workers.

It is likely that Flanders would also have been disappointed with the turn of events at Fawley, particularly since management, instead of embracing a spirit of union participation and integration, came to pursue a strategy of de-unionization. Rather than embracing collective bargaining and union participation, Fawley management sought instead to pursue a 'strategy' – in the form of a staff status programme – which would eliminate collective bargaining rights from the site. The 'individual' was to take precedence over the 'collective'. The case study revealed, in fact, that Fawley management had never really embraced the notion of 'integration' as a serious strategy in the first place. Fundamentally, productivity bargaining was used at Fawley in a 'unitarist' way. It would almost appear to be the case that Flanders had, in some ways, read into the Fawley situation what he wanted to see. His own ideology may have got in the way of his understanding of productivity bargaining. The use of productivity bargaining as a strategy of pluralism was found to exist more as myth than reality.

It should be noted, however, that the case study findings do not in any way deny the value of the reformist prescription of Flanders and others, that is, that reform would be best achieved through the integration and direct participation of the union and workers into the management decision-making process. The reformist prescription has not been tested simply because Fawley management never really used productivity bargaining in a 'pluralist' manner to begin with. Productivity bargaining at Fawley, in other words, did not constitute a deliberate strategy to integrate unions and workers into the management decision-making process.

Furthermore, the Marxian view that productivity bargaining would increase the exploitation of labour turned out to be totally unfounded. The Fawley case study also demonstrated that much of Marxian writing, both that written directly on productivity bargaining and much of the early labour process work, may have given management too much credit in terms of its ability to act strategically in the management of industrial relations.

The application of the political approach to industrial-relations strategy at Fawley has been of considerable value in understanding the complex problems associated with the design, negotiation, implementation and maintenance of a rationally based strategy. Productivity bargaining was an inherently unstable strategy due to pressures not only from subordinate groups but also to tensions within the supervisory and managerial groups. At Fawley, problems and contradictions were seen to be rife throughout the productivity bargaining process.

Finally, the application of the symbolic approach to the study of industrial-relations strategy has provided important insight into the reasons for the perpetuation of productivity bargaining. A puzzling

232

question throughout the research was always 'why did management continue to use productivity bargaining in spite of its failure at the rational level?' – the symbolic approach has gone a long way towards uncovering some interesting answers. Although the symbolic perspective has not yet been applied directly within the industrial-relations literature, it is hoped that my research has demonstrated the value of applying this type of analysis to the study of industrial-relations phenomena.

Using case study analysis, this research has attempted to look systematically at the meaning of strategy for industrial relations. The results have pointed out the grave dangers of simply assuming that stated management intentions become translated into reality. It has also been demonstrated that there is a need to go beyond rational analysis to take advantage of the insights offered by both political and symbolic perspectives.

Bibliography

Allen, W. (1964) 'Is Britain a half-time country, getting half-pay for half-work under half-hearted management?', *The Sunday Times*, 1 March.

(1966) 'Britain in blinkers', *The Sunday Times*, 12 June.

Armstrong, P. and Goodman, J. (1979) 'Managerial and supervisory custom and practice', *Industrial Relations Journal* 10(3): 12–24.

Atkinson, J. (1984) 'Manpower strategies for flexible organizations', *Personnel Management* 16(8): 28–31.

Atkinson, J. and Meager, N. (1986) 'Is flexibility just a flash in the pan?', *Personnel Management*, September: 26–9.

Bamforth, J. (1966) 'The price of productivity', *Personnel Management*, December: 208–16.

Bassett, P. (1984) 'TGWU warns BP Chemicals on staff deal', *The Financial Times*, 6 December.

(1986) *Strike Free: New Industrial Relations in Britain*. London: Macmillan.

Batstone, E. (1984) *Working Order*. Oxford: Blackwell.

(1986) ' "New forms" of work organization: the British experience', in Grootings, P., Gustavson, B. and Hethy, L. (eds.) *New Forms of Work Organization and their Social Environment*. Budapest: Vienna Centre and Institute of Labour Research Budapest.

Batstone E., Boraston, S. and Frenkel, S. (1978) *The Social Organization of Strikes*. Oxford: Blackwell.

Batstone, E., Ferner A. and Terry M. (1984) *Consent and Efficiency*. Oxford: Blackwell.

Batstone, E., Gourlay, S. with Levie, H. and Moore, R. (1985) *Unions, Unemployment and Innovation*. Oxford: Blackwell.

Batstone, E. et al. (forthcoming) *New Technology and the Process of Labour Regulation*.

Behrend, H. (1957) 'The effort bargain', *Industrial and Labor Relations Review* 10: 503–15.

Bennis, W. G., Benne, K. D. and Chin, R. (1961) *The Planning of Change*. New York: Rinehart and Winston.

Bensman, J. and Gerver, I. (1963) 'Crime and punishment in the factory: the functions of deviance in maintaining the social system', *American Sociological*

Review 28(4): 588–98.

Benson, J. (1977) 'Organizations: a dialectical view', *Administrative Science Quarterly* 22: 1–21.

Biggs, N. (1970) University of Manchester Institute of Science and Technology Foundation Lecture, delivered in January 1970.

Blackler, F. and Brown, C. (1980) *Whatever Happened to Shell's New Philosophy of Management?* Farnborough: Saxon House.

Blauner, R. (1964) *Alienation and Freedom*. Chicago University Press.

Bolman, L. and Deal, T. (1984) *Modern Approaches to Understanding and Managing Organizations*. San Francisco: Jossey-Bass.

Braverman, H. (1974) *Labour and Monopoly Capital*. New York: Monthly Review Press.

Brewster, C. and Connock, S. (1985) *Industrial Relations: Cost-effective Strategies*. London: Hutchinson.

Brewster, C. and Richbell, S. (1983) 'Industrial relations policy and managerial custom and practice', *Industrial Relations Journal* 14(1): 22–31.

British Broadcasting Corporation (BBC) (1967) 'Esso work to rule', Transcription, 10 October, 5:55 p.m.

Brown, W. (1972) 'A consideration of "custom and practice"', *British Journal of Industrial Relations* 10(1): 42–61.

(1973) *Piecework Bargaining*. London: Heinemann.

(1974) 'Productive of change', *New Society* 30(632): 420–1.

(ed.) (1981) *The Changing Contours of British Industrial Relations*. Oxford: Blackwell.

Bucher, R. and Stelling, J. (1969) 'Characteristics of professional organizations', *Journal of Health and Social Behaviour* 10: 3–15.

Burns, T. (1961) 'Micropolitics: mechanisms for institutional change', *Administrative Science Quarterly* 6(3): 257–81.

Cicourel, A. (1964) *Method and Measurement in Sociology*. New York: Free Press.

(1973) *Cognitive Sociology: Language and Meaning in Social Interaction*. Harmondsworth: Penguin.

Clegg, H. (1972) *The System of Industrial Relations in Great Britain* (2nd edition). New Jersey: Totowa.

(1976) *The System of Industrial Relations in Great Britain* (3rd edition). Oxford: Basil Blackwell.

Cliff, T. (1970) *The Employers' Offensive; Productivity Deals and How to Fight Them*. London: Pluto Press.

Commission on Industrial Relations (C.I.R.) (1973) *Industrial Relations at Establishment Level*. London: HMSO.

Corina J. (1967) *Forms of Wage and Salary Payment for High Productivity*. International Management Seminar. Versailles: OECD.

Cressey, P., Eldridge, J. and MacInnes, J. (1985) *'Just Managing'; Authority and Democracy in Industry*. Milton Keynes: Open University Press.

Crozier, M. (1964) *The Bureaucratic Phenomenon*. London: Tavistock.

Cyert, R. and March, J. (1963) *A Behavioral Theory of the Firm*. Englewood Cliffs,

Bibliography

New Jersey: Prentice-Hall.

Daniel, W. (1970a) *Beyond the Wage-Work Bargain*. London: P.E.P.

(1970b) 'It's still worth making productivity deals', *The Times*, 28 September.

Daniel, W. and McIntosh, N. (1973) *Incomes Policy and Collective Bargaining at the Workplace*. London: George Berridge and Co.

Day, R. and Day, J. (1977) 'A review of the current state of negotiated order theory: an appreciation and a critique', *The Sociological Quarterly* 18: 126–42.

Donovan (1968) Royal Commission on Trade Unions and Employers' Associations, report, Cmnd. 3623, London: HMSO.

Edwards, P. (1984) 'The management of productivity; a preliminary report of a survey of large manufacturing establishments', discussion paper, Industrial Relations Research Unit, University of Warwick.

Edwards, R. (1979) *Contested Terrain*. London: Heinemann.

Edwards, R. and Roberts, R. (1971) *Status, Productivity and Pay: A Major Experiment*. London: Macmillan.

Eldridge, J. (1971) *Sociology and Industrial Life*. London: M. Joseph.

Ellis, J. (1975) 'Pressure for a new type of productivity deal', *The Financial Times*, 14 May.

The Financial Times (1984) 'Above-average cutbacks boost Exxon confidence', 25 July.

The Financial Times (1985) 'Achieved increases not ill-defined aspirations'. 19 November.

Flanders, A. (1964) *The Fawley Productivity Agreements*. London: Faber and Faber.

(1966) *Collective Bargaining*. London: Faber and Faber.

(1968) 'The case for the package deal', *The Times*, 9 June.

(1972) Preface to B. Towers and T. G. Whittingham (eds.), *Bargaining for Change*. London: Allen and Unwin.

(1975) *Management and Unions* (2nd edn). London: Faber and Faber.

Fox, A. (1966) 'Productivity bargaining', *New Society* 8(208): 446–8.

(1971) *A Sociology of Work in Industry*. London: Collier-Macmillan.

(1974) *Beyond Contract: Work, Power and Trust Relations*. London: Faber and Faber.

Friedman, A. (1977) *Industry and Labour*. London: Macmillan.

Fyall, A. (1968) 'Jack's pay packet is bigger – and that's good news for Britain', *The Daily Express*, 17 May.

Gallie, D. (1978) *In Search of the New Working Class*. Cambridge: Cambridge University Press.

Gospel, H. and Littler, C. (1983) *Management Strategies and Industrial Relations*. London: Heinemann.

Gottschalk, W. and Towers, B. (1969) *Productivity Bargaining: A Case Study and Simulation Exercise*. University of Nottingham: Department of Adult Education.

Gouldner, A. (1954) *Patterns of Industrial Democracy*. New York: Free Press.

236

Bibliography

Gowler, D. (1969) 'Determinants of the supply of labour to the firm', *Journal of Management Studies* 6(1): 73–95.

Gowler, D. and Legge, K. (1983) 'The meaning of management and management of meaning', in M. Earl (ed.) *Perspectives on Management*. Oxford: Oxford University Press.

Groom, B. and Goodhart, D. (1983) 'Enter the jack-of-all-trades', *The Financial Times*, 17 August.

Hawkins, K. (1971) 'Productivity bargaining: a reassessment', *Industrial Relations Journal* 2(1): 10–34.

(1978) *The Management of Industrial Relations*. Harmondsworth: Penguin.

Hill, P. (1976) *Towards a New Philosophy of Management: The Company Development of Shell U.K. Ltd*. Epping, Essex: Gower Press.

Incomes Data Services (I.D.S.) (1970) 'New agreement from productivity bargaining pioneer', Report 100, October: 6–7.

(1977) 'Review', Report 263, August: 2–3.

(1979) 'Statistics', Report 318, December: 31–2.

(1980) 'For and against . . . opposition to single status', Study 227, October: 1–4.

(1983) 'Closer harmony with national agreement in Fawley settlement', Report 413, November: 5–6.

(1984) 'Why change at Fawley', Study 322, September: 17–19.

(1986) 'Flexibility at work', Study 360, April: 1–24.

Industrial Relations Review and Report (I.R.R.R.) (1981) 'Productivity bargaining part 4 – are commitments enough?' Report 239, January: 2–5.

(1982) '8 per cent increases for Esso Fawley workers', Report 282, October, P.A.B.B.: 2–3.

(1982) 'Oil industry – Fawley leads again', Report 282, October: 11–15.

(1983) 'Job losses fund productivity gains', Report 288, PABB, January: 2.

(1984) 'Flexibility agreements – the end of who does what', Report 316, March: 2–9.

(1984) 'Flexibility agreements – the impact on procedures', Report 317, April: 8–11.

(1984) 'Flexibility package at Mobil Coryton – exploring new frontiers', Report 323, July: 7–12.

(1984) 'Productivity bargaining: 2 – profitability and flexibility', Report 332, November: 2–8.

Jacobs, E. (1975) 'The great productivity myth', *The Sunday Times*, 20 July.

Jones, L. (1967) 'Guidelines on productivity bargaining', *Personnel Magazine*, January: 22.

Kinnie, N. (1985) 'Changing management strategies in industrial relations', *Industrial Relations Journal* 16(4): 17–24.

Klein, L. (1976) *A Social Scientist in Industry*. Epping, Essex: Gower Press.

Knights, D. and Willmott, H. (eds.) (1986) *Managing the Labour Process*. Aldershot: Gower.

Lawler, E. (1981) *Pay and Organization Development*. Reading, Massachusetts: Addison-Wesley.

Bibliography

Legge, K. (1978) *Power, Innovation and Problem-Solving in Personnel Management*. London: McGraw-Hill.

(1984) *Evaluating Planned Change*. London: Academic Press.

Lévi-Strauss, C. (1963) *Structural Anthropology*. New York: Basic Books.

Littler, C. (1982) *The Development of the Labour Process in Capitalist Societies*. London: Heinemann.

Lupton, T. (1966) *Management and the Social Sciences*. London: Hutchinson.

Lupton, T. and Gowler, D. (1972) 'Wage payment systems: a review of current thinking', *Personnel Management*, November: 25–8.

Maanen, J. and Barley, S. (1985) 'Cultural organization – fragments of a theory' in Frost, P., Moore, L., Louis, M., Lundberg, C. and Martin, J. (eds.) *Organizational Culture*. Beverly Hills: Sage.

McCarthy, W. E. J. and Ellis, N. (1973) *Management by Agreement*. London: Hutchinson.

McKersie, R. (1966) 'Productivity bargaining: deliverance or delusion?', *Personnel Management*, September: i–viii.

McKersie, R. and Hunter, L. (1973) *Pay, Productivity and Collective Bargaining*. London: Macmillan.

March, J. and Simon, H. (1958) *Organizations*. New York: Wiley.

Marsh, A. (1972) 'The contribution of employers' associations' in Towers, B. et al. (eds.) *Bargaining for Change*. London: George Allen and Unwin.

(1981) 'Employee relations from Donovan to today', *Personnel Management*, June: 34–6 and 47.

(1985) *Employee Relations Bibliography and Abstracts*. Oxford: Employee Relations Bibliography and Abstracts.

Mintzberg, H. (1978) 'Patterns in strategy formulation', *Management Science* 24(9): 934–48.

Mitchell, C. (1983) 'Case and situation analysis', *The Sociological Review* 31(2): 187–210.

Morgan, G. (1980) 'Paradigms, metaphors, and puzzle solving in organization theory', *Administrative Sciences Quarterly*, (25): 605–21.

Morgan, G. (1986) *Images of Organization*. Beverly Hills: Sage.

Morgan, G., Frost, P. and Pondy, L. (1983) 'Organizational symbolism' in Pondy et al. (eds.) *Organizational Symbolism*. Greenwich, Connecticut: Jai Press.

National Board for Prices and Incomes (N.B.P.I.) (1966) *Productivity and Pay During the Period of Severe Restraint*, Report 23, Cmnd. 3167. London: HMSO.

(1967) *Productivity Agreements*, Report 36, Cmnd. 3311. London: HMSO.

Nichols, T. and Beynon, H. (1977) *Living With Capitalism*. London: Routledge and Kegan Paul.

Nightingale, M. (1976) 'The Sociology of Productivity Bargaining'. University of Bristol, Ph.D. thesis.

(1980) 'U.K. productivity dealing in the 1960s' in Nichols, T. (ed.) *Capital and Labour*. Glasgow: Fontana.

Nystrom, P. and Starbuck, W. (1984) 'To avoid organizational crises, unlearn',

Organizational Dynamics 12(3): 53–65.

Parker, P., Hawes, W. and Lumb, A. (1971) *The Reform of Collective Bargaining at Plant and Company Levels.* London: HMSO.

The Petroleum Economist, August 1981.

The Petroleum Times, February 1982.

March 1984.

Pettigrew, A. (1972) 'Information control as a power resource', *Sociology* 6: 187–204.

(1973) *The Politics of Organizational Decision Making.* London: Tavistock.

(1977) 'Strategy formulation as a political process', *International Studies of Management and Organization* 7(2): 78–87.

(1985) *The Awakening Giant: Continuity and Change in ICI.* Oxford: Blackwell.

Pfeffer, J. and Salancik, G. (1974) 'Organizational decision making as a political process', *Administrative Sciences Quarterly* (19): 453–73.

Pondy, L. (1983) 'The role of metaphors and myths in organization and in the facilitation of change', in Pondy, L., Frost, P., Morgan, G. and Dandridge, T. (eds.) *Organizational Symbolism.* Greenwich, Connecticut: Jai Press.

Pondy, L., Frost, P., Morgan, G. and Dandridge, T. (eds.) (1983) *Organizational Symbolism.* Greenwich, Connecticut: Jai Press.

Poole, M., Mansfield, R., Blyton, P. and Frost, P. (1982) 'Managerial attitudes and behaviour in industrial relations: evidence from a national survey', *British Journal of Industrial Relations* 20(3): 285–307.

Pressman, J. and Wildavsky, A. (1973) *Implementation.* Berkeley: University of California Press.

Purcell, J. (1981) *Good Industrial Relations: Theory and Practice.* London: Macmillan.

(1983) 'The management of industrial relations in the modern corporation: agenda for research', *British Journal of Industrial Relations* 21(1): 1–16.

Purcell, J. and Sisson, K. (1983) 'Strategies and practice in the management of industrial relations', in G. Bain (ed.) *Industrial Relations in Britain.* Oxford: Blackwell.

Roeber, J. (1975) *Social Change at Work: The ICI Weekly Staff Agreement.* London: Duckworth.

Royal Commission on Trade Unions and Employers' Associations (1966) Report 39, 'Memorandum of evidence submitted by Esso Petroleum Company Ltd', May.

(1967) *Research Papers 4: 1. Productivity Bargaining, 2. Restrictive Labour Practices.* London: HMSO.

Salaman, G. (1981) *Class and the Corporation.* Glasgow: Fontana Paperbacks.

Schein, E. (1985a) 'How culture forms, develops, and changes', in Kilmann, R., Saxton, M., Serpa, A. and associates (eds.) *Gaining Control of the Corporate Culture.* San Francisco: Jossey-Bass.

(1985b) *Organizational Culture and Leadership.* San Francisco: Jossey-Bass.

Schumacher, C. (1981) 'Personnel's part in productivity growth', *Personnel Management*, July: 26–30.

Bibliography

Scott, W. R. (1981) *Organizations – Rational, Natural and Open Systems*. Englewood Cliffs: Prentice-Hall.

Smircich, L. and Stubbart, C. (1985) 'Strategic management in an enacted world', *Academy of Management Review* 10(4): 724–36.

Smith, I. (1973) *The Measurement of Productivity*. Essex: Gower.

Smith, O. (1971) *Productivity Bargaining: A Case Study in the Steel Industry*. London: Pan Books.

Stettner, N. (1969) *Productivity Bargaining and Industrial Change*. Oxford: Pergamon.

Strauss, A., Schatzman, L., Bucher, R., Ehrlich, D. and Sabshin, M. (1963) 'The hospital and its negotiated order' in Friedson, E. (ed.) *The Hospital in Modern Sociology*. New York: Free Press of Glencoe.

The Sunday Times (1975) 20 July.

Thompson, G. (1982) 'The firm as a dispersed social agency', *Economy and Society* 11(3): 233–50.

Thurley, K. and Wood, S. (1983) 'Business strategy and industrial relations strategy', in Thurley, K. and Wood, S. (eds.) *Industrial Relations and Management Strategy*. Cambridge: Cambridge University Press.

Timperley, S. (1980) 'Organisation strategies and industrial relations', *Industrial Relations Journal* 11(5): 39–45.

Topham, T. (1969) 'Productivity Bargaining', in Coates, K., Topham, T. and Barratt-Brown, M. (eds.) *Trade Union Register*, London: Merlin Press.

Towers, B. (1972) 'The nature and development of productivity bargaining', in Towers, B., Whittingham, T. and Gottschalk, W. (eds.) *Bargaining for Change*. London: George Allen and Unwin.

Trice, H. and Beyer, J. (1985) 'Using six organizational rites to change culture', in Kilmann, R., Saxton, M., Serpa, R. and associates (eds.) *Gaining Control of the Corporate Culture*. San Francisco: Jossey-Bass.

Tushman, M. (1977) 'A political approach to organizations: a review and rationale', *Academy of Management Review* 2(2): 206–16.

Wedderburn, D. and Craig, C. (1974) 'Relative deprivation in work', in Wedderburn, D. (ed.) *Poverty, Inequality and Class Structure*. London: Cambridge University Press.

White, M. (1981) *Payment Systems in Britain*. Aldershot: Gower.

White Paper (1965) *The Period of Severe Restraint*. Cmnd. 2639. London: HMSO.

Wigham, E. (1967) 'Fawley – Stage III', *The Times*, 19 July.

Williams, K. (1982) 'Oil majors face declining U.K. markets – head on', *The Petroleum Times*, November.

Willman, P. and Winch, G. in collaboration with Francis, A. and Snell, M. (1985) *Innovation and Management: Labour Relations at BL Cars*. Cambridge: Cambridge University Press.

Wood, S. (1982) 'Introduction' to Wood, S. (ed.) *The Degradation of Work*. London: Hutchinson.

Wood, S. and Kelly, J. (1982) 'Taylorism, responsible autonomy and management strategy' in Wood, S. (ed.) *The Degradation of Work*. London: Hutchinson.

Index

Index

Index